OURSELVES, *Inc.*

OURSELVES, Inc.

The Story of Consumer Free Enterprise

by

LEO R. WARD

Essay Index Reprint Series

 BOOKS FOR LIBRARIES PRESS
FREEPORT, NEW YORK

Nihil obstat

Arthur J. Scanlon, S.T.D.
CENSOR LIBRORUM

Imprimatur
✠ Francis J. Spellman, D.D.
ARCHBISHOP, NEW YORK

INTERNATIONAL STANDARD BOOK NUMBER:
0-8369-2208-5

LIBRARY OF CONGRESS CATALOG CARD NUMBER:
79-128327

PRINTED IN THE UNITED STATES OF AMERICA

Contents

Preface

THE co-ops begin to reach the stage where they speak for themselves, and that is what for the most part I propose to let them do in this book. But in the first place what is a "co-op"? Is it not just a lot of people who get together to run their own grocery or oil station? Is it not just another form of business, and a trick for making or saving money?

It is questions like these that I want to answer, and always within the concrete situations where the people are co-operators. Put bluntly, however, my reply, to be developed as we proceed, is that co-ops are not just a device for making or saving money. The vital point is to see *how* and *why* the co-ops do what they do, and to see the way they begin to be linked with the whole of our educational and political and religious life. That is what we are to consider in many actual cases.

Around the year 1800 and for a generation afterward many co-ops were started, but they died almost as soon as they were born. Especially in England, people had it in their heads that something could be done in the co-op way, and at last by making careful studies of co-op corpses some weavers at the town of Rochdale had by 1844 worked out principles and methods that, if carefully followed, make any co-op almost foolproof.

These weavers are called the pioneers, and their principles are taken as the charter and gospel of co-operation. Number One: One member, one vote. This principle means that the rich man and the poor man are put on the same voting level in this enterprise, and the co-op is committed to true democracy. Number Two: No profits, but if any savings are made they are returned, after allowing for reserve, to the patrons, and in proportion to their patronage. Out then go money-making and profit taking and monopolies and cartels, and the State trying to catch up with the miscreants. Through this rule the co-ops are of immense relevance to our times. Number Three: Open membership. This means that any

person of good will is eligible to join. Number Four: Neutrality
in race, religion, and politics. Such a provision saves the co-op
from race wars, and nationalistic and religious and political wars;
and above all, the co-op can never become a political instrument.
Number Five: Trading for cash, and at the going market rates.
This protects the business and the people from the evils of debts
and installment buying and of competitive price wars. Number
Six: Limited interest on capital. No 10 per cent or 12 per cent, and
no 36 per cent or 42 per cent, for anybody's money. Number
Seven: Provision for the unceasing education of the members.

The Rochdale Pioneers did not see, though we so easily see now,
that they were marking out a procedure that goes far beyond a
possible saving on the grocery bill. The social effects of any
economic and industrial technique that is commonly used have
to be enormous. Not every participant knows this at the outset.
But as we proceed to view many American co-ops, it would never
do to omit the fact of social rebirth implicit and often actual.

The co-ops in our country and abroad arise in every kind of
circumstance and with every sort of sponsorship. This is natural
within co-operative democracy. And the name "co-op" is at times
attached where it should no longer be, or should never have been;
if the unit, for example, is partisan and nondemocratic. But we
do find real co-ops everywhere, no matter which part of the country
we might pick, or which state or city. The cases studied in this
book are typical of successful and fairly successful co-ops in both
our country and Europe. Because of time and traffic problems,
however, the cases used are mainly within eight of our midwestern
states, and it is a matter of justice to say that a thousand persons
have helped me, and without stint or suspicion or reserve.

Any Rochdale co-op is an economic democracy and a social democracy. It cannot tolerate the financial dictatorship of monopoly,
corporationism, cartels, and absentee landlords. And it has no
occasion or use for the political dictators. Its principles of open
membership and "one member, one vote" say "no," and its practice
in every country says "no" to any form of dictatorship. No voting
by shares or proxy or money, and no precipitating a demand for
political bossism. The Rochdale co-op, which is the truest and most
successful, is of the people and by the people and for the people.

And I have every reason to say that in fact I have found the co-ops, both in this country and in Nova Scotia, completely open, frank, and democratic. They are the people's business, and often the people's club and the people's college. Democracy is theirs from first to last. And it is evident in theory and practice that no dictator can abide them.

The Rochdale Pioneers set up in an effective way on December 21, 1844. Would it not be the marvel of their second century if the co-ops were able to stand between the old capitalistic individualism that has been so hard on the people and has kept the State on the run, and the new collectivisms that are dead set against our human freedoms? Would it not be great if the co-ops could protect us from each extreme, and also protect the State from the individual and the individual from the State? I believe that this is the co-op's place. In positive terms, the co-op is the people's, and makes for freedom, ownership, and community.

Because the co-ops go directly and consciously for the people's good, I need not apologize for taking an occasional slap at attitudes and practices that at best are only incidentally with the people. This I do merely in passing and to make clear the nature, techniques, and effects of the co-operative movement. The word "co-op" is used because it is the people's word and is by this time a thoroughly good American word.

Of and by and for the people. Why, then, should we not be for and with the co-ops? The only question is whether they will work, and to this question we cannot give an answer in advance. The truth is that they do not and will not automatically work; they have to be worked. And here we are confronted with part of their real and persistent problem. People get into ruts, grow apathetic, at times fold up in conditions that are unsatisfactory and yet remediable. That is the way Pa and Ma did, and that is the way the world runs. To take vigorously and intelligently hold with the neighbors and to run the world—that is another matter. We Americans are independent, everyone going it alone, and so we have been, for over a hundred years. Nevertheless, during that same time the co-ops have made their way, one must say progressively and against odds, in country after country and in commodity after commodity. What has gone so far in such circumstances will go farther. Possibly we are not yet in a position to say how far they can go. What is already clear is that once they begin to control from 10 to 15 per cent of trade in any line they begin to exercise a humanly beneficent leverage on that whole business.

All these matters will appear as we proceed now to visit a great variety of co-ops in our own country and to mention their success also in England, Ireland, Sweden, Denmark, Italy, and throughout prewar Europe, and also in South America and China.

L. R. W.

Notre Dame, Indiana
January 4, 1945

OURSELVES, *Inc.*

.

One

MINERS' DECLARATION OF FREEDOM

1

ON A Sunday afternoon in the middle of May I am going by bus across Ohio toward the town of Dillonvale. For weeks it has rained, but today the sun is shining on the little towns and the fields that rise from the feet of muddy hills. In spite of warnings about week-end jams, this bus runs along half full and the driver finds time to talk to the passengers.

At Dillon, as the natives call it, I am to see the co-ops. But I am wondering this afternoon how far the co-ops could take over businesses whose names are in public places. Here is a list picked from signs as we pass through towns. "Cochocton Hotel." I suppose co-ops could do hotel work, which after all is not abstruse and is done by people. "Kroger's." "Gamble's." The co-ops now run food stores in many towns of many countries, and it is their chief work in Dillonvale. "The Church of Christ." The question might be asked here how truly a church is a co-op. "Dr. Alvira." Of course, the co-ops have gone into medicine. "Buckeye Body Shop." They have also, in recent times and in our country, begun to try their hand at running a variety of factories. And so when I read "Shell" and "Sycks Bros. Bakery" and "RR crossing" and "E. K. Jacobs, Contractor," I know that the co-ops have oil wells and refineries, and that they run bakeries and build houses.

To ask whether all these can be co-op is only to ask whether two or three or more can pool and work together in furnishing themselves the corresponding services. The answer is that often they do, and that men in larger groups, say ten, a hundred, ten thousand, have for a century done such works for themselves.

At Cadiz, a short word with the accent on the first syllable, this bus stops for good, and I must either wait till morning for a tiny bus to Dillon or look up the one car that will take me there. Just now the square, on a steep hillside and today's wind like a gale, is full of people, for across the street from the co-op store they are dedicating a board, one might say a fence, with the names of all the boys and the one girl in the service. The list is incredibly long, even if we are now among farmers and miners, people who have big families. The bands are from several towns, and the boys and girls are in red and black and white suits, and as they all play at once there on the gusty hillside, their instruments shining in the sun, it is as if a hundred Gabriels had come to blow the last trumpet, and all of them were doing it. Traffic is stopped by four men whose insignia is a red, white, and blue fez made for the occasion, or it is routed through an alley that goes straight down.

As things ease off, I talk to two men and a woman. The men know nothing of the co-op, though the glint from its sun-hit window almost knocks our eyes out. The woman knows it, and does not too much like it. "They say it ain't any cheaper, not a bit. Umumph," she says in an accusing tone, her body listing a fraction toward the guilty co-op.

The one man who will take me to Dillon is found, and away we go. To him gas and tires are nothing, as long as they last. We jump over these big hills or little mountains, and jerk around corners. At each turn it is as if he shoveled me to the next, and as he meets someone at a narrow bridge he goes straight on, and I say to him, "Can you make it?" "We'll soon see" is all he says, and he blasts by the astounded people and keeps scooping the two of us past every obstacle. I see only the worst things, and there are quite bad things along this road. What caved that house in? "A gas truck blew up, two hundred feet away, and two men in the truck." No breath and no slackening of pace as he says this. The condition of these great hills, at the outset good for little except grazing, but now charred and useless forever, is explained in two words: "strip mining."

2

In Dillonvale they started a co-op half a dozen years before World War I, and it has first and last stood firmly on its feet. It is what we call a consumer co-op, which means that in it and through it the people furnish themselves with goods and services. It is much more than a self-serve, and more than a self-help unit.

In reality and as far as it goes, it is in this sense of "self" a self-make, self-direct, self-manage, self-own, and self-serve. That is, the people themselves in Dillonvale set up the co-op, and it is they who through local persons named by them direct and manage it, and it is owned by them and exists to serve and only to serve them. In every way, it is their own. No foreign or alien capital has any control over it, and no rich man in Pittsburgh or poor man here gets one iota of profit from it. This co-op, as any co-op, is strictly nonprofit. And what does it serve the people, or more properly what do they serve themselves through it? Coffee, sugar, carrots, beans, potatoes, meats, gas, shoes and shirts and dresses.

But we must first notice how it got started a generation ago, and how through all kinds of weather it has ever since made its way.

Without doubt it started as an American-Bohemian enterprise, its founders not long from the old country. In 1908 Dillon was physically as it is now, some miners in a long crooked crease among the hills, and in terms of men's attitudes and hopes these miners were even more cornered than they are now. Their co-op arose because men badly needed it and had the intelligence and courage to set it up; in other words, for exactly the same reasons that their unions arose. The co-op may be looked upon as a union, and the union as a co-op. Their ends are the same; what they aim at is the freedom of men who otherwise are far from free; and the men who set up one set up the other. Neither union nor co-op alone can do the work, but together they can and do go a long way.

Now among these miners perhaps the Bohemians, lately come to our country, were among the poorest, unless we count their intelligence and courage. The tall hills were not theirs, nor the good soft coal under them, nor the houses into which the immigrants crowded. Even their physical integrity would soon suffer, with an eye gone, or two fingers, or a foot. In 1904 some people dared to set up a little store, and because that failed the odds were against enthusiasm for a consumer co-op. And still it was in just these circumstances that in 1908 they set up their store and made it go.

So four of the thirty-three original members, the four hardy survivors, tell me. Ten dollars, as much as thirty-five or forty dollars would now be in Dillon, was the cost of a share. It could be and had to be met "on slow payment," since the miners were working about half time. The local lent them one hundred and fifty dollars, and one miner was able to lend them two hundred and another three hundred. That was the sum of their starting capital. The manager, a young man, was paid ten dollars a week.

I suppose that was for part time and that he also mined coal. "No," he says, "that was about what miners got, and I took it to be even with the miners." He was a good manager, and for thirty-five years they have had him through thick and thin. The co-op was set up in December and by March an inventory showed a gain. That same year the men tried to buy a carload of flour, and "found opposition." They needed one thousand dollars, and credit would not be given. The manager then went from house to house and collected the money. At first they handled hardly anything but groceries, but soon they were into shoes and other merchandise. Up to 1914 they were gaining ground, and then set in a miners' strike that lasted over a year. "That nearly killed us. We were lucky to go through." After that bad time business increased, and dry goods were added and a bigger meat market. In 1917 a big building was put up alongside the store to serve as a hall and recreation center. The next year the miners tried in five or six places to organize stores, but these failed, "because they were looking for big commercial gain." It is true that three of them were saved, but only by being received into the bosom of the Dillon co-op.

The next few years business was good and new buildings went up, one of them at a cost of fifty thousand, subscribed by the people. If anyone thinks that sum is little, we may remind him that Dillon has never had over twelve hundred people, most of them miners. We have to remember too that poor men in a small town trying to free themselves in ever so small a measure are not popular. Those in high places, in churches and politics and local business, make it hard on them. Only after more than a dozen years did the miners in Dillon win honor. The dark, quiet man telling me these things has himself been through them, and the record of a long struggle is in his words when he says simply, "After that we were recognized."

In this town they say that in 1927 they had the biggest co-op business in the United States. It went up to three quarters of a million. Now Dillonvale was at last established, it was on top of the highest wave to date and could ever after take things for granted. That is what the uninitiated might think. But if Dillon thought so, it shortly learned a lesson. The trouble was the common trouble of miners, the persistent labor problem. That year of 1927 the miners went on a strike that lasted eighteen months. As they say at Dillon, "We lost that strike. Never found jobs for three or four years. That hurt. Still, we stayed, and our business increased." And with the general hard times, co-operation was needed more than ever, and the Dillon co-op began to spread over the county. "Two new branches were opened the same year" (1932). "The co-op in the town of Neffs has its own history." It was started and operated by the Polish people of that town. "But in 1934 it combined with us." In the past few years other locals have joined what we might call the central local at Dillon.

In 1935 the people put up a slaughterhouse and packing plant "to supply stores with pork and sausages and so on." Just before the war made the materials too scarce, a warehouse was put up at a cost of ninety-five thousand and with a floor space of twenty-six thousand feet. "All the money subscribed by our people." In fact, it was oversubscribed. And in that same year the business at Dillon and its subsidiary co-ops went for the first time over a million dollars.

3

That is the beginning of co-ops in Ohio and it is in a real sense their beginning also at Dillonvale, since they can and will be developed here in half a dozen additional lines: In the people's credit or bank, called a credit union and not yet brought to its peak in this locality. In medicine, too, which as a rule is too costly and therefore for the most part is done without in poor places. In insurance, which is well started even now through the Farm Bureau: "as a unit we are a member of the county Farm Bureau." The next step at Dillon will be a people's bakery, "because we already have customers and establishments." Branch stores will continue to multiply.

The miner's wage for hard, dangerous work has been and is low; about ten dollars a week in 1908 and thirty-five a week in 1943 with prices stopped only by high ceilings. The families normally are big. And often the work is five, six, or seven miles distant. When the miner gets to the tipple or portal, he has in some of the local mines and in nearly all the old-style mines to go down into the earth and often to travel underground for an hour before he comes to his work. After that he is paid by the hour. Naturally he demands underground portal-to-portal pay. In a broadcast Mr. Roosevelt said that the striking miners should for the duration give up the demand, and we must say that his speech, from his eminence and at the war-moment, was wonderfully appealing to the public. But the miners at Dillon did not see it that way. He and not they had prestige and a national hookup, and his argument ran like this: You miners, go back to work! Go back till we get this job done in Europe and Asia. If you don't, you are traitors! And your sons and brothers in Africa and the South Pacific would say to you: Go back! The miners at Dillon said this was sentimental and unfair.

Like all laborers, these men ask equality, dignity, and freedom. And that is all they ask. On the other side are those we call the "operators," as if they were on the same power-level, and were scarcely responsible for wages or conditions. And while the operators have taken the miner's strength and labor and also our underground resources, they and others, at Dillon and elsewhere, have taken the cream of the trade-profit. The miner could not be allowed equality and a person's dignity and freedom. The mine was not his, the times of employment were not his, the product going out on little tracks in car after car was not his. The bakery, the meat market, the store was not his, or the medicine or banking or the undertaking parlors. At Dillon for a long time, as to this day in many places, the house he lived in was not his, but the company's.

Not much chance for equality, dignity, and freedom. Not much chance for a person's life. Not much chance for family life and community life. And not much chance for a real and effective political freedom. It is not easy to believe that God and nature meant human persons and families and communities to be so limited.

Two facts are at once obvious. The co-operators have achieved something against odds, and if they cannot safely go faster they can certainly go farther. And it can easily be made obvious that miners and all laborers need co-ops just as they need unions. With the two they can advance their cause. In fact, the co-op at Dillon has made its way along with the union. Of course, the union and at times the strike are necessary, but alone they are not sufficient. Here and elsewhere if the control of finance and the houses and rent and the stores is under the thumb of the company or banks or the chains, an increase in wages in effect means little: it can be absorbed overnight in interest and rent and prices.

In helping to establish the proper corelation of unions and co-ops the Dillon experiment has been important. It is a kind of single-handed co-op that, starting alone, was until recently isolated even from the general Ohio co-ops. And to date it gives incomplete returns, since it has worked only in terms of groceries and meat and not in terms of housing and production and marketing and medicine. Yet it is exceedingly solid and we may look on it proudly as one of our American achievements in the past generation. And the more so because when our co-ops were all this time working almost exclusively as marketing co-ops, this one more than any other began to suggest what could be done by consumers. For its twenty-fifth anniversary in 1933 the head of all co-ops in this country said that it was well managed and had competent co-operators as directors. "It is one of the outstanding examples of successful co-operative mercantile business in this country." And he said it could go on being an inspiration so long as it elected as its directors only men who knew their business and had a conscience. Another said that its record is one of success "in the face of great obstacles. The reason for this success, I believe, is that the co-operators of Dillonvale and vicinity are *co-operators for life*. Co-operation is a part of their culture. They would not fail to co-operate any more than they would fail to educate their children."

A main source of strength in this co-op has also been a main source of weakness. Its beginning was with a body of very courageous Bohemians, and their national oneness gave it unity and consequent strength. But the Dillon co-op has had a hard time in getting beyond that body. It tends to remain Bohemian, and no co-op can afford to be merely Bohemian or merely Polish, or merely Catholic or Hebrew. On the other hand, the feeling that long existed at Dillon between church people and the local co-op is undoubtedly in large part the product of mutual misunderstanding. Of course, Dillon has had some church people who were against the co-ops and thereby in effect stood against what could serve both the Church and the people. Some co-op people, too, were willing, at least in such case, to bypass religion. But I think that in this matter a much better day has dawned, and the old feeling is hardly more than a memory.

Just a word on the more concrete attainments of the Dillon co-op. It set out with thirty-three members and now runs to about fifteen hundred. This means seven or eight thousand persons, as almost every member stands for a family. The first two years it could only finance itself, but in 1911 it returned nearly three hundred dollars to the then few member-families. It gained consistently until the great strike of '27-'28 when the patrons' dividends fell below what they had been in 1913. And even so, in its first twenty-five years it furnished to the member-families dividends of nearly a quarter million dollars, and kept as reserve fund half that amount. If we may be generous and suppose that on the average it has had five hundred families, then in the thirty-four years so far accounted for—including its first penurious seasons—it has returned to each family over twenty dollars a year and a total of about seven hundred dollars. This of course is nothing to wealthy men, but at compound interest it runs into something and in 1908 and through the lean years of 1927 and the thirties it was enormous for the families of Dillon.

"What is the success due to?" I asked one of the old leaders. "To loyalty?"

"To loyalty and honesty," he said. "Loyalty in the members, honesty in managers and directors." But we must say in the strongest terms that co-ops do not promise or afford fortunes to anybody. They are a way of community life and community good, and not of profit. If a man is out for money, if that is the way he is trained in his home, his school, his college, his community and his church, he had better avoid the co-ops. These, set up by the people and for the people, are not meant to make anybody's pocketbook fat. The co-op man's blessedness, whether he be member or leader, is not to be counted in millions, but in the people's good.

4

"At least 60 per cent" of the people at the town of Dillon and a smaller percentage from surrounding villages are into the co-ops. Into a bit of meat processing, and a bit of banking and in a lively way into what are now called the food stores. In all perhaps they do not do much of the business in this county; in terms of dollars, just a million's worth each year. But it is in their hands, and this fact may be as vital as the savings effected by and for the people. And as some good students of co-ops think, it may be that in towns and cities and among laborers co-ops best develop around the store. This tends soon to include dry goods and shoes, and then a meat market, and possibly gas and oil at the door, and also at a desk in the corner the office of the local credit union that helps to finance the people trading here, and then a people's bakery because "customers and establishments" are already had. And within the same body of people medical and hospital and burial groups can form, and parcels of people ready to build their own houses.

As I visit the Dillon store, there come to us Václav, aged seventy-nine, and his wife Antonina, aged seventy-four, seeking the pension. An old-line co-op official they ask to sponsor their cause, and he kindly asks me to come along just to see this not untypical local event. The man Václav was trained in the Austrian armies in the nineties. Did he ever fight, ever kill in war? Naw, he says in a broken tongue, there was no one to kill; just practicing. He has now mined coal, shaft and drift, for thirty or forty years, and his hands are empty. The old woman is brighter and sprier, and she attests that a son has given them "five or ten a mon', or whatever he was able." Does the old man do any work at all? Naw, she says, "just crutchin' aroun'."

Possibly they brought themselves to this unenviable state of asking for relief and pension. In general, governments might bring them to it, and wars also, and big industry and big profits. But not the people in the co-ops. At least the people in the co-ops may be trusted to go a long way toward getting on their own feet and staying on them. At Dillon the present average refund is about thirty-three dollars a year. Even without interest this would run in a generation to a sum sufficient to take care of Václav and Antonina.

5

These mountains or tall hills are underlaid with coal, and it is said that far beneath the present level of coal is another and better deposit. And they are full of people's stores. At Smithfield they did thirteen hundred dollars' worth of business on one payday this summer, and last week they sold up to $3,819. Keeping up this rate, Smithfield alone would work toward a quarter million in 1943. One thousand of last week's was spent on meat for these working-men. Big Mike pants sell at $2.49 and Strong Man shirts at $1.69. They cannot keep potatoes, the demand is so heavy. Wire is hard to get, and the last screens were sold this morning. Two schoolboys have helped, but one is leaving in two weeks and the other before a week. "They were in and took their physicals Sunday. They worked here after school hours two years and were getting to where they were some good, as good as men."

This and all the stores are well kept and well patronized. They are clean and bright and their goods carefully shelved and ordered. In them are fresh fruits and vegetables, and at Dillon fresh pineapple and some asparagus at sixty-five cents a bunch. In the store at Piney Fork are a man and wife shopping, he not more than forty-five with bony face well marked, she big and rotund. Her trouble at the moment is that she cannot find a slip big enough, though the price of $1.21 pleases. To the girl's "Here, how about this?" she replies, "It's a nice slip, and long enough, but not big enough the other way, around."

It is almost time for the four-o'clock shift, and a great ball of a man, only his face white, the rest of him in coveralls and a striped and long-beaked cap, goes up the hill and over the ridge to work. A woman hurries into the store where she can buy packaged and sealed sandwiches, and little one-bite pies for six cents. Coke bottles, yoked in sixes, stand at the door.

At one store we learn that the manager went to the war. "This man we have was the butcher. A good butcher, and he's making a good manager. His assistant is that little woman. Her husband went to the war, and we hired her. She's quick and smart." The store will go well.

The stores are at the foothills or a few rods up the sides of the little mountains. For years these mountains have been alive with miners, and at this moment a shift of a thousand men is in them or on them, and in twenty-four hours three shifts of seven hours each loads out thirty to forty cars, each car carrying from fifty to seventy tons of coal. Till a few years ago the men worked by the ton and did what is called shaft mining and in a few cases drift mining: in the shaft type a hole is dug straight from the surface to the coal, and in the other type the men work into the side of a hill. Now a new type of mining called strip mining is commonly used in this area; the steam shovel with mechanical power is the tool. A team of twenty-three men, and now because of man shortage eighteen men, handles it. All the evil words said about this destroyer of our natural resources are just. It wrecks the soil forever. During many centuries a thin layer of fertile soil has formed. On these roughest hills of Ohio that layer may be only two or three inches, but in Illinois where, conservation programs notwithstanding, strip mining is also used, the layer may be as much as two feet. Thick or thin, it is gouged into and buried beneath a hill of clay and rock. And while this desecration occurs in the interest of profit, where are those men whom we pay to see to conservation? How about a little co-operation in the interest of the people?

When the men worked by the ton they had to put up props every so far to protect themselves from the fall of slate and also to watch out for accumulations of what they call "bug dust," a fine coal dust that is highly inflammable. All this they claim they did with no pay.

Piles of slack keep burning the year around. "Them piles," says a miner, "they're a nuisance. Them fires burning." How long—a month or more? "A year. Five years that one is burning, and it's only halfway up." The smoke from them eats the paint off the houses. "Look at this yellow house here. It was yellow, and now it's like that. They peel off." He says this circumstance hurts the sale of co-op paints.

6

"Till the co-ops came here," says a housewife, "prices were away beyond. Just for an example: meat you couldn't hardly get for two and three cents more. But once the co-ops got started, their prices are about the same." In fact, she'd say some things are too high at the co-op. "I know there are different kinds of oranges, and sizes.

But seventy-nine cents, that's too high." No, she does not know at all how a co-op is set up or operated. "We just trade there, well, most of the time."

Another, a soft-faced woman with thin whitish hair, speaks without accent. "Came over here seventeen years ago," she says. "We're sold on co-ops. Three children, and I have to buy a good deal; only if you'd see my garden: we'll can a lot this year, if we can get jars. Some things, well, maybe they are too high at the co-op. Some complain it's clannish. But all are invited to vote on the hiring of new employees."

As I go from house to house, blackened men are coming from work, their clothes coal-dusty and loose and baggy. At his own door man just grunts to man, "S'long." Their work is mechanized, depersonalized. They do not discuss it or the product. Little sense of pride in their work, and no sense of possession. But their eyes are clear, looking out of these streaked faces, and no man is turning into the beer houses or in a hurry to return to them. They make straight for home, and the people at Dillon know by the hour the men come and go at which mine they work. "The P.R.," says some one, meaning the P. R. Nicholson mine. At this hour men could only be coming from that pit. And there, says a Polish woman, "they work old style; not the new machinery." She knows; she is a competent little woman, her house not like a coal mine but like a sunny field. Three sons she has in the service, one in Africa, one in the Pacific; "South Pacific, but we don't know where," and one learning to fly in Texas. "That's the one that's most danger." And a boy in school, "not eighteen yet." Her husband does work hard. "Oh, yes," she says, and her words, so simple and mature, express a lot of Dillon and mining life: hard work is expected and is nothing. The things that count are regular work and pay and freedom. The husband is on the night shift and leaves home at ten. Just now he is taking his sleep, and we can hear him snoring. The house is well furnished and precisely kept. The electric refrigerator is a small one. "One hundred twenty-four dollars," she says. And then seeing me look at the extraordinary radio she says proudly, "One hundred nine. One hundred nine dollars." I have no doubt, but do not dare to ask whether it was bought on the installment plan. In any case she likes the co-ops, for quality and prices. "I am satisfied with both: on the kind of goods and the refund."

Two

BEGINNINGS OF THE FINNISH EPIC

1

ANY home of the Finns in this country happens also to be a great home for co-operatives. This is only in a small part because some of them knew something of co-operation so well developed in Finland, and mainly because, like the Bohemian miners, they needed co-ops and had the intelligence and courage to establish them.

The Finns live in several parts of our country, but above all in the icier parts of northeastern Minnesota, and in the regions bordering on the north and the south shore of Lake Superior. The bulk of them came to us only a generation ago. They came deprived of freedom and not so simply expecting freedom as demanding it. They had been lately enslaved by the Russians, and if it is native to man to demand freedom and if the constant battle of modern man has been toward political and economic freedom, we may certainly say that no Finn ever turns his back on that fight. Man can be free, man is supposed to be free, man must, whatever the cost, make himself free. That, I think, is the declaration of independence given concrete expression by the Finnish co-ops in our Northland. All that north country is now full of co-ops. It is safe to say that we have over one hundred and fifty of them that are in great measure of Finnish origin. These of course are the locals, found in so many towns, though possibly in this or that case standing for a county. Then there is since 1917 a wholesale co-operative in the city of Superior, initiated by a few of the locals and now serving all of them.

This is the story that I get not only from several days of visiting with a live group of co-operators who work with the central, or wholesale, but also from going to half a dozen towns and seeing co-ops as they function. These live co-operators, most of them young men and women, are ready to lay the cards on the table for anyone who wishes to know the story of their co-ops.

Our Finnish immigrants of the first decade in this century did not find the freedom they demanded. They had only jumped out of the frying pan into the fire. Into their hands were put saws and axes to cut down our great birch and pine, timber that in its day, and this was not long ago, was some of the best that God's earth ever produced. But the Finns did not own the timber, and would never own it. So perhaps they were not free men after all. They were in someone else's hands almost as the saws and axes were in their own hands. The Finns were, as the axes were, tools to fell and without apology destroy a natural resource.

And for whom was this done—for the Finns? No more than for the axes. It was for the few owners. It does happen nevertheless that with the timber gone and the axes rusted and the enterprisers moved on into rubber and oil and war profits, the Finns and Scandinavians and Poles remain. And part of the story of their remaining is the story of the co-ops.

At first the Finns thought they could find out what to do, and could do it through political means. They were laborers, and became I.W.W. people and avid followers of Eugene V. Debs. The State and Labor could do whatever needed to be done. That at least for a while and among some Finns was the prevailing attitude. But what must first and last be said is that the Finns were then as now a wonderfully integral people, refusing to be torn apart, and also full of courage and of an intelligence applicable to the practical order. And though for a while some of them appeared leftist, the main body of them always remained patient and conservative.

In the thick of the woods the men established boardinghouses on a kind of union or co-op plan. But more significant was their perpetual reading and study and discussion. It was not just the random occurrence of talk and argument at work and around the fire in the evening. What was really the mark of our early Finnish life was cultural activity and folk spirit and a practical reading and study that looked to social reform. This lumber country was a wild land and into it at best led nothing but "corduroy roads, and there's lots of corduroy stuff still buried there." Houses or shacks were built of logs, and then, of all things, at every crossing of these bull-country roads went up an opera house! The Finns must have a place to meet and discuss and to act out the ideal life. "Drama has played a very important part in the cultural life of this region." In these opera houses built of logs the people studied together and read together and had their plays. A co-op leader of the second generation tells me that his father simply lived by these social events. Here men working together would learn how to get access to the bounty of the earth. "Temperance societies were the earliest development, but always it was the study-action approach." The ideal was by no means to work for another, no matter what the wage, but to be on the land, to own land and to be free. The people could reach this end only by study and action, and it was supposed from the first that this to be effective must be community study and community action. Here was and is the ideal of the Finns, to cut their way, no matter through what Northland snow and ice, to human freedom. They got up bands for their own music, and formed literary and reading clubs. "Miners and farmers, especially, read and read." Two things they were doing: serving as hewers of wood, and at the same time reading in little groups to find their way out of that servility. "They were reading books together, chapter by chapter."

What was it they read? Marx certainly, and the works of Eugene V. Debs. Then early works on co-operation, such as the principles of co-operation by their own V. S. Alanne. This in Finnish, and also in Finnish many books on history and economics and science.

"Study-action *was* the early program." This was for four or five or as many as ten years following 1910. Out of such a matrix grew most of the present co-ops in the region surrounding Superior and Duluth and sometimes scattered nearly three hundred miles from these cities. First the sympathy in the main was in the direction of socialism, and this feeling has not yet died, nor has it failed to go over into action, in Upper Michigan and Wisconsin and Minnesota. It went, for instance, with the Farmer-Laborites and then to a notable degree with the New Deal. And it was found after World War I, among some of the Finns, to be ready for communism. But not for long.

2

The earliest of the co-op societies were on their feet by 1910. These were stores or consumer co-ops, and they multiplied so that by 1917 they numbered about forty, "their stores dotting the clear-ings and the mining towns from Sault Ste. Marie westward nearly to the Red River Valley." No doubt the people were not getting much, though something real, into their own hands. They were insistent and "radical," but the chance for a truly human life was all that their radicalism demanded.

"The philosophy was this"—and I may say it remains "this"—"a strong faith and idealism, faith in the rightness of what they were doing. Even if it means sacrifice, we are building and we must stick."

But conviction and philosophy by themselves would not save people. It takes practical arts. For instance, "lack of bookkeeping gave rise to failures during the war, and therefore bookkeeping, that's all!" Other protection also was needed, such as auditing, legal advice, and educational direction. And a very practical step had soon to be taken. The stores bought where they could and as they could. How about some co-operative control over wholesales, as they already had over the retail stores? One control is good even without the other, but it is not good enough. Thus in 1917 the whole-sale was born in the city of Superior which is a convenient central point. At the outset this was regarded as only a kind of office to give advice, and of its patron societies, namely, the locals, only one was a paid-up member. Even at that, in its first timorous and formative year it had sales running to twenty-five thousand and it showed earnings of 1.07 per cent on sales. Before ten years its annual sales went over one million dollars, and now they are above five million, and the Central Cooperative Wholesale handles for its patron mem-bers hundreds of articles, all under the co-op label.

The wholesale is there to furnish goods and services to the local, and precisely those goods and services that cannot be got or can hardly be got by the local on its own. And yet it is on its own that the local must go. It is founded by itself with no more than advice, even if expert advice, from the wholesale. It must rule itself and finance itself and through its own neighborhood own itself, with no more than advice from the wholesale. That is to say, the co-ops grow like a tree or a plant from the bottom, and not in an authorita-tive, dictatorial way from the top. The local society is radically responsible for its own success or failure. It is exactly at this vital point that co-ops, in this region and everywhere, have something of the first importance to teach Americans. It is this: Things and services needed for the local people can for the most part be best provided and done by the local people. Security, yes; but the best and ultimately the only security is local and community security. Recent history as well as the history of all highly centralized governments proves that security provided by the State leads in a straight line to dictatorship by the State.

Hence the eminent wisdom of these and all other co-ops in their insistence on local control, local government, local ownership, local and neighborhood security.

Of course, the wholesale remains of decisive importance. It roasts coffee, a service we cannot afford to have in every small town. It offers all the time to every co-op an auditing service, to see that books are as they ought to be. This also is decisive and vital, since co-ops, like any business, can fail at this point through failure to take care of themselves, and not every little town can afford to maintain an auditor. Says a leader, "Because lack of bookkeeping gave rise to failures during the war, therefore bookkeeping is provided." So of legal advice.

Most crucial of all services is that in the line of education. Advice on setting up a co-op and on keeping it straight and balanced is of course educational. So is advice on new branches of the co-op or on types of co-ops new in the particular neighborhood. And for co-operators and everyone else nothing more salutary than a little education "on the evils of credit trading." As the co-operators put it, in installment buying "you pay and you pay." You pay, and then some! "Installment buying is slavery." That is the truth. But the people have to learn it, and for mankind it will be a bright day when the co-op or some other educational body will have taught the people this elemental lesson. From the outset, the wholesalers saw the irony in "Our Friend, Credit Business," and the wholesale at once declared for credit unions or people's banks "to help solve the credit problems of co-operators so that they do not need to use their stores as banks," that is, to be running into debt at the local store; also "to get them into the saving habit," and to provide funds on which the store itself could draw in case of need. To the 36 and even the 42 per cent interest legally taken on small loans in these states, no tribute! To Wall Street, directly or indirectly, no tribute! So, besides the credit unions, these people have set up in Superior their own bank. On credit buying, and we must surely note on the problem of fire insurance and life insurance, a ceaseless educational program is needed.

Advertising in its blatant and costly form is gone. But informational publicity is used, and is hardly separable from educational work. Consumers need an immediate practical learning, need to be "wised up." Otherwise the advertisers "sell" people. To protect themselves the co-operators in and around Superior have for some years used the co-op labeling system, and also the CO-OP label, this latter devised by the Superior wholesale and retained as its own registered trademark until given by it to all our American co-ops. Here and elsewhere the co-ops try to carry nothing now unless it is grade-labeled, and they usually manage not only to keep up to the levels as marked by federal standards but to keep several scores above these. The highest grade of goods wears a red label, the next a blue, and the lowest a green. In this way people can now know without inspection or argument exactly the grade of goods their money buys.

To keep the people in the locals informed, the wholesale at Superior and the locals have, as a separate organization, a busy printing press of their own.

Besides all this, the educational department has various schools to train people to be co-operators and also to train some few as local managers and assistants or even to be department heads at the wholesale. The schools meet often, for periods of two weeks or four or six weeks or longer, and aim to discipline young people in the needed practical arts, and also, and not last and least, in the principles and ideals of co-operation. Unless a local body knows what it is doing and why it is doing it, the chances are that it will go to pieces.

The problem is to keep the local co-op squared, as nearly as possible, with Rochdale orthodoxy. A particular creamery was set up with the notion that it was a genuine co-op. But though it once had over five thousand members, and sales mounting to three and a half million, its people had no intelligent interest and not more than 3 per cent of them attended the monthly meetings. Even when a dance was to follow the business session, they waited an hour and came merely to the dance. Sums were then spent on education, but they "never reawakened interest. It was set up too fast, without educational basis." Another co-op tried to proceed without paying patronage refunds, and another with disrespect for the principle of "one member, one vote." All these are matters for the educational men at the central to correct, if the local people are amenable.

3

"It has been a long development, and not always entirely peaceful." So says an older man who has seen all of it. Among the problems have been the following three: First, how to get non-Finnish people to join this supposedly Finnish body. Second, to keep the sons in the good co-operative footsteps of the fathers. And, third, how a few years ago to cure the co-ops of an undeniably Communist infection.

The Finns brought in the co-ops. To the Finns let the co-ops belong! That is the way the attitude in this region tends. As a matter of fact, people come honestly to feel that the co-ops exclude non-Finns. "For years," said a farmer, "I thought it was a Finnish store." For him the co-op was lost in the nationality. And a young Catholic working now in the shipyards said the same or even stronger to me. "Finnish, Communist, and co-op—they're all the same thing!" He himself knew the identification was unjust, but he said it was the usual popular way to take the three and that to his own mind when co-op was mentioned the other two recurred. A man in one of the villages said, "I think some are under a kind of impression that co-operators are kind of Red, somehow or other. Even Evelyn here, she says she doesn't know why, but she just does. Of course some of them around here were. So I suppose that's why." A dog with a bad name might as well be hanged! In Duluth a Catholic of distinction told me that next door to him lives a co-operator. And wonder of wonders: "Do you know, he's a good neighbor, and has a good family, and owns his home."

Beyond a doubt the all-Finnish color of the co-ops has also been a barrier. The older Finns organized the co-ops, and this they did for Finns, and they spoke only Finnish as they did it. Thus it hardly occurred to them that they were setting up a limit and hindrance to co-operative development.

That barrier is being broken down by the young Finns, those of the second and third generations. For some years the co-op schools have been conducted only in English. This at once encourages the young Finns to take over, and invites non-Finns to be a vital part of the co-op movement. The Finns are great democrats, in every sense: political, economic, and social; and the result is that the young Finns are in many cases excellent liaison officers between the co-ops and the non-Finns.

What, then, of the second-generation problem? A leader replies: "I think we have that licked, to a certain extent. Because we have had our youth camps and kiddie camps. A woman at Cloquet gives all her leisure gratis to show the children what co-operation means. And at Brule we have had a four-week camp; now three-week or two-week; and this teaches co-op sociology, and economics, and philosophy, and history. I believe that is about the best job we have done. I say that, because through it we have young people who are quite definitely interested in the implications of the co-op methods and movement. The school program has done it. Still, the older generation tells us on many occasions that we haven't the old spirit. Well, I am sure the young people are coming through. Many managers are young and are second generation. In some towns the manager and his wife are as if on a pilgrimage, co-ops are so important and vital to them. Take the case of Estowac over here. The manager was a young man within the draft age, but the draft board said they couldn't let him go: he was too valuable a man in the community. That means the co-op is accepted there and also in many places as a community builder. And where our older men give the responsibility to younger men and ask them to deliver, they do it. When you go out to the locals, you will find some co-op societies in the hands of the younger generation. As for the all-Finnish limit, they are taking that as a co-op problem to be solved."

The Communist nut had to be quickly cracked. Otherwise it would have disintegrated the whole work. It was in 1929 that the scare, and something more than a scare, arose. A Communist fever had beyond doubt affected some members for at least a dozen years before that date. Says a man who lived through "this Communist scourge": "1929, late in the year, when the panic started, heralding hard times, the Third International evidently gave the order, and Communists in this country gave orders to those on our board to get complete control, and as test demanded five thousand dollars, claiming that they had worked for years to build up the co-operative." Were any members really Communists? "Some were, that is true. Some high officials were Communists. Some I could name left the Communists and are good co-operators now."

But was the money to be openly given over? No, this would not do. Some subterfuge must be used, since the record must be shown on the books. "Well," said these Communists, "that's a matter of bookkeeping. Give it another name!"

The question was whether the Communists would or would not control the co-ops. "Fair and unfair, they lined things up" in preparation for the annual meeting in March of 1930. After a struggle of a year and a half the Communists lost and were ousted. But it was a war, and in no war can either side win. For if the genuine co-operators held their ground through thick and thin and in that sense may be said to have won the final decisive battle, they also lost. A dozen co-ops broke away, a dozen of the ninety that had been united in 1929, and a volume of trade was lost. Much worse was the bad feeling at least temporarily created. Hatred and conflict are not good co-op soil. Says one of my friends, "A lot of energy was spent," and the memory of that "scourge" is not sweet. "Energy and a lot of enmity." Another says, "It fanned enmity and suspicion." The Communist group published in Finnish a magazine called *Tyomies*, and to this day continues to publish it.

Nevertheless, the number of loyal co-ops kept growing. The radical bodies had little success, and one by one almost all of them have asked to return to the fold. "They are let come back if they show themselves loyal and also patronize the wholesale. But we do not receive them by a global decision or as a global movement. This Communist scourge made our work for the time much more difficult." The leaders know what they are talking about when they say, "The scars from that battle are still evident."

4

These several troubles belong to the past. The present sailing of the co-ops in all this area is comparatively smooth and prosperous. While I am visiting the co-op people in Superior, at their shops and offices and in their homes, a wet cold wind off the lake sweeps the wide streets of the city. As I wait in the rain one day for a bus, a ragged man tells me war is wrong because Scripture says we shall not kill and he says his brother is overseas with some kind of gunners' crew. "But he hates all this fighting. I'm sure surprised at him." Why so? "Because when he was home he was always into fights. Sure does seem strange, him not liking it." On the Sunday and in the same protracted rain, a big man who has his feet on the ground says his work has made him miss Mass. "But see, I carry this to protect me, and it always brings me luck." He wears a crucifix against the walls of his body. Another day the driver of a milk truck picks me up. It is at the shipyards he works, ten hours a day. "It is easy work, but particular." The sides of the ship are built piece by piece, so that if one section is bashed in, just that one hole need be repaired and the ship is saved. Extraordinarily particular work; it must be exact. If a bit of it is out of line, it must be knocked down and made right. "We have to fair it up." What does that mean? "True it up. You see, fair it up." The long hours on the farm and in the yards can be borne "because we are in debt."

As I leave town to study the locals, the co-op people in Superior continue their search for new ways to make such a man independent. What they look to, at least for the postwar era, is a complete terminal. This would help fisherman and farmer. "The fishermen do own some trucks now. They truck into Duluth, but then turn the fish over." They should have a processing co-op, a trucking co-op, and a marketing co-op. Then they would control, and their herring and trout would come to something, and no government would ever have to try to take over and to save these people.

So of the farmers on the shores of the lake. "The diversified approach would save them." This means cream, poultry, mink, potatoes, and berries as their products. "What we want is a marketing program and a quality program. The berry growers think of marketing through their own terminal this year. And we need a constant educational program. To get WPA relief some actually sold their cows. Think of that for shortsightedness! You just can't reverse a trend like that, once it's started. Pooling of farm machinery, trucks, and threshers—that's needed. Is science going to by-pass agriculture? Blight simply took the potato crop in 1942. The Agriculture Department says, 'Lack of spraying.' And it could be afforded. It would be simple; of course, not for one or two men, but through the co-ops. Any neighborhood could go as a co-op and buy a good sprayer and in no time do the work. The department has the science. But it's useless. They are still ignorant of what a local co-op can do.

"And that's the work of this educational office up here—bringing in new ideas. What good are the co-op stores, if the people have no income and cannot buy from them?"

HOW MINNESOTA CO-OPS GROW

1

At the town of Virginia in the heart of the Range, or iron country, we are having tonight a regional session. Almost, one might say, in the enemy's country. For iron, as the lumber before it, has not been owned by co-operators. Who, then, does own it? Not any of these Finns or Poles or Slavs whom we see in the streets, but some men who are mysterious, powerful, silent, and likely present on the Range not once in five years. Absentee landlords.

So much is true. But in the people's words and minds even this ghost of the personal is absent. It is The Company that owns and operates and ships, and makes the profit. That is the strange economy in every region of this sort. In a way several companies own our iron in this Range area. United States Steel, for one; or at least so people say. Then above this and above all others, the Oliver Mining Company. And who is Oliver? They say he was one of several sons, each given iron mines by the father, and this boy, eventually topping the others, was named Oliver. "A few independents, besides. But they don't amount to much. Pretty much monopoly-controlled."

Whoever owns, an army of men is now working in these mines, and every day we see moving toward the Twin Ports trainloads of rusty-colored iron ore, sixty, eighty, and a hundred cars making up a train, and one hundred and fifty thousand pounds to the car. By other men it is dumped into ships and steams off to the steel centers and is made up so as to serve man.

Today they are stripping with machinery, to get to the ore which is at various depths. Some is at the surface and on this they can use open-pit mining, and likewise on other ore down to thirty or forty feet. But they can also strip the ore even if it is down one hundred or two hundred feet. Where they are now stripping, the boulders roll down the earth-wall to the foot. Roads are built on terraces at several levels, and along each road new little trees, well dust-covered, are planted, to help hold the roads and walls. Alongside the pit are gray rocks and, at the end of May, grass and trees that are just showing green at the tips. The walls bared down into the mine are of many iron shades, purplish iron, and black and brick iron, and a coal gray-black iron. Two hundred feet below us the trucks crawl like iron-brown bugs toward the "pocket" where they dump their loads of ore. This is then brought on a revolving belt up the walls and out through a tunnel in the earth and loaded into cars on the surface.

At Virginia and Eveleth and all the towns the co-op men live by such work, and by a little trade, and on the land. Virginia has a Co-op Center that might be the pride of any town, but only the co-op people will enter it and not all of them because some feel that some co-operators have taken the social life of the co-ops as a religion. Beside the Center is the co-op store which is closely looked to and does a good business. And at the foot of it is the people's mortuary and funeral service, for here and in many places throughout the Midwest the people now have co-op undertakers and co-op burial. Nor is this at all strange if we believe in co-op weddings and co-op dances, that is to say, in the community and in human solidarity. The dead man still belongs to us and we to him, and we will give him a co-op funeral. And have not most cemeteries been co-op for many centuries?

This local burial co-op has been busy and has had great success. Today the body of an old woman lies here, a woman "born November 3, 1872, in Finland, and came to this country 41 years ago"; she is said to have suffered greatly and to have been like a saint. The stuff and make of her shroud give her the look of the Third Order. And here also is the body of a young man killed in the mines. "Arvid G. Pryatela, 33, of Hibbing was killed in a cave-in in the Agnew mine Monday, May 24, 1943. Pryatela was born in Elcor and had worked in the Hibbing mine for about one year. Details of the accident were not available."

To the surviving widow and two sons it makes a difference that burial arrangements are in charge of the co-op. The difference on the average, so we learn at the mortuary, is from two hundred to three hundred dollars. In this case the widow, no doubt with little insurance or property, would have nothing short of the costliest funeral, and the saving is said to be about three hundred and fifty dollars.

The Range Co-op Federation also makes insurance available to the people "at cost." Why should the people not have insurance, and since they foot the bill why should they pay more than cost for it? Why should Finns and Slavs and Swedes and Poles on the Iron Range in Minnesota either do without insurance or pay tribute to companies in New York and Hartford? These cities do not pay; it is the local people who pay. To them, then, should go the whole benefit. That ideal of "insurance at cost" is what the co-op tries to approach. Of course, the insurance is on cars and buildings and life. Lately the people in some local co-ops have chosen to try a new form of life insurance which already is a standing success in England. If a family that is a member of the local co-op store suffers a death, a stipulated percentage of its trade last year at the co-op goes automatically to the survivors. There is no "premium" or charge, first or last, from a family, since the co-op bears the cost. The amount depends on the amount of the family's trade at the co-op and on the percentage accepted by the co-op board. In the case of a father's death it is usually 40 per cent of the trade.[1] The following letter suggests what this insurance may well mean to poor people.

Tower, Minn.
April 26, 1943.

Gentlemen:

I am returning this receipt as you requested, and I do want to thank you so very much. Until the day your man came here with the blanks to fill in I didn't even realize the insurance existed. Truly this check is like a gift from Heaven, especially at this time with doctor bills, hospital bills, and the funeral expenses. He had been in such good health until three weeks before his death, so you can see what a shock his going was; one ray of lite I shall always remember is this kindness on your part.

Sincerely
Eleanor Strom.

[1] For details, write Cooperators' Life Insurance, 2233 University Ave., St. Paul, Minn.

The secretary for the co-op had added these notes:

age: 47
total purchases, $224.88
percentage, 40%
benefit, $89.95
member of Embarrass Cooperative
death due to Oprebral hemorrhage following operation
died April 13th 1943.

As I visit the secretary, a Finn comes to see about his car insurance. He is a strong, ironish man, his face wrinkled and the wrinkles themselves twisted. He holds his head on one side, his little watery blue eyes rolling around. But he jokes in Finnish and smiles, and to this day the confidence and firmness of this man does me good, there in his "Pay-day" overalls and a tie to his gray work-shirt and his hat pulled down far as if the wind were blowing a gale in the quiet, sunny office.

2

"Men can hardly come to meetings with A cards, and if there is any red tape about getting gas, the older element just won't come."

Perhaps that is why only vigorous people under fifty come to the regional session this evening at Virginia. They are office men for co-ops or managers or members of the home board, and like the fieldmen many of them think co-op and readily talk co-op. One justification for the new plan of co-op life insurance, they tell me, is that it "brings increasing co-operative loyalty." The main problem for this evening is how to find man-power in these times, and in the informal talk at the outset I hear a pale young man say, "They used to say you couldn't make a good co-operative employee unless you were a co-operator." I ask someone what good the credit union is to them, and he says, "After the store is founded, to help us lick the credit problem. Banks and installment buying—that's too costly." Another is saying, "Ya, ya. Mixed, like we got now. Some private business, and government, he help some, and co-ops."

To the session come about fifty persons, men and women, almost any of them dressed better than I am. Usually they are people strong and square in build, and I have a picture of twenty women only two of whom most of us would not call plump. One tall rough clean man is smiling. A lean black man thinks himself quite a talker. An overalled man merely looks in at the door. A red-faced man stands, the face creased a bit, face and hair and the whole top of him except the white and blue of his eyes reddened and bronzed, and the man himself with the look of a minister-prophet. The men mostly range along one wall, the women along another.

The discussion leader says that outlines have been sent in advance. "We are here to study some of the major problems that face us right now, and first of all the manpower shortage and the training of new men." They are to break up into groups of ten to allow discussion, but the Finnish-speaking body gets eighteen. "How would you train them? We have tried managers' schools and book-keepers' schools. But with industry and with boys overseas and in camp we are scraping the bottom of the available candidates."

Each group appoints chairman and secretary and gets to work, the Chair of our group in a kind of clipped accent reading the points for discussion.

Chair: "How best meet the manpower problem? The floor is open for discussion."

Member: "We haven't been able to do it. There—it seems there are two problems, manpower and training on the job. But since we have to train anyway, there's only one problem."

Member: "So far as this business of training goes, why not finance a man for the correspondence school?"

Member: "We have to take a man, all the training he's had is running the truck. It seems to me this correspondence course would be just the thing for him."

Member: "I believe if a man is interested and a co-operator, and has the chance to get his toes in, he'll work out all right. But if it is going away to school—we just can't do that, you know, now."

Chair: "Would we suggest that a man be given the course?"

Member: "Yes, if the directors think a man has the stuff. It's for them to judge. If they think he's worth using, he's worth teaching. And if a man is taught, he'll be an asset to the store. He'll do his work right."

Member: "These war plants put a man in school for a year, and pay him besides. Now we'll have to sacrifice."

A white-haired young man is nervous, his knees knocking and his fist to his chin as he says: "I move we go on record as favoring the correspondence course, with the federation paying all, or part if they don't see their way to pay all."

A deep-voiced woman says: "We haven't said anything about wages. That's why they go, only the ones that are drafted."

Member: "Good men are just as valuable now as ever. I think small stores may have to run in the red for the duration. We are cutting our own throats by trying to hold the wages down. Boards and directors have always considered that wages aren't so important. But today, what kind of spirit has a man toward his work when he knows someone else is getting twice as much?"

Member: "You can't hold workers by wages. We said to our manager, 'Is it wages you want?' And he said, 'No!' We were willing to pay him twenty-five per cent increase, and he wouldn't stay."

Woman member: "Our clerk wanted to leave. We raised the salary, and she said, 'It ain't the money question. I want to join the Wacs [Wex].' And she's a Wac today."

Member: "If they have the co-operative idea and really believe in it, they will stay with us."

Chair: "I-think-we-take-the-next-point." The language tends to be like that, each syllable equal to any other: "the-cheapest-book-keeping-there-iss; it's-been-first-a-buying-clupp."

But above all, ideas are kept straight, and when we have had coffee—Finns want coffee all day and all night—these calm, methodical, and civilized storebuilders and storekeepers bring together the results of their separate discussions. People must see things for themselves and know what they are doing; these are their stores and they must not only know how they are run, but must run them. The decisions, then, are two and are precise: A good manager can look after two or three stores and need not spend the whole day and every day in any one. Every co-op can afford to put someone through the correspondence course and get him in line to be a tiptop man.[2]

[2] The course contained in V. S. Alanne's *Administration of Cooperatives.* A course in twelve lessons, with questions and assignments.

3

At Floodwood by good luck we run into the leading local co-operators and hold an informal meeting. We are out of the iron area now and into cutover country where men are trying to clean up the wreckage left by the lumber kings and to make dairy and general farms. Dairy products are first, then chickens and potatoes and mink and some sticks from the next crop of timber. The land is far from poor, but it is too far north and all grain has to be bought, an almost intolerable overhead in the dairy business. A survey of over three hundred farms showed an annual income of from six hundred to eight hundred dollars. One-third of the farmers were forced to accept relief in the worst times. The poorest sold their cows in order to be eligible for relief. "What they should have been doing," says one of the Floodwood co-operators, "was cutting off the scrub timber and developing the land. In 'thirty-three you could get a great big cow for twelve dollars, and now you'll pay one-twenty-five for her. A ten-year-old sold the other day for one-ten, and she probably won't fetch more than one more calf. That's the way men were fooled: the relief was all going to be over in a moment."

Even during that period the sales in the Floodwood co-op store increased. The co-op creamery too had a steady growth. "It was a good time to build. The store went up for fourteen thousand, and we now have invested twice that much from the accumulated capital, and fifty thousand from the creamery."

We are sitting—and one might say uninvited—in a co-operator's house, and it is better to be indoors, for this county is divided, half co-op and half antico-op. The credit union came right along with the store. "The bank," says our host, "couldn't answer the purpose in the depression. Poor men needed little sums, and borrowing them at the bank is robbery. The biggest reason was that people needed financing at the co-op store. We couldn't extend credit here —it was against the principles; and we thought this was the answer, and it was. Ain't that true?" The question is asked of the former manager.

This silent man only says, "We stayed on a cash basis."

The credit union started with thirteen hundred dollars. Now it has six hundred members—quite a distributed ownership in a small bank. And it has sixty or seventy thousand in circulation.

The ex-manager says, "It was like home to come to Floodwood back. Made many friends here. And enemies. Well, it's natural; they are people." The store grew in spite of and against the most concerted opposition. The opposition is in the town, but has used or would have used the poorest farmers for its purposes. Yet at present eight hundred and fifty families are members of the store co-op. And at that, "the marketing side is more important here." It is the creamery that counts most, and with it, that is to say with the same membership, the people could begin to promote woodworking. "If we get individual [individualistic] business here, they'll do like they did with the pine." "That's true," says the head of Floodwood's schools. "And it'll have to be continued with conservation; in co-operation this anti-isolationist policy is something we've got to learn; we've still got elm and ash and poplar. One forest, and the best we'll ever see, was destroyed for profit. Everybody who has any stake at all in the community will benefit from co-op control. We have a lumber market, and we only need a mill and a depot for lumber."

Of course, these men and women, though excellent co-operators, cannot simply keep to the one topic, and I hear talk like this, running through the co-op talk: "Kuola, what is that port on the Red Sea? Well, that is where he is. Lanto had a card from him." Then I discover that he it was who designed the self-service at the co-op. They make enough maple syrup for their own use. It takes about twenty gallons of sap to make a gallon of syrup, and the earliest sap makes more syrup and boils down faster.

Says the farmer Kuola, "This feed proposition [for the cows] is going to be a tough one to crack. It might be better to get it all from the West: have a mill near Fargo somewhere and ship it all in here." This year the co-op is going to do some experimenting with Canadian peas, and with what I get as a "Laurentian type of rutabagas," also from Canada. And "if we're going to develop poultry raising, we've got to have a co-op hatchery."

The co-op creamery pays its patrons nearly half a million a year. One of its great tasks now is the production of powdered milk for overseas. This has to be denuded of cream, since with fat in it the powder would not keep. Then subjected to heat and pressure the skim milk reappears in its original color but with the appearance of ashes made from paper. Says a workman at the creamery, "How much is 26 times 200? Well, that is the pounds we do a day." It takes one hundred pounds of milk to make eight and a half pounds of powder. Five churnings are done a day, with (I believe) twelve hundred pounds of butter to a churning, and a million pounds in the year.

The co-operators have put up their own locker and quick-freezing plant. "Three hundred lockers taken now, and going like hot cakes. New demands every day." The lockers cost a family eight to ten dollars a year, with additional cost for killing and dressing and smoking meats. For example, the charge was $7.78 for killing and dressing a hog that dressed over three hundred pounds.

This is part of the story at Floodwood among farmers whose land is yet only in small part made and whose income is low. They are common men taking their economic life into their own control. The store is theirs, and the creamery and the locker plant, and a bank that is big enough to take care of minor needs at least and keep them from being gobbled up by loan people who in Minnesota are allowed up to 36 per cent on small loans. Burial services are available to them on the co-op plan at a neighboring town. The same is true of insurance; and the hatchery and the woodworking plant will in all likelihood be under the people's control. It is a blind man that does not see the need the neighborhood has, here and in many places, of such an interlocked body of co-operatives, or does not see what those do toward providing and protecting the physical basis of the people's life. And it can do and even here is probably beginning to do wonders in making communities human and livable. For it no longer leaves every man to go his own economic way with at best only the negative thought that he does not legally injure his neighbor. Quite the contrary, it gives men a chance to do in a real way what we are to do: "Thou shalt love thy neighbor as thyself." And think what in terms of man and in the human-divine terms of men following Christ, forty or fifty thousand completed Floodwoods, in our rural areas and in our Chicagos and New Yorks and Detroits, would do to make our people Christian, self-respecting, and free!

4

Starting on the way to the model co-op town of Cloquet and on toward those called Moose Lake and Kettle River, one reads history and current events in certain nonco-op signs. Twin Ports horse market: draft and logging horses. Men's choice: Royal Bohemian Beer. Goldfine's coal and feed. Zalk-Joseph Co.: everything in steel. Pittsburgh Coal Co., dock No. 7. Gospel Tabernacle. Phillips 66.

The town of Cloquet is co-op through and through. Its own people number just seven thousand, and its co-ops half that many member-families, which means that in and around the town about one-half the people, or fifteen thousand, belong in a direct way to the co-op community. Here they have nearly all forms of co-ops, such as co-op gas and oil and farm machinery, a co-op service station, a burial co-op, a main co-op store with three branches, a co-op electrification plant, co-op insurance (so someone assures me) through the Mutual Auto and the Mutual Fire, and a big membership in a co-op creamery at the next town.

Through it all has been the rugged old man John Mattila. He says, "I built this own house. Tooken nearly two years. Started 1919, dig basement. Built it all myself and thought it up-to-date then. We had eight our own," he says, "and we raise two grandchildren. Eino, Mike, John, Tyne, all marry, and Karl he in war, and Helen's man and three, no, four grandsons." On the table is the Bible in Finnish, and on the piano a copy of *Jesus Only Songs*.

"It was thirty-three years ago, about this time," says Mr. Mattila, "we think if we could better conditions a bit. Ah, we had an awful difficulty. The people were afraid, and the merchants all against it. But still we didn't stop. An' we didn't give no credit. No; no credit.

"You understan' me?

"I was on the board of directors, and it was the second year. We started about this time; it was 1910. Had to put up a building; we made kind of team like, two men in a team, and went around. It was all wolunteer and no compensation. The people start for nothing, first years all wolunteer.

"Well, we make stronger and got a little more people. Then we make a big yump. It was 1921 or '22, and there was labor trouble and a paper mill strike. The man we hire him, he went around, especially on Monday and Tuesday when he wasn't busy in the store. Everybody know him and have faith on him, and he collect three thousand dollars. The worst year we had was in 1921. I didn't put that down and it's quite a while, too. This last depression we never feeled it here. It was going ahead and expanding and getting more capital. This building here, it was built after the big fire. This here, No. 2, it's a big building.

"I don't know what I done with my last month's report. Ah, ya, they keep me on the board yet, and on the Trico board. They think I have nothing to do. I think about a thousand of our cooperators are scattered all over the world; some gone to the war. That make a difference, the war. Some departments—hardware—it's down; and some is increased yet."

In the food stores the sales for the one month of April, 1943, ran well above one hundred thousand.

"I was a lumberyack. Most was lumberyacks. Ten dollar shares. The fire gave us a setback. We didn't have enough insurance to cover it, and after it they said they were only worth thirty-five cents. More than ten now; I think it's twenty-nine dollars."

We ask him whether he is free to go with us to visit a farmer. "Well," he says, "I can't see that nothing yust holds me back. I'll go. Maybe the two of us together could remember a little. Drove twenty-five thousand miles in a car, me and my wife, but not since 1936."

He and farmer Tikkanen go on with the story. Cash it had to be, says the farmer. "There was not thirty days, sixty days, ninety days: they had to be paid."

But it was hard to build again after the fire. These two men went around "at twelve night, and called a meeting of the directors, and we gave all the money what we had, to pay the wholesale."

The farmer sees me look toward his barns. "Thirty-three cows," he says, "one thousand chickens, three hundred pullets, and lots of young stock." He and his wife and a daughter milk the cows by hand. "That's her, Dorothy," he says as she appears mopping up the porch in order to get a look at the strangers. "Her husband's in Ireland and might be home any day. Did you see old Kojo?"

he says to Mattila. "He's in six crooks already. He's this way, and like this!"

"These English-speaking people," says Mattila, "they're afraid, they're afraid. They start no co'peratif."

Tikkanen says, "There was no drop waste. We never paid too much, only what was cost merchandize, and how much is the dividement I couldn't say. I was working in the paper mill, and I had to buy one window 24 by 26, and just think of that! $2.25 the co-operative price, and $3.50 the private company! And we were getting a profit of gross profit two and one half per cent. If we didn't have no co-operative, I think it would be different prices in Cloquet."

As we go home, we meet a co-op truck. "Six delivery trucks," says John Mattila, "small and up to eight ton, and one what you call a pickup. Here is our yunkyard. They bring scrap and rubber and throw it in here. We play ball with them."

Then as I depart he has advice and blessings for me. He is angular like a burr oak growing on the point of the hill, solid and not rotting away. His words are: "If you want to build something good, go slow and make yourself sure. Well, good-bye and good luck, and God bless you!"

5

"Ah, ya," says John Mattila as I leave. "You should visit Mrs. Wilson and Mrs. Tuominen. They teach the kids co-operation from the diapers up."

Everybody here is into the co-ops, Jews and Catholics with the Lutherans and naturalists. Mrs. Dan Jones is enthusiastic and talkative. "If people would go to the co-ops and throw personalities out! I was asked to go to the annual: they wanted someone neutral—as if I could be that! Some said the Finns were the whole movement. They're not; any more than Father Robert is the Catholic Church. I know myself how it has helped here. The profit system—we're taught that in school. They'll sell you anything, the capitalistic system, on time, and get you in bad. 'It's only five dollars a month, or maybe ten cents a day.' The co-operative system, they don't try to sell you anything, but just what you want, and as far. I have a friend. I worked on her gradually for three years till they actually see they are in a better system. A woman compared prices and found the co-op store more reasonable, but her mother always traded at the other store. Another man and woman, they always were carried, and didn't like to change over, although they paid up."

Mrs. Isenberg, a big strong woman, busy in her garden, only looks up as she says, "It's the sanest approach to business. I don't know how far it will go."

RISING OUT OF THE ASHES

1

WHEN it is clear between the long rains of this spring, the lovely blue sky of Minnesota seems light years away. Then white clouds appear, and rain pours again to wash trees and grass that already are as clean as a Swede's face.

Today we are going to visit a grocery store at Moose Lake among the Larsons and Olsons and Andersons. But it is not merely a store among these Swedes, but run by them and entirely for them. For "the Swedes are good co-operators." That fact and formula are known to co-operators the world over. The Swedes in Sweden can co-operate. There the co-ops are among and by and for farmers, of course, as for a long time the co-ops in our country tended exclusively to be; but the co-ops in Sweden are as if prorated throughout the whole population, and professional men keep up co-ops step by step with farmers and laborers. In this country, too, the Swedes know how to co-operate, and when we find a co-op managed by an alert Swede we are sure that this unit can hardly fail. On the other hand, it is granted that many of the Swedish co-operators in this country lack something of the co-op spirit, and are less alive to what co-operation can do to build or rebuild a community and to what co-operation can do toward building the national order.

2

The grocery store is a quietly busy co-op, around the corner from the main street and up a slight slope with rain falling on it this second day of June. Across the street are Gambles Stores and also Lumby's Appliances and Furniture. At its back and down two steps is a lean-to that serves as the co-op hardware, and beyond a muddy alley littered with broken boxes is the back of a drugstore where everything is sold except cars and stoves and potatoes, and alongside this is the post office and in sight is the station where trains stop every day, and not far off the co-op creamery.

The co-op store is busy even on a rainy day in midweek. Last year it did a business of one hundred and twenty thousand. This sum may seem big for a country store, but the sales at any store with life in it are incredible to the layman, and in the local store, which includes meat and light hardware such as knives and saws and cream cans, the turnover ran to about four hundred dollars a day. Its earnings, after allowing for wages, taxes, rent, repairs and depreciation, came to eight thousand and something or nearly 7 per cent of the sales, and in the ordinary store this amount would go to the chain, the "businessman" or "the house," but in the co-op it returns in some form to the patrons. The net earnings here, which, according to a survey made by the U. S. Bureau of Labor Statistics, are above normal for co-op stores, are not up to the very best co-op practice. The net earnings for 1942 were 1 per cent above those for 1941, and the total sales showed a pickup of over 35 per cent. I need not say that even in wartimes this gain is extraordinary for stores of any type.

The chain store, of course, is dull and mechanical and de-humanized in large part. But this co-op store need not be, and is not. It is a small-town store where people meet their neighbors and friends, and it is their store, and all of them can be more or less at home together in it. This latter fact alone, economies being equal, would justify the co-op.

Here they come, then, people talking and visiting and at home. A narrow-bodied black man is taking a second look at the hat he'd like to wear. "This," says the salesgirl, "is $1.65." Now why this poor man, no doubt a farmer, should think of a new hat is not clear to me. He has a good gray-green hat on his head, and to his back an all-leather hunting jacket, and on his legs brickish pants. I cannot think he is less than well dressed. He pulls at the hat as he looks into the glass, and smiles a little, surely more within him-self than at his appearance in the new hat. Only experimenting, that is all he is doing. He says the hat is too small; he throws it down, picks up his parcels of meat and vegetables, steps over the self-service rail almost as if he hurdled it, and at one stride this Gundar Hagg is out in the street and the rain.

A big blond girl of twenty with a pink bow on her head is buying all-white anklets at 35 cents. "I guess I better take 10½'s. But my feet don't look that big." She will take a dress, too, at $2.35. But it is hard to fit her. Each time she goes behind the curtain with the dress looking new and folded on her hand and her wrist, and then reappears with it hanging limp from her fingers. "No, this won't do."

The girls do not try to sell the dress to her or the gray-green hat to the man. Nobody is selling anybody anything. Nobody running after anybody to unload goods on him. Nobody stealing a money-look at another's eye to see whether "ten cents off" or "terms" will sell what the other only more or less wants. No pressure. The reason is that this is the people's store, and it is up to each person to buy just what he wants. As Mrs. Dan Jones of Cloquet says, "Just what you want and as far." Not a soul tripping our Gundar Hagg as he hurdles the rail. No suave girl merely hired to be nice and to make sales and to be sure, for the sake of her own salary, that she waylays the big blonde. No bonus for pressure and sales.

A farmer is scraping change into an old purse, and talking to his neighbors as he does so. Says he, "And then a dollar on top."

In general the people seem not to be run down, out of cash, or poorly clothed. But a ragged man and woman, almost the sidewalk apart, go past in the rain, he with a slightly blinded, stumbling look, she fat and baggy. The rain is coming in sheets now, and the lilacs are halfway out. In the window, no doubt left from last season and to stay till the rains are past, are men's and women's straw hats.

Clop! Clop! goes the butcher's ax. "Do you know," says the grocer to him, "that eggs went up two cents?"

There is a great air of freedom and yet of order about the store. People are not watched as they shop around or as they arrive at the cashier's desk. For a country town, this is a big store, with the main part lighted today to make up for the lack of sun. Men wander into the hardware whether or not the clerk is present. Almost all the things sold are brought from afar: the hats and sweaters and children's dresses and garden seeds; and the meat, if possibly raised here, is shipped away to the Twin Cities to be processed and shipped back; the journey, and then the special merits of a great center, put quality into meat and something of an overhead on it. As an Iowa farmer, surrounded by corn and cattle and hogs, lately said to me, "We can't get good meat here." Where, then, can you get it? Only the tomato and cabbage plants are raised in the neighborhood.

A little pocket of men surrounds the cashier or the butcher and keeps up a barrage of jokes and mild laughter. It seems to me a jollier crowd than I ever saw in a Finnish store, with more freedom but not so sure or firm an order.

The store is advertised, that is to say, the sense of going co-op and trading co-op is recommended. But the goods are not advertised. They are merely marked, a tag giving people the needed information. On the bulletin board are chalked up notices of items not sold here but found now in the neighborhood. For strawberries see John E. Johnson, for little pigs see Mrs. Matureski, R.R. #4, for team and harness see Mrs. Lejeski.

A man as wet as the street says, "I planted between the raindrops. But, by gosh, I believe I shouldn't have planted at all."

A boy arrives trailing a river of rain. Says a wry fellow, "What you should get, Axel, is boots that'd go up around your neck."

So they carry on. Farmer is almost as if trying to sell a coat to farmer. Says he, "They're swell coats, real good."

"How you, Jake?" is the only response he gets.

"Not bad," says he, a plump front on him. "Weather can't please ever'body. So I pick this as my kind of day. No, I wouldn't do it," he is soon saying to a clerk. "You can't please us all, and a limited supply is all you can put in, in a store like this. . . . It's luck. But you can't stay in business on luck. *And* you don't make ends meet." It is the plumped-out Jake who is giving these pieces of advice and wisdom, a cigar in his teeth now, his hands buried in his overalls. Doubtless he is a director of the store.

3

It is only a few miles to Kettle River, a town purely Finnish and purely co-op. Here an official at the co-op store has its record and standing by rote. It had some sort of start in 1913, but was incorporated only on October 22, 1922. Its authorized capital now stands at forty thousand, the par value of shares at five dollars. Its members are four hundred and fifty-seven, and its employees six persons. The sales for 1942, in groceries, meat, feeds, and gas, went to one hundred and forty-six thousand. Last year its earnings went up to nine thousand five hundred, and that was about 6.5 per cent of the sales. That was the amount which, minus a safe margin left for reserve, went directly to the patrons, who on the average got a dividend of about twenty dollars a family. The operating expenses were 8.75 per cent, and—as at Moose Lake—the increase in sales over 1941 was incredible; it was 21.66 per cent.

How much was charged against "receivables" in that same year? How much was lost in bad debts? None, I am told point-blank. "No receivables. All-on-cash."

That is perfection in one of the elemental Rochdale principles. Goods are sold for cash. That is Rochdale law. The common causes of failure in stores are two: incompetent management and selling on a promise. And whenever we are in Finnish territory we know that these, as well as the minor causes of lapses, are reduced to a minimum. Said a visitor to this co-op town of Kettle River, "They do lots here with little. We don't do so good with lots."

"While I think of it," says man to man in the store, "oats is climbing."

It is time for coffee, and with a break between rains we go across the street to the one place where it can be got. This is a café and accordingly nonco-op, and the fat little maid has the tables worn away with shining.

"Split Rock is here," says one of the men with a finger on the table. "That's all Polish and Catholic." But they have no co-op, do they? "Oh, sure. Oh, no, they have none at Split Rock. But in the Kettle River co-op creamery, they're all into it; they gave a good response, very good right off the bat. And here's Kettle River. See! And Moose Lake is here. That makes a triangle, all close together, Polish, Finn, and Swede." His point is that any and all persons and peoples can co-operate. But the store, that's different; they have a private man, "their own, they patronize at Split Rock."

Kettle River comes perhaps as near as any town we yet have in America to being the complete co-op town. Besides the store with meats and shoes and light hardware, and the immense creamery, we have at this town a co-op gas station, a garage, and the C-A-P Co-op Oil Association. This last, its letters standing for three counties, "pioneered in trucking oil." It looks to quality all the time, and "is controlled through consumer ownership." The people also have an REA co-op, a rural electrification unit bringing electricity to the town and to the farmers through a local co-op and at a rate that laughs the private companies out of business.

"Pretty near all business of all kinds is done through the co-ops; probably in the nineties: ninety-some per cent of the total." That leaves not much in private hands. "One private store here, a small one, and the taverns are owned private. The rest in this place is co-op."

The REA is a regional distributor, the local co-ops in five counties holding the shares. For labor and maintenance the cost is relatively nothing, but the cost of construction and of equipment is immense. For instance, among its assets are listed "Poles, Towers and Fixtures: $342,383.83" and among the liabilities "Special Construction Obligation: $630,722.82."

They have also for the five counties a special trucking co-op, a kind of union having its directors and annual report. In the co-op library I notice these volumes: *The Robber Barons*, by Josephson, donated by J. Vorhees in March, 1934; *Franklin D. Roosevelt*, by Ludwig; *The Black Tanker*, by Pease; *ABC of Cooperatives*, by Richardson; *Mein Kampf*; *White Fang*, by London; *Growth of the Soil*, by Hamsun. But I would be far from suggesting that the co-op or other library in this or ordinarily in any of our towns is much worn with use.

The co-op garage has lately had its ups and downs. It is new, but with the rationing and "the loss of our best mechanics" it closed during the winter. In the spring it had, one way or another, to be opened to service the farms.

4

Out we go now and across town to the creamery. Here we meet a stream of persons, the dairymen being obliged, rain or shine, to proceed with their work. Sometimes we have three or four, sometimes eight or ten men and women telling in a sort of connected way the story of co-ops in Kettle River. A man comes by and stops a moment in the crowd like a bramble catching along the bank and then loosing itself and going on with the current.

"We were in the timber, lumberyacks," the men say. "All of us at first, and we make ties and everything like that." There was only one store, "and in spring we were told we were in red: we were in debt from the private store."

To escape this hardship and possible injustice, the families started a buying club, and it promised to succeed, with the members taking turns at management. But it is said that the merchants in the area were soon in collusion and effectively stopped purchases from any convenient wholesale. "That's no legitimate procedure," said they: it is a store without a store building, and business without a capital investment.

"That's where the C.C.W. [the wholesale at Superior] came in," says one of the men. "We said we would start business, ourselves. We had only eighteen dollars, and we phoned C.C.W., and heard they'd ask a commission, 10 per cent or something. That's where they started accumulating a little themselves, a little bit capital." Near by was a co-op creamery, "likely a real co-op; but it went under. Right after the fire that co-op was in the red through bad management and offering credit on feed."

"Ya," another confirms the record. "They elected a local manager; because he was from a good Christian family. But he didn't know the business—no experience; and it went into the hands of receivers."

They needed the expert help of the wholesale. So they called on CCW for aid, and on advice they started bookkeeping and auditing. A man came from the wholesale and everything got a going-over. Still, it may not be said that to date they had got far, and the local merchants, with things under control, are said to have raised prices; for example, flour jumped a dollar a sack.

"That made the people so determined," says a Finn, "we collected three thousand and paid fifty cents on the dollar. We had been in debt, and from that we went to five thousand in black, in three years." This is a square-built man, his muscles free and loose, his hair thin and the wine color so common with his people. He stands there, and quite a weight could rest on his shoulders, and on his head for that matter, so firm and so settled is he in mind as well as in body.

The Kettle River people next started talking about a creamery.

Every man was asking his neighbor, "Why not one of our own?" Says the strong man, "Moose Lake said they'd take the cream of the farmers." That did not suit, and the people subscribed up to three thousand dollars. "When we started in, we actually had two thousand in cold cash, but the people co-operated and gave free labor."

"Boosted prices on cream six, seven points," says a Pole, forgetting his counters. "We thought we'd ship to New York on the open market, and not through Land o'Lakes. There we learn somet'ing."

As though he would explain the history of cream, a man says, "We already had a co-operative telephone association."

Then followed the oil association and the gas station: "Right by the creamery, for the farmers when they'd come in," and the service station, and garage with the Chevrolet agency, and the REA. This last came through the efforts of one man, a Finn. He'd say, "Why couldn't we have electricity?" They got it with over five hundred miles of line, and it now serves about twelve hundred farmers.

"The Finnish people," says one, "have that, like: they start from a small square," cupping rather than squaring his hands, "and build. We paid our bills every year." Then with the bills paid, he goes on like a good dairyman, and says, "Sixteen cents for butter fat, that's the lowest we ever paid; in 1933. Some was paying only twelve cents. We have our own trucking association. And the men and women belong to the Dairy Workers' Union, No. 32. Robert Roney of Duluth was the organizer of the drivers; now he's refrigeration man for Arrowhead Creamery."

The best type of co-operator, one of the men says, is the man who believes in criticism: "not kicking, but constructive." For a while this man was with co-ops in Saskatchewan and he often argued on co-ops with an Englishman. "Him and I would fight like a cat and a dog."

The farms here support dairy herds, eight, ten, and fifteen cows. "And some of them have twenty or thirty head of cattle. But there's no three hundred and twenty acre farms, or anything like that."

The co-op movement seems to build up "other things. Like at Besco's Corner, they have bands, and national cooking honors, and 4-H clubs and Future Farmers of America." Everywhere they "talk about dividends and the like, and even those that are opposed to co-operation, get the benefits of it." One man knows about "that Nova Scotia movement, you know. Father Tompkins wouldn't tell them what to do, and they got busy and built a road, and they got thirty-five dollars for lobsters, for what they used to get seven dollars. And the credit union supported a sick man . . . the sense of feeling that everything was going good. I think that was the most sensible piece of helping each other I ever heard."

They talk about a town in Wisconsin where it appears things have not gone well. This is a company town, "run by one lumber company, and still cutting virgin timber."

"They have a company hotel," says one, and the others add their parts: "And a company hospital." "And company houses." "And a company store, and the profit for 1942, on the books, on the financial statement, was twenty-eight thousand!"

"And, naturally," I say, "they dominate the schools, the government, and the churches." This is so evident that the men only grunt at it.

5

What is "the fire" that recurs so often in the story of places like Cloquet and Kettle River? It occurred in 1918, a forest fire, and over an area of several counties it destroyed towns and farm dwellings, and despite every effort from within and without, it killed four hundred people.

Co-ops had started in many places among Finns and Swedes and mixed populations before that date. Along with everything else, the co-ops were wiped out. The railroads and eventually the government then operating them were charged with the fire, and at last the government made some kind of settlement with the people. But new and badly needed co-ops and revived old ones were planned before the smoke died down.

A man who had arrived from the old country in 1878 barely escaped with his hide and that of his family and neighbors. The fire came on them, and came faster than they could go. Running with no possessions but the rags on their backs, they leaped into a little lake. Even this would scarcely save them, and they had to keep their wet clothes over their heads to avoid being scorched to death.

This man had pioneered, and now everything was gone. The story is that the next morning a man who had made easy money in liquor said to him, "What in the world will we do now?"

The nude pioneer said, "The one thing we can do: start over again." The people, brought to a financial nothing, found reserves of courage and faith, and were soon going together stronger than before on the co-op road. One of their greatest co-op builders has been that old pioneer.

With the old man as he talks to or stays with us are his daughter, a heavy, square, dark woman always jolly and smiling, and her girl Mary Adelaine who will be five next Wednesday. The little one in blue jumpers is an actress. Her ice-cream cone is soon gone, and a farmer asks what has become of it. She only shows her empty hand and says, "All gone." But where is it gone? She looks overinnocent and says she doesn't know. Someone says part of it remains on her chin, and she does not act as she reaches far out to wipe the chin with her tongue. Of course, in this town, she is a co-operator, and a conscious one. Asked where she got her new red shoes, she says, "At the co-op."

Five

PEOPLE STARTING A STORE

1

BETWEEN apathy and ignorance and our habitual Occidental drive for profits, many of us are in attitude unprepared for co-operation. We shall have to learn what it is and what it can do, and also to discover in ourselves the really native demand not only to be loved but to love and to give ourselves in love to our neighbors. In that way a really human economy can be built, and also a community. That way, too, possibly lie health and security and stability and peace at home and abroad. But before we come, in the next chapter, to a tentative statement of the many goods available through the co-ops, we wish to see a few model co-operators, persons who have found it more blessed to give and to be one with the neighbors than to get and to take.

On the way to see the co-ops at Alberta Lea and the neighboring town of Twin Lakes (accent sharply on the "Twin"), we meet an old woman, round and short and jolly. Scot-born she is, and strawberry red.

"Lusten!" she says, "an' I'll tull you m'story. I had been bourne with a desire to hullp other people. And consequently I was always poor. I was just married, at twunty-two. And a young friend, she was just married too. She said one day, 'Do you see that van coming?' and I said, 'Do you thunk it's worth while to follow?' and she said, 'Yus, and I will go.'

"We went, and I can't give it for truth, but I think it was a quarterly meeting we went to. I went to this meeting, and I was certainly interested to hear: there was a dividend! That was in Scotland, and I wondered because I thought it was charity. I come home and said to Dad, 'Oh, I've found something and I thunk I'll like it. They call it cu-operation, and I thunk I'll join it.'

"I was just about a year married or so. The women's guild was going, and I joined. There was a man whose name was a household

47

word, Andrew Young, and it made me shudder: he was a Socialist, and I a Catholic! But he inaugurated classes for women. I went and admired him, oh, I can't tell you how much, but always wanted to tell him not to be a Socialist. But I'll never forget the words that Socialist man said: it was just my sentiments about people and about the poor. And I told the hubby.

" 'You just be careful of those fellows,' he said.

"At the guild we were always discussing co-operation *and* socialism, and I was afraid. But that's the way I learned co-operation, by study and discussing all about it. Now this is what it meant and still means to me. First, it was something I could not do, myself. Second, it was a body of men and women, together, and not regarding man's religion or race. Third, it was the closest I ever saw to carrying out the second commandment, 'Thou shalt love thy neighbor.' "

2

The next co-operator we met also got his lessons by hard knocks. He is the young undertaker in a town along the way, and his wife learned step by step with him. He was born a co-operator, if we may say that of a human being at all. And I think we may say it. For man is born good and not "corrupted," born with a tendency toward good and toward all good. The trouble is that he has not the strength and the light to go fully and effectively with that native bent, and himself weak and with a thousand bad traditions and object lessons around him he is soon growing into a man that is as selfish as sin.

Now, the co-operator I mention did not develop in that bad way, nor did his wife. But in their work they did not yet see how to work for the total good of the community.

He needed a job as undertaker, and the new burial co-op at one of the towns needed a man. Here was the chance for each to "profit"; that is to say, for each in the name of God to serve and to be served. No gouging of man by man, but each looking to the good of the community.

Till he was hired by the co-operators to run their establishment, this man knew only the word "co-operation." The thing as it worked out was a revelation to him. Every man is born to love man and with a tendency toward this great, central human good, and thus toward co-operation with man. But here was a man who above most was capable of love, and yet was a grown man before he saw how he could offer his professional services in love for others. And that is to say that a well-developed capitalistic system, schooled into our bones, will hardly allow us to be Christians at our work. As an old priest-co-operator said to me, "I am sick and tired of seeing men go through life half killing themselves for money and half robbing others, and then at the end by five minutes of confession and sorrow trying to square it up."

This undertaker and his wife are Protestant and deeply religious and for that reason grateful to have the chance to go co-op. They do not look for sumptuous funerals, but have contracted to serve as undertaker for fifty dollars a funeral.

The town and countryside in that region have not simply gone with these people. Old interests believe in profit and not in man. Co-operation is maligned, said to be bad, illegal, and officially a nuisance. Local people made it "as hot as they could" for the new co-op. They sued it and wanted it declared unfit for the town. It is said, too, though possibly as a joke, that in the state an argument proposed against burial co-ops was that in any co-op the members must be capable of benefiting, and the dead can get no refunds. And at one town I ran into a rock wall of opposition, and was even run into it by a scalawag of a seasoned co-operator. This good man for the fun of it took me to the next town to meet "a great co-operator." What I met was a mayor who had told his people that not one of them would be buried via the co-op. But the people this time got out of hand. As one of them said, "He nearly went beyond his power."

3

At a bus station on our way to Twin Lakes we see people huddled against the wall. For, though it is June, they are windswept as on a deck at sea. Two girls are seeking shelter along a brick wall, so that their blond curls won't be blown out straight. We are in Norwegian-Danish-Irish country, and the girls' faces are between clabber-white and pink and their eyes a baby blue. The face of an unshaved gray man has only a couple of wrinkles, but these are so deep that his face looks cut and scarred. A boy of thirteen is reading a book, his hair dark red and clipped short, his face scaly and freckled. A woman with white in her black hair says something to him; the flesh of his cheeks runs up to the whitish eyes and his mouth puckers, but he keeps his gaze on the book.

A few of us go to Twin Lakes today to help set up a co-op store. I ask an Irishman how big the town is. "You see the percentage of it," he says. "I don't know what they call it for population."

We must make an inventory of everything, for the co-operators are in the act of taking over an old store. Of the following we must render an account and mark down how many units of each and how much per unit: Crackin' good crackers. World's Fair toothpicks. Hollywood spaghetti. Standby mustard: of this there are seven glasses, twenty cents a glass. Campbell's tomato juice. Betsy Ross—it's better bread. Holsum potato (a kind of bread?).

Then some of the items, though it is not clear what they are, have lively ads. "Drink a bite to eat—Dr. Pepper good for life— at 10—2 & 4." "Folks, now they're richer in Vitamin B, the energy vitamin. Kate Smith."

Perhaps the articles are as many as two hundred in kind. They are five or six, a dozen, twenty or thirty in a pack. No wonder we are long into the night at them, and are tired looking up and taking down, and are weary of our exacting little marks. Often, besides, the matter confuses most of us. "Seven large," someone is saying. "Let's see: there's a difference here." That means that the one really competent person we have, the fieldman from the Midland Co-op in the Twin Cities, must give up what he is at and come to handle this problem.

"Three-pound jar. What would you say this jar is, here, by itself? Hardly a pound?"

All the workers are co-op, all the time is volunteer and no-pay, and no one expects coffee or a cigarette for his trouble. It is not business. It is co-op. It is the people's store, and it won't hurt them to find out from the inside and by way of donated labor what is in it. At any rate, that is what they do, and they certainly enjoy doing it. Ruby Jensen is here, and Al, too, a big Dane, but after working in the corn all day he is not much help. Tony Maloney is up and down and at last brings a whole shelf of things down on himself.

Marge Ryan is important, because she is treasurer of the new co-op. A man unloads his wife at the door and says, "I'll be back and help when the chores is done."

The talk is quiet, firm, and open to everyone. "We should 'ave got some, maybe."

"Oh, that'll go quite a ways. . . . Let's see now, I didn't get the suckers. . . . I've got that written down somewhere here, for the kerosene."

"Three dozen root beer barrels. . . . six times four is twenty-four pounds of lard; and eleven cottage cheese. Did you mark that down?"

"Yes, but how many ration points? . . . Betty go to the show tonight?"

"Um-hum." The mother who answers in this positive way is as busy as any. She stands with one knee against an old chair which she intermittently rocks, and in her hand is a notebook. "Isn't that the berries!" she says. "I know I had those bills." In a moment she is asking, "Did you say we have to count these points?"

By eleven the inventory is fairly well completed, and newspapers are tacked up to blind the windows. Aren't we going to paint, at least the front? No, we can't, now.

A woman stops with jars of something in her hands and gestures with both the jars and the hands. "What's he think we been doin'? Plowin' it under?"

"Ya," says the reader, never looking up from the paper. "An' it says: 'The wheat crop was indicated at,' let's see, this is millions: '730,524,000 bushels, or 26 per cent less than last year's crop.'"

People are running and are up and down with things, but Jensen says, "Wonder how they figure it out so close?"

Late in the day we touch up the store with ads for co-ops. One bold ad says, "Protect and build Democracy through a Co-op." Another, used in many co-op centers, tells an important fact about the neighborhood and co-ops: "Neighbors built America. Today Neighbors are building Co-ops." "Quantity buying is out! But you can buy quality. Buy co-op!" Then a sign tells us of co-op flour. What it says is, "Co-op Flour. It's tasty." Isn't this a case of an ad not for co-ops, but for goods? Not exactly. For between the first two words are the vital little words, "red label," and these, on a co-op product, mean the highest quality. And just at this moment when in our national life the general producers and distributors have won against the consumer and no longer have to tell the quality or lack of quality in their goods, the co-operators have won a much greater victory. For the co-ops have managed to keep to labels that tell the quality of goods.

While the co-operators are setting up the store, some people in the village and round about it are friendly toward it, some indifferent, and a few hostile. Boys are trying to peek in at the corners of the paper-covered windows. But I do not think they want to jeer at us, as the people in Toad Lane are said to have jeered, and surely were on all ordinary standards justified, when in 1844 the twenty-eight pioneers opened the co-op store at Rochdale in England. What could these people of a century ago do? They hadn't a thing to recommend them. But these men, after all, did succeed. The main thing they did was to find the formula for co-op success, the now famed Rochdale principles. At Twin Lakes they will learn to follow those principles, or they will fail. What has given them heart are the following three matters: They have studied and now know what has been done at Rochdale and in many places. Right in their neighborhood, at the town of Emmons, they have a consumers' co-op society. A few years ago this was on the rocks, but by better management and by going down the Rochdale lane they now do an annual business of one hundred thousand in groceries and chicken feed and cold meats and women's dresses. Most of all, in studying so as to see their way and in taking over the store, the people at Twin Lakes have had the fun and joy that come with finding and reawaking the spirit of the neighborhood. And if some continue to stand off or to sniff, or are afraid to say "yes" or "no" on any new project, the co-operators may bypass these, and to make the progress they deserve they must be patient and wait for those who are slowly converted.

Of course, I do not pretend that the co-op at Twin Lakes was made when the door was opened that Friday morning in June, but only to suggest some of the plebeian and humble steps that co-op people have to take in getting started at all. They have had to study, and in fact have spent months in study; presumably they are studying and will have to keep studying. To say nothing of this budding co-op, any big old-timer has to be vigilant. If not, it is soon badly managed and is going to the bowwows. It neglects Rochdale law and pays the penalty. It becomes sectarian and is a store only for Catholics, or Norwegians, or farmers. It begins to abandon the principle of "one member, one vote," and inevitably passes into autocratic, monopolistic control.

What it came to do is lost. What it came to do—to be man's, to belong to everyone, to be by and of and totally for the community. To know no Jew or Gentile, no black or white.

For if a co-op is born for anything, it is born for democracy, for the whole body of local people, to provide plenty—and this can be done from the resources of that community; and also to give the people a chance, in economic and industrial matters, to be a people, to love and to be loved in an effective way. Local control. Control by the people and for the people. That is the co-op way. The unity and solidarity of all the people for the common good. That is the co-op way. Dictatorship, absentee landlordism or any absentee lordism—that is antico-op.

It is platitudinous, but we must say and repeat that the main tendency of the century is toward dictatorships of various kinds, toward siphoning off the earnings of every little Twin Lakes for the profit of some John D. or other and for the profit of greatly inflated bureaucracies, and at the same time toward siphoning off the local spirit and spending it on some megalomaniac State. In these circumstances, Twin Lakes here and everywhere has a great task before it, if it is to save its own soul. "Deliver us from evil," says a sign at Twin Lakes and at every crossroads.

At exactly the time of my visit to Twin Lakes, people were meeting at the neighboring town of Albert Lea to take care of postwar unemployment. "This community went to work Thursday on its biggest problem of the day—finding a job for every man who wants one when the war is over." And what did the "12,000 gathered around the conference table" propose to do? "The problem, as they found it, was in two parts." First, to find out how many available postwar workers there will be, and then how many jobs. It is as simple as that, because with these data the citizens' committee will have the "necessary information for determining what Albert

Lea must do to make the two points come together." An official of the Minneapolis Federal Reserve Bank told the group what is "the biggest problem today": "each man can produce" so much now that we are all likely to suffer and possibly to starve. If we are to use the stepped-up ways of production that "have made America great," he said, then our big production of 1929 should look small to us and we should aim to increase it by 60 per cent.

They say that in oil well drilling the science of the best geologists is sometimes fallible. These men can tell whether a pocket exists in the rock, but it is always possible that a hole or crevice has let the oil escape. So of our big production. This conceivably can make that of 1929 look pygmy. The people at half a million Twin Lakes can produce the goods, yet because of some hole or crevice the people can be cold and ragged and half starved.

The co-operators say they have found the hole and can plug it. This book sets forth with the help of a hundred concrete settings what is the co-operators' simple wisdom and what is their real and effective procedure. That is why it mentions Twin Lakes where a baby co-op has seen the sun on this June day and where with ever so careful nursing it may in time grow into a lusty child of God and man.

4

It is with a farmer and leading co-operator that I stay while at Twin Lakes. This man, who believes so much in the land and its value for human life, and in a home on the land, and in the good of his community, has a big family. A daughter-in-law is here today, bringing her things to wash and herself to help with the wash, and with her is her son of seven months.

At night it is clear, at least for a time. Where is the farmer's son, "the one at home"? Surely he is not gone to town, paying rural tribute to Hollywood? No, not this time at any rate. He is in the field, plowing corn at night. The farmer is proud of this boy of sixteen. "He can easy do it, with the tractor and with the two lights turned on the corn rows. The machine runs easier at night, even if the man, watching so close, gets tireder. The boy that's in Africa has done up to forty acres a day, late in the season."

By nine at night, War Time, the calves, after nibbling at the dew-filled grass, settle down comfortably for the night and begin chewing on what must look to cows like minor cuds.

This farmer and his wife tell me that their children, as well as themselves, have been interested in co-ops. Why is this? The farmer, as he replies, seems not to miss any of the realities or of their relationships. "Well," he says, "take Mildred and me here. If it was only the cash we got out of it for the work we've put into it, it wouldn't be worth while. Only we see it different."

Doubtless the wife has her way of putting it, too, though it is not far from his way, since the members of any real family, and above all the man and wife, form the elemental co-op unit. So, on the co-op business, this farmer and wife are one. In what "different" way, then, do they see it? In spite of labor shortage, he has to pull down a cow barn that otherwise will fall down, and he has to rebuild. Do the co-ops carry him over this labor problem? Not at all. "We see it different. It could help to make the world a better place to live. That's why we do it."

They are old-time co-operators. The creamery at Twin Lakes, however, that is not co-op, is it?

"Oh, yes. You bet it is. It certainly is. Without that, well, that is the main thing, co-op or otherwise. Cream is the chief business of these farmers, and most of it in this county is handled through the co-ops."

The first co-op service station in our country was established at Cottonwood, Minnesota, in 1921, and five years later the first co-op wholesale for gas and oil was organized in Minneapolis as the Midland Cooperative Wholesale. Until 1926 the people in the area of Albert Lea got their oil and petroleum products in full dependence on the old-line companies. Then, determined to make a stand and aware of what others in Minnesota had done, they put up a service station at Albert Lea. From the first it has made its way, and in 1929 paid a dividend of 16 per cent, and all in all is the most obvious co-op success so far in this county. By the end of 1943, it and its branches had refunded to the people and thus kept within the community half a million dollars that otherwise would have gone to help create multimillionaires and for absolutely no value received. It may be that the people, here and among most of our co-operators in the Midwest, are mainly activists, people who by pot luck and good will get things done, and may not be highly intelligent orderers of the social and economic life. That is, they may understand little of what they do and of why they do it. So far as it is so, they cease to be genuine Rochdale co-operators, missing the democratic procedure which can be justified, and in fact can be, only on the ground of persistent study, and dodging the rule that part of the earnings be given to educational ends.

No doubt the co-ops at Albert Lea and Emmons and Twin Lakes have begun to do great things for man, things that certainly need to be done. Yet a local man has said to me, "We have a number of thriving co-ops in this county, but I'm afraid—so little educational work is being done—we're growing too fast in a commercial way." For co-ops, in Minnesota and everywhere, that is a perpetual danger.

5

Says a great co-operator of these parts, "All my life I've been looking for *the* co-operator. I mean the man who truly and fully is a co-operator."

What does it take for a man to qualify? Not good looks. Not health and strength, though these could help for co-ops as for anything else. Not money unless this is kept within co-op law and made subservient to the community. And not even good will, since this if untutored can upset things.

What, then, is wanted? Everything! So says the man I just mentioned. And yet just three qualities, he says, fill the bill: A man must have business ability, he must have honesty, and he must have the co-operative spirit. Happily we may as a rule take the honesty for granted. Not so with the other requirements. Only twice, says my friend, has he "really found this combination. A man may have business ability and seek himself—" a fact that centuries of modern history make clear. Or he may be a co-operator and not be much of a businessman.

An old Norwegian whom I visit has had what it takes. "All my life," he says, "I've been struggling for co-operation. And now I'm seventy-seven. My motto is, 'We'll do this together!'

"Oh, I'm on a close diet. No fruit or vegetables at all, but I can take grapefruit juice. Well, I want to live, and I enjoy living, if I am seventy-seven."

How long has he lived here? "All my life, seventy-seven years. I'm on the farm I was born on and always lived on." His eyes and ears and mind are keen, and he is interested in today and tomorrow. "Henry Wallace was saying on the air, couple nights ago, that the Scandinavian countries had co-operatives and the most progressive governments in Europe before the war. And they *are* great co-operators—Sweden and Norway—that's my country—and Denmark; they are great co-operator countries."

When electricity came this way, twenty-five years ago, our friend was offered a line to his house and farm buildings. " 'Are you interested?' they said. 'I certainly am!' 'How far is it?' they said. 'Just a mile. How much for that?' 'Seven hundred dollars.' 'And I'd own the line?' No, they didn't do business that way. 'And how much per kilowatt?' 'Sixteen cents straight.' I said: 'See here, I been reading how the people in Ontario all got light at one and a half and two cents a kilowatt, and I'll be interested at four or four and half, and maybe up to five cents.' The fellow laughed."

What do the people pay now under the REA? "Five to six cents."

As I leave, the old man is repeating his motto: "Let's pull together, for the new day and the new dawn!"

CO-OPS AND THE ORGANIC COMMUNITY

1

WITH the help of cases we begin to know what co-operation is. We get some glimpse of it as a procedure and also as a result or product. Before we go on to the expression of the co-ops in rural living and in medicine and housing and education and oil refining, we want to suggest some of the significance in the data already had from the case studies.

Man lives by bread, even if not by bread alone. Hence the easy and oversimple way of seeing co-ops, which are a process of getting bread, as only an economic or bread-getting enterprise. This is the Marxian and materialist error with regard to any human endeavor. As to such a view, it would be enough to say with the farmer at Twin Lakes that if that was all there was in co-ops— a dubious bit of breadwinning—or in life, for that matter, then neither the co-ops nor life would be worth while. We need the earnestness of Marx, but we need also a total vision. The real trouble with the narrow outlook on co-ops is that it is false; it leaves out the neighborhood, and any and all wider aspects. For example, what co-ops can do, and in fact do, for the national being, what relevance they might well have for adult education, for democracy, for health, for morals and religion, for security, ownership, and stability. In other words, the economic view taken in isolation falsifies the picture and almost totally misses man.

All the same, when we say that the human procedure involved in co-ops is not merely economic, we do not thereby say it is everything. Co-operation, for instance, is not religion or the virtue whereby we worship God. It is not any moral virtue such as justice or charity or purity, though of course dependent on and expressive of many virtues. It is not any scientific knowledge, though it depends on many sciences. It is not any art, though it uses many arts. It is not, in any land, the educational system though as had in Nova Scotia it is justly taken to be one in essence with adult education, and in Denmark, where more than anywhere else it is integrated with letters and culture and religion and patriotism and tradition, it could perhaps be stretched into a complete educational system. It is not politics or the State or the national government, even if some persons vaguely think and one great proponent of co-operation argues that it could supplant the State and give us a co-operative democracy. Nor is it democracy, even if for democracy it may be of elemental importance.

So far we say something of what the co-ops are not. But on the positive side and in their interrelationships, what are they? The question breaks up into half a dozen questions.

That man should have food and covering and shelter—that is an obvious demand. It is fair, then, to ask what the co-ops have to do with that demand, and in that way with the industrial and agricultural and economic processes and results.

That man should worship God and should try to live decently and positively as a person and as a member of the community—these are primal demands of his being. What have co-ops to do with these demands, and consequently with religion and morals?

That man should learn some degree of skills and of wisdom and prudence—here is a demand for learning wished on man in part by nature, and in its fuller reaches by his own desire and by circumstances. What do co-ops have, or what may they well have, to do with this natural demand and this chosen and socially developed demand?

That man should own property and productive property, and that he should be secure in his time and place and relatively self-secure, and thus stable and not like an Arkie or Okie—this is a natural and not an artificial demand, and we should like to begin to suggest in this chapter what the co-ops may well have to do with that demand.

That man should be a neighbor and have neighbors, and should effectively love and be loved, not merely in his family but in the wider community—that is a natural demand, and man is no good unless he fulfills it. "Man is naturally a friend to man." But, then, does man in all circumstances go with that native push? Just don't hate your neighbor! Just don't consciously exclude him when you say the "Our Father"! No tolerable society could be built on such neutral ground, nor of course on the hatred of man for man. Now, on that problem I shall not ask about co-ops, but assert from the start that co-ops have something real and genuine to say.

That we should actively love our country is a demand given within us, and native at least in the sense that it is necessary. And that we should not expect our country, or more properly its government, to keep going along breaking its back in the effort to bear all our economic burdens—this is a condition of the State's welfare and of our welfare. But that really is what all States now increasingly try to do, and just as if they and we had never heard of history and its vital lessons. The movement toward statism and the lust for statism are the strongest of all movements and lusts of our times: witness all forms of collectivism; for example, state socialism, which often is called social security, and then fascism, and nazism, and bolshevism. In other words, witness the State borne down now and crushed in all countries under an unnatural burden: in Russia, and Germany, and Italy, and France, and England, and the United States. Now our puny question. What have the co-ops in them that may in any measure boost us out of that badly unbalanced condition?

Freedom and the human person and society have suffered in the countries and the conditions just named. The acceptance of collectivistic statism is already a serious human defeat. If the co-ops, then, have any positive energy in them on that subject, let them, by the grace of God and man, speak and act!

But that condition, bad as it is, may possibly be less elemental than another. In any case, it is to date less prolonged than the proletarian condition. This is the attenuation, the neglect, the destruction of freedom. Men are not allowed to own. Men are not allowed to control and direct. Men are not allowed to decide. Men are, in this condition, not allowed to love the things they do, the acts they perform, their work, the materials, the processes, or the results. Not that some ogre stands up and says, "Don't! You must not love these!" It is simply that in the condition their nature disallows that love. In other words, persons are disallowed the right to be free and to be persons. Naturally, they resent this condition, and do and shall make war on it. At this point we only indicate the problem, and the proletarian attitude or psychology—which, we repeat, is justified, because natural and necessary. Later, but not now when we deal not much with Labor but with the Land, we ask what the co-ops have to do relative to that problem.

This book, written in defense of man, is of course written in reply to such questions as those enumerated, and on the ground of cases already covered we wish to suggest the answers and thus to suggest also the social significance of co-operation. Certainly at this stage the questions should not appear remote, or romantic or academic.

2

Many persons and groups want to save man, but are not alive to opening up techniques whereby man might possibly save himself. They are of all creeds and races and nations and philosophies, and no one may doubt their good will. But they want quick results. In their view society is always in a crisis, and man is helpless. Not a thing can man or the local neighborhood do. All must be done for them. All must come down on them in an overwhelming way from the top. In short, some collectivity must act as savior.

I often repeat this matter because, though it is obviously the most important problem before mankind in this century, most of us go in a fatalistic way for collectivism. Also, I had taken my present position before Pope Pius XI said in 1931 that whenever a smaller body can do as well what society needs done, it is better that such a body do it. Anything else is "a grave evil," "a disturbance of right order," and runs to tyranny. "This is a fundamental principle of social philosophy, unshaken and unchangeable and it retains its full truth today." Now, in the co-ops it has seemed to me from the first, and more and more as I have seen them in action, we have potentialities for social good that we have hardly begun to sense, let alone to realize. Let us see what these possibilities are, at least for the country community.

Here is a town called New York Mills and located a hundred miles west of the Twin Cities. It is Finnish, and therefore has a tremendous belief in man's powers and freedom, and can hardly be taken by any collectivistic invasion. At least I would as soon

bet on a Finnish community as on any to be in this connection the
last holdout.

And after all is not this the American faith and dream—this ideal
of freedom, this ideal of man building up a world where family by
family mankind should be free and possessed of productive property and thereby fairly self-secure and stable? Is not the top-down
collectivistic method alien to us, fit for an autocracy, but never for
American democracy?

Here, then, is what looks to me like a healthy little body of families on our Minnesota prairies. They are, as it happens, just con-
cluding the annual reports and sessions of co-op managers and
directors. Certain bits of their economic life they are running: and
such a load as they at once take off the almost broken back of the
State!

When I get off the bus in their town, it is late in June and the
sun is beginning now to come down straight and full on their flat
fields and the little shelters called houses and stores. Why is this
village placed on the prairies called New York Mills? The people
here appear not to know, and I do not learn when I have asked two
or three likely ones and also tried to find out from the people in the
next town. It just is, that's all! At the town of Wadena my bus did
the trick common to midwestern buses: it circled a block; and
among the obvious signs were these: Cudahy Co., J. C. Penney,
Bigelow's Land Office Loan Company, and the Minnesota Cooperative Wool Growers' Association. At the Mills I ask people about
this last. Is it truly a co-op? They know nothing of it. How about
the loan office, and Penney's, and Cudahy's? The people only
smile. They have in hand such matters as loans and cream and
notions. Economic or politico-economic dictatorship cannot get into
their town.

Why not? They have built up a wall against these. At least they
have begun to build it.

This is the way they work and proceed—and they do take their
time, since they are farmers and Finns. They start a store, put up
a gas station, run an elevator and a creamery. All this looks little
and innocent, and it really is; but it is effective for the people, and
therefore big. And it is, strangely enough, not innocent. So local
antico-op people have said. Co-op marketing through the elevator

and the creamery, this is all right. But not co-op stores. Why not? The people need gas and sugar and dresses and overalls and meat and coffee. Why should they not have these the co-op way? In the Midwest at least, it is still said they should not. Evidently the shoe pinches somebody's foot. So says a private businessman in a Minnesota town. "If they can do it better than we can, let them do it!"

For a small town, the store at New York Mills is in fact enormous, and so of the trade at the four main co-op units. I have the "report of audit" for the store or Co-op Mercantile Association from June 29 to December 31, 1942. Putting together for that half year the sales of merchandise and produce and hardware and meats and in the service station, we get the staggering small-town total of $132,342.28. That is big talk, after all: it is well over a quarter of a million for the year. And managers and directors meeting together now informally in the store, and their wives and smaller children in some cases with them, tell me that the total co-op business last year in this little town was over a million dollars.

Now, I don't care for big figures or big business, but I want to know what this co-op turnover means for the people.

The earnings in the store for that half year came to $8,570.78. Suppose that the even eight thousand went as refund to the people, leaving the rest for educational purposes and reserve. Suppose, too, that the other co-op units were in effect as good servants of the people for that period. In that case we had going back to these farmers about sixty-four thousand a year. How much thus goes back per family and per farm? That depends on the number of families, and I have not the figure. Suppose four hundred, and the sum is one hundred and sixty dollars a farm family, and since for dairying in Minnesota these farms are small, running only to forty acres or so, the return is four dollars an acre. Even if we double the figure, the return is two dollars an acre. Think what it is in five or ten years, or in a generation.

In one generation it might mean the difference between free farmers and enslaved farmers. The farm family is in most places, and wherever the co-ops do not protect it, paying an immense tribute to alien forces, and these in effect exercise a dictatorship over it. How much is the annual tribute? A dollar an acre, two, three, four or five dollars an acre. In thirty or forty years this is the difference between freedom and slavery.

And it is pure tribute. It goes for no value received. Of course it goes from other than farm families, but it is only of these I now speak. Out goes the tribute day by day and week by week and year by year. This is the direct road to economic slavery, and whatever other forms of slavery there may be, this form is elemental and is sufficient. For with or trailing this form, the other forms will mostly appear. Out goes tribute to the big oil companies. At the farmer's tank stops the big red truck. Surely this is "service"! A bill of eight-fifty today. Surely that is next to nothing, the service considered. But since the co-op oil stations started—it was in Minnesota, in 1921—we have learned that it is about 10 per cent too much. This farmer pays about 85 cents too much today, and so does his neighbor. Let every farm family in every part of the nation keep doing that, and a link of a chain is being formed around the farmer's neck.

Let the same go on in the store. Then to a mixed lot of owners, for example, local storekeepers and minor chains and big chains, every New York Mills is paying a tribute of sixteen thousand a year. And so on. Grain companies, no doubt centered in Chicago, Winnipeg, and Liverpool, ask their bit of tribute; say sixteen thousand a year from each country community. Some packing companies also want that sort of "cut" on cream and in general on dairy products.

That is hardly one-half the economic story, taken merely as an economic story. For we have many other ways of paying tribute to persons and groups alien to our little communities. Take the obvious case of interest on loans—and are we any longer wondering why the mortgages are so high and are so slow to get any lower? In fact, with the inflation during and after the war of 1914-1918, people were too ready to lend on land and too ready to borrow on land. The result was that a special and high tribute started going out to banks. Many of these were local, and with agricultural depression in 1922 they began to go down. But the mortgages were picked up by larger banks and by insurance companies. And much of the tribute keeps going out. In many instances the big banking units own the land now, and we have absentee landlordism. This comes to a special type of local slavery, and I only suggest here that people's co-op banks might in the future learn to protect us from such a fix.

Think of other tributes. On machinery, and on cars. On doctor bills, perhaps, and on drugs which form rather effective material for chains. Sometimes on burial: they say in Minnesota, the ordinary tribute in this line is about 30 per cent. And on insurance, whether this be for people's lives or their crops or cars or other property. And on meat packing and on the canning we get people to do for us, and on lockers and freezing plants. And think of the nice tribute on entertainment that every New York Mills pays to Hollywood.

We all complain of sales taxes, but these are as nothing compared with our ignorance tax, our stupidity tax, and our inanition tax. And the part I speak of is for absolutely no value received. If we were to put together the tributes just named and add them up with those more concretely mentioned above, we would begin to see something of what co-ops can do for people.

Is there some mystery or sacred seal that keeps us from having co-op insurance? But we already have it! Or from having co-op medicine, co-op stores, burial co-ops, banking co-ops, processing and shipping and marketing co-ops, and co-op entertainment? But we already have every one of them!

That way, then, possibly lies considerable leverage for the people, if they really want to be free. It is conceivable that by hard work economic freedom can in that way be had for American farmers—and, as we shall see, to a notable extent for other Americans and all peoples. What it takes is intelligence and courage and initiative and sacrifice, and what I do not want to allow is that Americans have not these qualities. It takes a working up from the bottom and a working inch by inch. Perhaps that patience required by the democratic process is what we are traditionally short on and what we do not like to learn to supply.

3

So much at present for the economic effects, the actual and possible ones. Our position so far is that, given a chance, the co-ops may have it in them to protect the economic life of the American farmer and the American people. On the other hand, the methods we have for some time progressively used, the commercialized and centralized and corporation methods, are good for making a few millionaires and many poor men.

But the economic is not the end of the story, unless man is to be stripped of all his human quality. Let us look briefly at some other implications of the co-ops. Beginning in the pig lot and the farmer's kitchen and going on from farm to farm and house to house, the co-ops could perhaps do as much now as any unit namable for the re-creation of the country community. Wars, speedy travel, the loss in some cases of faith and its practice through the little old church; and chain stores, chain banks, chain drugstores, big machinery, and Hollywood—all these have done wonders in tearing apart the life of the farm neighborhood. If the co-ops can go a little way toward rebuilding that life and our whole life into what "A.E." called "a true social organism," we ought by all means to have them.

And this they can do. We have seen them working in this direction among men and women at Twin Lakes and at half a dozen places and later we shall see the same effect especially among the Ohio and Indiana and Kansas co-operators. Said "A.E.," the true social organism remakes men and society, whereas highly specialized production "only develops economic efficiency. The evolution of humanity beyond its present level depends absolutely on its power to unite and create true social organisms."

Democracy, the neighborhood, faith in God and man, the love of God and man, and the moral life as expressed in charity and justice—it is possible to see that these are distinct from each other. But they are not separated, and not easily separable. And it is here that the co-ops come alive and discover their own soul. They achieve economic good. But see how they do this. It is the people themselves that achieve it, the people planning together and working together and thus brought closer and closer to each other in their social and educational as well as in their economic and industrial life. That is what co-ops properly are, the people living together and effectively forming "a true social organism." That way we make no wars on each other. That way the tooth-and-nail theory of man's nature dies the death it deserves. That way man loves his neighbor, perhaps not in blatant words, but in reality. That way man can carry on his social and his economic life for his neighbor and with his neighbor, and for and with his neighbor honorably and we may say proudly worship God.

Then poverty and pauperism need not haunt us on the land or in the towns. Then land and homes, to date defaulting so regularly to banks and insurance companies, may be kept and owned by the people. Then instability and insecurity may possibly stay away from the door of every man who believes in God and his own neighbor. Then that fear that is so hard on people may be past. Then sickness and disease may be reduced, and that unintelligible condition, hunger and starvation on the best food-producing land, may never again be known.

Then bureaucracy may be unheard of, and the State be relieved of those unnatural and impossible burdens which Pius XI knew and we all know that it everywhere now tries to and perhaps must try to carry. Then the family of isms that fall under collectivism may no longer be spawned in every European country and brought as aliens, and I would say as enemy aliens, into America. The omni-component State might be interred, and men incidentally begin to be as free as God and nature meant them to be. Imperialism, whether of power politics or of power finance, might be of another century. Our economics and sociology and their many men of good will might be more realistic.

If that series of statements is anything like the true picture, it is no wonder that great believers in man and in God, such men as Bishop Grundvig and Luigi Sturzo and Pope Pius XI, have been strong for the co-ops.

4

Is all this good of co-ops, which possibly by intelligence and time and hard knocks can be worked out—is this good only for the country community? If it were only for men on the land, we ought to be working for it since we depend on the land, and not only for food but for men. The landmen pour into the cities. Even if they go too fast in that way now, still some must go, since the land is prolific and overproduces people, and some of these the city must have if it is to survive at all. But, then, what sort of people? I for one want them, in cities or on the land, to be men of such freedom and intelligence and initiative and neighborliness as the co-ops could help us to produce. Then we might continue to have a core of men with love for their neighbor and active care for his good, with freedom and the manliness that is its mate, with security and ownership and hope, and above all with faith in God and man. Think, on the other hand, of men without this faith, without hope and ownership and relative security, without freedom and its values.

If, then, the co-ops and their good were limited to men living on the land, we should nevertheless go all out for them. The fact is that there is no law of psychology or economics or geography or history that so limits them. In England the co-ops are mainly and almost exclusively in the cities. In Sweden they are everywhere. In our own country they can make their way with labor. This we have seen in the case of the miners in southeastern Ohio, and we shall see it in the case of other workmen. We shall see that they are at home also in Detroit, Cleveland, Chicago, in Boston and New York, in Washington and Philadelphia.

COMMUNAL WORSHIP

1

It will do anyone good to visit the Benedictines at St. John's. And when a person is a friend of the Abbey, and it is a day in June and the eve of Pentecost, what could be finer? The abbot and monks will receive any guest as if they had been waiting for him to arrive and had not another thing to do.

They really do have something else to do. We might say they are to sing the Office and to perform the liturgy. But the work is more vivid and real and at once more personal and communal than those words suggest. The work is a work they do together, and it is the praise of God. Several times a day they bow before the altar and say, "Holy, holy, holy, Lord God of Hosts!" And they bow low to say the "Our Father" and to sing the "Gloria Patri."

But are they co-operators? In an elemental and inclusive sense, yes. And also in the narrower sense of that word. These matters we shall see. Just now we want to see how St. John's Abbey and University, truly a center for study of the co-ops, lives its own life. For St. John's in Minnesota was the home of Virgil Michel, a man who studied co-ops here at home and also in Nova Scotia and wanted to know their place in an integral program for Christian society.

Pope Pius X called for the "active participation" of lay people in the acts of worship, and a constant work at St. John's is to teach others to worship God, and to carry out the liturgical life. This means their taking part in the prayers and chants, and above all in the Mass. It means, too, their use of Sacraments and sacramentals: for example, the blessings for fields and shops and houses. In that way, man's home and work and domestic life and his study and play can take on a new meaning and be lifted out of what would otherwise be its natural self.

The monks invite all their guests to come before the altar for the

69

acts of worship, and on the eve of Pentecost the Vespers are lovely. Now, one must say that it is hard to sing them well, and not many of the monks get every iota of the Gregorian, the chant that comes in part from the famous St. Gregory I (d. 604). But all in all the effect is wonderful. Think of song-prayers like these, done with the sublimity of the chant by men dedicated to the work. Laudate, pueri, Dominum: laudate nomen Domini: praise the Lord, ye young men, praise the name of the Lord. Let the name of the Lord be blessed, from this time now, and for ever. From the rising of the sun till its going down, worthy of praise is the name of the Lord. High above all the nations is the Lord, and above the heavens is His glory.

Another work of the Benedictines is to cultivate the soil and live by it. Sugar they have from their own maples, a famous black bread from their own ovens, milk and cheese and butter from their own dairy, pork from their own lots, and a wine made by themselves. In that way land and trees and cattle begin to take on a new dignity and a kind of revered quality. Even above "the heavens" is God's glory, and also above man are the angels. But next is man. And "by nature," as Virgil Michel liked to put it, all things else are subordinated to man.

It is best, however, to bring food and drink as directly as feasible from God's earth and sea. Then we will not forget to reverence them.

These men, then, have the work of teaching others the love of the land and the love of prayer-song and the turning of labor and cultivation into a vocation with its own nearness to the divine. And teaching them also in history and arts and sciences and philosophy and theology, and in the highest reaches of these.

One work I have noticed especially among these Benedictines, and one may say it is the central work of the present Pope. This is teaching men human unity and human solidarity. Pius XII has been Pope since March, 1939, and from the first his purpose was human unity based on human and divine love; his peace aim, so consistent and so persistent, is an item within that purpose. Whatever of that question, it is a delight to see at St. John's an interest in everything that makes for common human good, and to see Jews and Negroes in the act of becoming Minnesota Benedictines.

2

We might find co-operation in more special and technical senses at St. John's. But I prefer to study it mostly in terms of Virgil Michel who gave the energy of a keen mind and fiery will to a study of Christian social reconstruction,[1] by no means excluding co-ops. The worship of God and the common good of man—that, in short, was his program.

The program demanded study, and an integration of special studies. It required the study of philosophy, for instance, since the reconstruction of the human person's role in the good society makes no sense till we know what the person is, and what man is, and society, and the common good; and that is only a fraction of the philosophy needed. Then we need many sciences, and especially the social sciences: sociology and economics and politics and history. And arts, and letters, and theology. And we must bring these together and order them justly in the light of nature and grace. Besides, we have the more practical arts to develop and use, such as house building and home building and child rearing. Nor does this ordering of our world, and this being thereby like to God, occur in some unperturbed spot, some sort of vacuum, but in a world turned upside-down many times, by many modern movements: by the Renaissance, the Reformation, the Enlightenment, by Comte, by Darwin, by a perpetually new science, by wars, and by both the old individualism and the new collectivisms.

Now, to keep making and remaking a map of a truly human order fit for man's nature and his life in Christ—that is the task of every social philosopher worth his salt and of every social scientist. Of course, that was Virgil Michel's task, the bold attempt to work out such an order in theory and at the same time to keep his mind and hand not far removed from practice. The last ten years of his life were spent above all at this task, and I cannot easily name persons in this country who were more zealous at the work or more effective in doing something toward its achievement.

Is his work therefore to be called co-operation? In a broad and a literal sense, it is, since it supposes and demands a vast amount of collaboration and the integration of many special findings and of

[1] See his *Christian Social Reconstruction.* Milwaukee: Bruce Co., 1937.

all our theoretic sciences and practical arts. In the ordinary and narrow sense, it is not "co-operation." Still the two can be brought together, this wider and total integrated life-knowledge and co-operation in its limited sense, and for our social salvation they should be brought together. To Virgil Michel that was a fact as clear as daylight.

In passing it may be said that Virgil Michel repeatedly scourged the two extremes given in our times, the old individualism and all the new collectivisms. "The contemporary heresies of gross individualism and stupid materialistic collectivism have replaced the fundamental ideal of the Christian brotherhood." This is his summary. But his mind was constructive, and his interest was in a new and vital Christian order.

3

In an article on ownership and the human person,[2] he said that for thousands of years ownership as an institution was in theory derived from and also took its practical cues from the human person. But now we tend to make the person a sort of derivative from property. What is man in this case? A factor in production, "a hand, a unit of cost or expense." Politically, man is not much better off: he is "a mere abstract mathematical unit" that on occasion punches a voting machine.

That is the way for the vast majority in economics and politics, their character as persons deflated. A few are superpersons, and the will of these favored ones is the law.

Society itself becomes a kind of joint stock company set up in the interests of the relatively few property holders.

On the correct view the human person is rational, the most perfect and precious thing in all nature, and is not subordered to other men, but is to be treated as on a par with them and as sharing an equal dignity. The fellowship or society of persons is based not on blood or geography, but on the social nature of man, and the germ cell of this fellowship is not the individual, but the family.

Things become personalized and are a quasi extension of the

[2] "Ownership and the Human Person," *Review of Politics*, v.1 (April, 1939), 155-177.

person. This of course is not true when ownership is absentee or is a drop in an ocean of stocks and bonds. But it is true when the person spends his hopes and plans and activity on the goods, and even more so when he and those close to him do all of this together. What are goods owned for? Only "for the good of the human person." And how much is to be owned? Enough for personal needs and personal growth and also to look to the advance of culture and civilization.

Through the "corporative order" we shall get to social reorganization: that is, in Virgil Michel's grasp of the matter, "through the joining of individual men into immediate groups sufficiently small for the individual men to count in them and to contribute perceptibly to the common good of the group. Larger groups may be composed of these smaller groups, but . . . the small groups must retain enough autonomy of their own, so as not to become mere mechanical elements in the larger organism."

In this position of his, it is evident that Virgil Michel is under the influence of many sources. For instance, the thinker Maritain and the social scientist Dawson and half a dozen liturgists such as Guardini and Cabrol; and the social encyclicals, and Catholic teaching in general; the thought of St. Thomas on the person and society, and the main tradition of the West on man. He is alive to present changes and human needs. The doctrine may be old and settled, but it comes up new and fresh in its meeting of today's problems. No radical and no quietistic deadhead can do any good thing that at once faces our situation and is itself able to stand. Now, this priest Virgil Michel was nothing if not vital. He saw a personalistic group on the Continent and was for it and with it. He saw a distributist-decentralist group in England and America and was for it and ahead of it. And it is true to say that he was at the center of the liturgical revival in this country.

4

Was he therefore for and with the co-ops? He certainly was! And St. John's, with him and following him and no doubt inspiring him, has been consistently for any and all good there is in co-ops. First, let us see something of his theory on co-ops, and on their inter-

relationship with the liturgical movement and with the papal doc-
trines, and then suggest how he had begun to look toward action.

I think it is just to him and to all parties to put down this ex-
clamation as if from him: Through capitalism or state socialism, or
a combination of the two, to a Christian personalistic society! From
the State down! It cannot be done! It must come, this society—if it
is to come—from littler and autonomous groups. It must work, if it
is to work at all, from the bottom up. That is the way of growth in
society. Individualism is bad, and God knows we were long enough
in finding this out and in condemning it. The Christian and the
personalistic cannot come from the bureaucratic and totalitarian.
To learn that fact we need not have waited till this century.

People must again learn to do and organize to do what the State
inefficiently does or tries to do for them. That, in Virgil Michel's
view, is the reason for affirming the smaller groups. "That is the
rationale of an organic construction ·of society, of a corporative
order."

That is also the reason for co-ops, and the good and sufficient
reason. But there are other ways to put it.

For instance, under the old individualism labor is hardly human.
It is rather "a cold market commodity, to be bought and sold" or
left idle and sterile. Under collectivism labor is an imposed task
which must be done. It can, however, be finer and human and
Christian. Under Christian solidarity, labor is "an element in a
social co-operative enterprise which gives the members a livelihood
and contributes to the common good. It is always a service to the
fellowship." That again is Virgil Michel, and if possibly he is not
speaking of co-ops in a literal sense, he is not far from mentioning
their place in a total Christian economy. And at times it is literally
of the co-ops that he speaks.

I must say he puts strongly the case for co-ops. A person belongs
naturally to the organic whole or fellowship called society, and is to
keep a balance between his own self and the social body. He must
allow due place to other persons and to the social body and to lower
nature and also to God. But man needs the help of God, which he
best gets through the communal and personal effort demanded of
him in liturgical worship. Now, vital though it is, this liturgical
movement goes in an important sense right along with the co-

operative movement. Each is an expression of the long overdue reaction against individualism: the old individualism in religion, in economics, in industry, and our whole life. And each of them, the liturgy and the co-operative way, calls for "an active return and exercise of the spirit of common fellowship and of mutual aid and support." At this point others may be as surprised as I was at finding Virgil Michel saying that each decidedly needs the other. For he says it could happen that the co-ops would partly or wholly miss the Christian way, their followers failing to achieve good "through Christ." The result would be a merely naturalistic and non-Christian effect. "And for that very reason it is eminently true that the cooperative movement, which in the domain of nature seeks to realize the ideals of Christ, needs the support and the help of the Christian spiritual movement that seeks to realize the ideals of Christ more fully in the supernatural domain of our spiritual lives. For us Catholics, this means in particular that the cooperative movement needs the help and the inspiration of the liturgical movement, and it necessarily means that the liturgical movement, under pain of remaining sterile, needs to flower out into ever increasing Christian cooperation in all the things of life."

But this effecting of an integral life, of an almost new life for person and society, a life of responsibility and at the same time of freedom—is anything like this now achieved? Does our education in high school and college build up toward this? Does it really teach boys and girls that their homes and their love and labor and play and their lives in their entirety can all and each be as human-divine incense before the All-Sacred? And do they begin to learn how to get out of our co-ops the good that is in them?

No, says Virgil Michel, and here he is spokesman for St. John's.[3] The schools fail to help build for America a total Christian civilization and culture. What, meantime, do they do? They support and advance the ideals of a bourgeois "*laissez-faire* liberalism." These ideals are easy money, bourgeois culture, ready-made things, a high-powered mechanical way of life, and the "mechanization even of Christian religious life."

The remedy is the same old one: an integral Christian life. Some

---

[3] See Virgil Michel, "Christian Education for Rural Living," *Catholic Rural Life Bulletin* (now *Land and Home*), August, 1938.

of its parts are the following: Sharing in the worship of the Church and in the lay apostolate. "A firmly grounded rational conception of life, and of the nature of things," inclusive "of co-operation [in the untechnical sense of that term], of personal social responsibility." Then for rural youth, the study of the possibilities in electrification, in "agricultural associations, producer and consumer cooperatives, credit unions. . . ."

It was just like Virgil Michel to fire away at the schools that have nursed us all. They are tame, he said, bourgeois, passive, routine, and mechanized, and not generally awake to the fact that adult education is here to stay. Such a country as Denmark with its folk schools could teach us a lesson. These are "integrally cultural," and we need them. The people with us have always gone to the school, but we now need the school to go to the people. This he said after his study of Nova Scotia co-ops and especially his discussions with Father Tompkins, the great inspirer of these. We need co-ops as education with their Nova Scotia development in study and discussion among adults, and their special winter and summer courses and their regional traveling libraries.

Would the Popes bless such endeavor? Well, two Popes did bless the Nova Scotia experiment. And, as Virgil Michel saw it, one of the greatest encyclicals on social rejuvenation has principles that simply require Catholics to consider co-ops.

In his *Christian Social Reconstruction*, Father Virgil made what, so far as I know, is the strongest statement ever made by an American Catholic for the co-ops. Look at his words:

All over the world the cooperative movement is growing by leaps and bounds, sponsored by persons of all different beliefs, and flourishing in particular in the Scandinavian countries and Great Britain and in the Catholic sections of other European countries. In recent years it has also made great strides in our country, and not least in Minnesota. No Catholic interested in the principles of the *Quadragesimo Anno* can afford to neglect the cooperative movement.

Then he gave what had been stated by co-operators as the chief points in their program. First, open and voluntary membership, with no limitation of color, race, or creed, and each person free to join the ranks or stay outside. Second, the old co-op rule of "one member, one vote," a rule that sees to democracy in every genuine co-op.

Third, the giving of purchase dividends, a method that takes profit seeking and profit making out of business and out of life. These points, said Father Virgil, though possibly limited to economics, fit with the aforesaid papal letter. Look too at these strong and well-chosen words:

> The cooperative movement is throughout a voluntary organization; it plays no politics; it organizes economic life for the purpose of consumption needs and not for profits which ignore the prime purpose of economic activity; and it exemplifies above all the spirit of mutual aid among all members of society—a principle upon which the civil state itself finds its basic moral justification. There are few movements or ideals in our day that harmonize so well with the ideals of Christianity as do the cooperatives.

However, he was no extremist and he was far from claiming that co-operatives are or could be a be-all or a do-all. His general conclusion was that men of all religions and all men of good will need to unite if we are to solve our social problems. The matter of social rebirth is a work for Christians to do, "and for all Christians in unity of effort." Its spirit therefore must be that of divine charity, since only this can unite all men of good will and achieve peace on earth.

5

The efforts so far made at St. John's toward action that would kill the old individualism and forestall the new bureaucratic collectivisms are at least of interest. The efforts are two, and Father Virgil was the moving spirit of each. The first is a local co-op in the sense of a people's bank or credit union. This on its fifth birthday had one hundred and fifty-five members and shares running to something over nine thousand and loans to date of over thirty thousand. Three loans had been refused, out of two hundred and forty-five applications, and not a cent had been lost in bad loans. The people had borrowed for fuel, and over twice as much for insurance, over three times as much for taxes and for clothing, four times as much for educational purposes, ten times as much to buy cattle and horses, fourteen times as much for medical and hospital care, forty times as much to pay off old debts, and fifty times as much to buy homes and farms.

In general, they were looking to their welfare, of course, and more especially to ownership and freedom. That is the way with credit unions. And what is important of credit unions here and everywhere is that the poor man who otherwise has to pay an exorbitant rate of interest—in Minnesota, 36 per cent, and in many states such as Illinois and Iowa up to 42 per cent—is able by cooperating with his neighbors to get money at a decent rate. The small group can in this matter protect and save itself, whereas the big centralized bank or loan company can only enslave the poor man.

While I was at St. John's the men took their second step. After long study they set up the St. John's Workers Guild: "in order to comply with the wishes of Popes Leo XIII and Pius XI as stated in their social encyclicals—namely, to establish vocational groups." The aims are these: to enrich the religious life of the persons through works of mercy and through charity between workman and workman and between workmen and St. John's; to aid each member in bettering his condition in body, mind, and property; to plan and achieve social security, adult education, and recreational and social life; and to act as a sort of labor union. And as I learned later, one of the first achievements of the Guild was to work out a statement of the wages sufficient and proper for the families represented.

Besides, Virgil Michel started an important Institute for Social Studies which aims chiefly at a deep understanding of Christian social teachings, and uses the co-operatives as "one of the invaluable techniques" to effect its purposes. He also had what I consider the grand idea of setting up a rural life school, a school for complete human living. This was a hope of his, and the hope was to bear fruit when in the summer of 1940 his confreres at St. John's established such a school. Says the director, "The cooperative movement occupied a very large place on the program of the first rural life school and has continued to do so ever since as the rural life school movement developed." The "movement" indicates that the idea of this short course in integral rural living has spread, and the school is now held annually in a score of places,[4] and always with great interest in the co-ops.

[4] The schools are set up with the collaboration of Catholic Rural Life (3801 Grand Ave., Des Moines).

Eight

THE PROFIT MAN AND THE CO-OP MAN

THE profit man, as we all know him, is in business for money. He is a busy man, since he believes that business is business and that money talks. His is the serious creed that money is to be used to make more money, and it is with such a lead that the economists have for a long time defined capital. The more pure of heart he is in this belief, that is to say, the more directly and single-mindedly he goes for money, the more perfectly he measures up to his type and also the more money he is likely to make. That is why he has to be sober and thrifty and industrious, in order to be free of interests that would distract him from his pursuit of profit, and the "good man" is understood to be the man who is down to business and misses no chances. The virtues are those habits that help him most in making profit.

In Western society he was, till the "stars" appeared, the most important man among us. This is because money tends to rule, to control in many fields, such as business, politics, education, and religion. Whatever may be said for the co-op motive and procedure, the case against is that in fact it cuts a slice out of the profit man's profit.

Now, no matter how much we might find to say against the profit man himself, it is evident that much may be said for him. It is in the age of the profit man, our own age, that a volume of goods amounting to plenty has been produced, and probably it never was produced before. Of this we might occasionally remind ourselves. As we go along now on a Jackrabbit bus toward the city of Sioux Falls, we recall that this bus is run for profit. The roads were built out of taxes, though no doubt someone made a good thing out of the deal. The railroads too were built by great, strong men, dynamos who were able to see and do a work that people wanted done, and able to get government help in the form of subsidies for doing it, and to "make" or take hundreds of millions for their trouble.

79

These men were the empire builders, lustful for prestige and power, honored as kings. So in many lines: the steel mills, the coal mines, the iron mines, the forests, the oil fields, the factories for making cars and tires and planes.

Money talks. These things could not be done unless the big man had a free hand to make big money. Industry and agriculture and finance can never be by and for the people.

That is one interesting conclusion from the history of industry and the profit man. Besides, a man who takes his time and lives quietly with his neighbors and perhaps to a notable degree for them is an unimportant man: for he does not make big money. It is Benjamin Franklin or Samuel Insull and not Francis Assisi who is the saint. Gain is holy, and is a sign of God's benediction on the man who makes it, on the family, too, that has a tradition of it, and the nation that goes in for it and makes it. A prosperous people is thereby known to be a good people and to have the true religion. Poor men are bad men, and poor men and poor nations have got what was coming to them. The man "well off" is the rich man, and the man "doing well" is not at all necessarily the man doing good for and with the community, but the man making considerable money for himself.

This attitude of money-making and profit taking is common to us in the Western world, and this identifying the making and the taking with goodness and greatness and divine favor is so much a part of our minds that it would require a jar for us to begin to think and live in other terms. A poor man perhaps begging for his bread, or at best working for it and never wanting or going after a lot of money—surely he cannot be much of a man. That has for generations been our attitude. Poor nations, like poor men, are retrograde and unprogressive.

Efficiency and big production are the main merits in an era given to money-making. And yet these, themselves not always achieved, are by no means good without qualification. Evils have arisen too. Big wealth for a relatively few, poverty for most people—no effective democracy, but a sort of plutocratic aristocracy. Also a mechanical world, not only because of the machine, but because of the hardness and injustice that often go with imperialism in finance and in politico-finance. A world open to war with all its destruction. A world that seems unable at times to distribute the plenty it produces. A world that as it goes on and develops becomes less and less a neighborly world, less a personalistic and familial world of justice and love, a world hardly knowing the neighborhood life, a life of family knowing and loving family, of fellowship and brotherhood in economics and agriculture and industry. Think, in that world, of neighboring, of sharing, of looking to the other's good!

In my native little neighborhood, no doubt narrow in many ways and at that time isolated, we used to know and love—or hate—the neighbors. When a new family came, we received it as a neighbor. Once, however, a man came who knew only money. A neighbor asked this new man if he would help him do some work—and of all the replies! The new man asked, "What is there in it for me?"

On that profit ground we can never hope to build a human community. And yet that has long been the proffered ground.

To try to manhandle this money-making world, we have got into serious difficulties. We have imperialisms, and collectivisms. These last could undoubtedly be worse, in Italy, in Russia, in Germany and France, and in the United States. But nowhere is collectivism too good, since in some degree it does and must make man the peon and serf of the State.

It would therefore be untrue to say that the profit man brings us unqualified good. And we do not want his unmanageable progeny—collectivism with its dictatorship.

2

We shall take a look now at some of the ordinary forms in which the profit man every day appears to us. It is his voice that we hear all day and all night on the air.

"Charm Curl permanent wave. Send today. Write a card to Charm Curl, station WAIT, Chicago." That is the tune we hear. That and many others, all timed to profits. "Morton's salt. When it rains it pours." Then from Morton's a moving story about war and peace, and always about the merits of Morton's. "Signing off till tomorrow morning and reminding you that American railroads are all united for victory." They certainly are, and have been, and it is possible that the several wars and the times of relative peace and the new needs and sufferings they bring do not alter the essential direction and aim of any business-is-business enterprise. Early in the day we are served vital truths about wheat and rice Sparkies: "They're immense . . . vitamins . . . the kind everybody needs to keep up wartime strength." Often that is the tune: what Uncle Sam wants us to eat, the vitamins he says we should have in order to be patriotic. Science and Uncle Sam and faith in God join hands to say we should eat this or that brand of salt or rice or should have just this brand of shortening for our piecrust. "The kind Uncle Sam says every man should eat . . . You know, Uncle Sam wants everybody to keep strong and eat plenty of good food." "Drene, D-r-e-n-e," does some particular good to us, and we should have it often. So of other recipes. "Forhans, F-o-r-h-a-n-s, Forhans . . . part of the wartime effort to declare for healthy teeth." "Loaded with whole-grain nourishment, as recommended by Uncle Sam. Remember, Uncle Sam says to everybody: 'Be strong, get plenty of healthy food.' "

So the chatter goes on, the man rarely believing the words he says and, we are bound to suppose, hating the work he does.

"C/o Victory Vitamins, Chicago, and enclose $1." Next, we are offered a fire extinguisher: "And your money back if you don't say this is the biggest bargain in years." Another says, "Twice your money back if your dog doesn't go for it. It has sniff-appeal in it." Between ads is a line or two of music: "All I do is dream of you!" Then we get Vitamins Plus with some wizard or other: " 'Yosemite!' Give that gentle-man eleven silver dollars!! . . . five seconds, please . . . all right: twenty-five dollars!!! . . . Founder of the University of Virginia. Oh [in an unbearably oozy voice], I'm awfully sorry." Then after a moment, in the most excited tone, "Give that lady ten silver dollars!!"

". . . and you will marvel at our ability to sell it at $2." "One spraying with XX moth powder lasts for a whole year. XX—remember the brand—XX." "Everybody needs these vitamins to keep on the beam. They're shot from guns and they're bang-full of nourishment. For your children's sake. . ."

"I wonder how many of you folks know that a Gillette blue blade is only 1/100,000th of an inch thick? And I wonder also how many of you folks know that Gillette is engaged . . . Gillette technicians have known this, right along. Make no mistake: Gillette blue blade! Brother, you can't think the kind of shave the Gillette blue blade gives you!"

"Contains more than enough vitamin B to convert itself into energy. And remember, doubly fresh. Wonder bread!" "The meals were tried by plenty of men . . . maple chiffon pie . . . short-cut recipe . . . Pet milk . . . two teaspoons plain unflavored . . . two teaspoons plain unflavored. . ." "And now, Road of Life. Dr. Agnew sat in his office looking out." "Daniel Bashes root beer! Daniel Bashes root beer!" "Sweetheart of Song!" "All the mamma beavers are going out to work alongside the papa beavers." "Super-Suds, Super-Suds! Lots of suds from Super-Suds! That's the way in South America and everywhere the girls are saying, 'Super-Suds . . . with super-do!'"

"Some swell buys at Siebold's. Six big stores. . . Last month the greatest sales in history: $7,500,000. We're mighty proud of that record. More music now, with Dick Harding singing, 'I'll pray for you.'"

Why all this talk? What is it about? What, after all, is it for? If the unprogressive man from Mars came and inquired, what would we have to tell him? It is propaganda. So far, no argument. Are these programs really patriotic and religious—to believe their tone—and scientific? Or have they some special axes to grind? Do these sweet voices really know anything about vitamin B and its possible existence and its relation to our personal and familial and national health? And do they really and truly care? When E-lec-tron-ic works us up quickly with tragic underseas tones in a battle to defend the freedoms, which of the freedoms is it so keen to defend and promote? In its own words, "What is the big idea?" When we get gratis a hurried drama with our own people trading their necks for candy bars of specified types, and we are so convincingly told that X chewing gum is keeping up morale on all fronts, what is it that in fact we are being sold?

Is all this advertising done for science and art and learning, that is to say, for truth and beauty? Is it done for religion and faith in God and Christ? Is it done for Labor and the rights and free-

doms of the common man? Is it done to save our honor, our traditions, our national soul?

In their sober moments, most people know what it is for. It is
for profit. Just at the moment I do not ask about its possible justification, and do not bother to contrast it with the co-op refusal to
high-pressure us into buying a lot of things we perhaps do not
need. Nor do I here emphasize the devotion of the co-ops to quality
and an honest label. For the task of this chapter is rather to set
over against the co-op man, whom we begin to know in part, the
old-time profit man, who is so close to us and so much within ourselves and our hopes as well as our past that we hardly ever notice
him. The little passage we now conclude only says: The profit man
is a propagandist for profit. He wants education in his favor, and
the law in his favor, and then in the normal case he will keep
within it. He is interesting and versatile. He will use any language,
that of science, or freedom, patriotism, faith or health, just so long
as it helps him to make a profit, and he easily identifies any of
these with profit seeking. In a word, his direct interest is in money,
and not in man or God.

3

On my tour to study the co-ops, I meet many typical profit men.
One man watches me closely and watches everyone closely as we
buy things from him. He sees a narrow circle all around him, and
within himself he is saying, "How do you know that this man
or that woman over there wouldn't buy another dollar's worth?
How best to hit this prospective purchaser—with talk of savings
or of quality? What little word would do the trick?"

In passing I repeat that the co-op stores and shops are not trying
to unload things on people, not trying to get people into debt
through installment buying, and after my visits to so many of them
in eight of our states I must say that their attitude as well as their
interest is rather that of neighborly conduct than of big sales. No
point to trying to "sell" a fellow when the store and the goods are
his own! Of course, we must not at once look for too much, since
the co-op people are almost all of them made-over profit people.
Yet it remains true that they have found in Rochdale co-operation

a technique that invites them to work for and with the neighborhood.

At a town on the prairies I am advised to call on the charming Brothers Keene, well known locally in business. At the door of their shop a fat little girl, not especially bright, meets me. Mr. Jonathan Keene is out just now, but Mr. Thomas Keene is in the office and—of all unlikely things!—will receive me at once. He looks me over, and keeps an eye on trade all the time. How wary he is, and how extremely careful not to commit himself to anything. He will let me hang myself, not only first, but first and last, and with no training or faith in diplomacy I soon have my skeleton swinging helplessly before him. But he does not smile. He only turns his chair slightly toward me, and his face with two watery blue eyes in it comes mechanically my way. No word about co-ops do I dare to breathe in his presence, for in the same block with this man the word "co-op," so effectively removed from profit, would dry up any throat. And I am so innocent on business for business that I never guess what he thinks I have come for. He thinks, of course, that I have come to sell him something and one way or another to get money out of him. Naturally, then, he is ready to meet any show on my part, and when he learns that my bus is soon due, he loads me into his car and is glad to see me off. He does not smile to anyone or speak to a soul in his part of the city. When people speak, he merely bows a stiff bit and tightens his lips, careful to commit The Firm to nothing and knowing all the time that business is business and not an item in neighborly conduct or properly for the economic good of that community.

All along the road we meet men of this type. On the Jackrabbit is a competent man of business, self-assured like a salesman in boom times. He is not tight-lipped or afraid to tell a thing or two, and we all soon learn that he's a Legionnaire and a successful hotel man. Business is not a bit good in his line, though he says that "this North Dakota here," pointing to it, is one of the best hotel states in the country. "Now you take the town I'm coming from— seven thousand people; and we have the best hotel in town."

"And no business?"

"What?" he says, surprised that anyone would interrupt his speech. "Oh, none; very little; poor business. Only we're diversified;

that's all that saves us. We go south into Nebraska and Kansas, and there our hotels, they're all packed. You couldn't get a room in them."

"The buses," I suggest, "have big business. Buses and railroads."

"Wonderful!" he shouts, with his whole soul lost to them. "And elevators, too; and if a man was into stores, and could get the stuff. You can't get things to eat." The hotel man says that his town in Kansas—pointing across the five hundred miles toward it—has some special concession, and though the town is "only as big as Sioux Falls here: 40,000, they got a plant that cost twenty million."

"Big business for a town of that size."

"What? Oh, great, wonderful!"

This profit man tells us about a wonderful rich man who must also have been a profit man. These are his farms we are passing, the Rainer Farms. He was a certain Rainer, owner of a newspaper chain, "built it up till he died two years ago." He had fields of Durocs and $80,000 worth of Holsteins and raised 25,000 turkeys a year, and had a lake and also rented all the surrounding lakes as a swimming pool for the mallards that he hatched in incubators. "Sorry he's dead," says the hotel man, "because many came from Wisconsin and New York to buy cattle and stayed at the hotel."

Then in the autumn all who advertised in his papers he brought to the lakes for hunting, and he had cottages for them and a chef and bowling.

"He made money out of that, too, didn't he?"

"He—what? No, _he_ made no money out of it. He charged them nothing, but it was his advertisers, and I suppose it paid out that way, and he was out nothing."

Such is the estimation of profit man by profit man, and he is not slow to eulogize the man who in these parts and in our times was the rich and successful man. We know his hero, we know in what he himself believes, and what he sees as the motive of conduct and the end of life. Competitive capitalism, says one of its national spokesmen, has made us free. The hotel man would understand this gospel.

He gets off then to see after the hotel business in some town, and leaves us to the evening paper where we read that a Cream of Wheat man died just yesterday. "A former Eau Claire man, Cliff

B. Reggy, jr., 89, a founder and former president of the Cream of Wheat Corporation, died Thursday night in his Chicago home." This man, found dead in bed, was a Vermont man who in 1882 went to Eau Claire "and opened a law office. Thirteen years later, after he had expanded his interests to include the farm mortgage business and grain marketing and milling," he hitched up with other businessmen and organized the corporation. Some years later he went into the big city.

Here, then, are real cases of profit men: the Brothers Keene, the hotel man, the lake-and-duck man, and the Cream of Wheat and mortgage man, all of them coming into my way as I cross the prairies. It is the profit man who has made us free. It is he who controls the hotels and the press and in some places the land and cattle. He is the gentleman who on occasion has taken over the farm mortgages and the milling and the marketing of men's grain.

4

It is hard to say how much better or worse the co-op man could do all these things, that is if in fact he could do them. What we know for sure is that here and there in one country or another he has done most of them. He and his kind have seen to housing in settled places, and in lumber camps, and in colleges. Sometimes, as in the case of some of our ten thousand credit unions, he and they retire old debts and manage to avoid mortgages. The marketing of grain has been a central business with him in this country, and he has helped men to own land and cattle. Could he have done the milling in the Midwest in the eighties and nineties? Why not? Could he set up a press, and have broadcasting facilities of his own? This is only to ask whether profit men will allow him free speech, and the reply to this question cannot yet be given.

Milling in the hands of the people—not for profit, but for the common good. Land and houses and lakes and cattle in the hands of the people. Grain marketing in the hands of the people. Banking and the "mortgage business" not in the hands of any one or two or three, but in the hands of the people. That bold program is the democratic and American program of the co-ops. Freedom—

the freedom of persons, of families, of the community, and the State, that is their program.

That is the theory. Naturally, it is not yet worked out, and perhaps it will never be worked out in anything like its fullness. Life is not so simple as ever to fit ideal theories. But something has been done to date, and it is likely that much more will be done. Here and there, too, we begin already to find a man or a woman whom we may dare to call a co-op soul. Not for gain but for human good is this person's life lived. I think that Joe Ryan, among many others, qualifies as a co-operator. This man I meet on a farm the day before I leave Minnesota, and with him are two or three neighbors, none of them far from the ideal.

Joe had to go co-op. As a boy of eighteen he went into Dakota to harvest grain, and I'd guess that it was nearly forty years ago. Some profit men, gouging the grain farmer, converted Joe to co-operation, or got him to find in himself his co-op soul. The situation was as follows. The grain was taken out of the farmer's hands and marketed for him. This was service, though at considerable cost, since it was done at ten cents a bushel (I believe these are the figures); just a ten-cent spread between the farmer's wagon and the Twin Cities.

The farmers said it was too much, but apparently they could do nothing about it.

Then they became daring. They got hold of a few elevators, and started shipping wheat, and at a spread of only six cents. However, they did not last long. The shippers took to handling grain at a four-cent and even a three-cent spread. Out of business went the farmers' elevators, because they could get no grain; nothing for them then but to be liquidated. With the pressure off, the spread on grain leaped up to its old level.

The farmers had been routed once. Would they come back for another fight? They certainly would, and they did. The boy Joe Ryan and a few men thought their way out that winter, and with the next harvest the farmers were shipping grain, and to this day they are shipping it. Joe, now these many years a Minnesota dairyman, remains quietly and effectively a co-op man. Grain goes from his county only via the co-ops. The farm homes and the barns are lighted via the co-ops. At first the creamery was nonexistent, because the town, as an old record says, did nothing but "a large shipping business in grain, flour, potatoes and livestock." But now cream is the main product, and the creamery, run for a while by an Irishman, then by a German, then by a group of businessmen, has long been co-op. The gas station, too, is co-op, and is operated by a man whose thought, if racy and with a way of its own, is nevertheless sound.

This station man is big and young and soft. Says he, "Someone said, 'Only 2 per cent of the members in co-ops understand.' I'd say 2 per cent is too high. If it happened they didn't get a patronage refund, they'd drop out, most of them. That's why I say education is the greatest essential need of the co-operatives. There's going to be lots of trouble ahead, but after this hog-wrestle, what's going to be a-popping, I'd like to see it."

5

Joe Ryan or any other co-op man believes in freedom for the people. He believes in and works for every family's having ownership and security and stability. But big profits and big centralized control that make a handful wealthy and the people poor—in this he cannot believe.

What the soul of the co-op man is, in contrast to the soul of the profit man, keeps coming to me as I leave Joe Ryan and as we passengers encounter the hotel man on the Jackrabbit. Till it is dark we can see for miles across these Dakota and western Minnesota prairies, even from the window of our little bus. Across the wheat are clusters of green trees, planted forty and fifty years ago to serve as windbreaks; and white houses, and red barns whose red at this distance looks like brick. For almost a generation the old individualistic farmer, pitted against Capital and latterly the State, has lost the ownership of this good land, not only here but far off in every direction, with the result that we have had the Oakies and Arkies "tractored out, burnt out, blown out." And the farmer, for all his good will and hard work, can never by himself regain ownership. He needs to go farther than his traditional habit of trading work with other farmers. He needs now to process with them, to market with scores of them, and with them by tens of thousands to have his own oil and coal and factories. Fortunately he has begun to do all this. We shall see that the urbanite even more than the farmer needs to take much these same steps and to become a co-op man.

AT THE GRANGER HOMESTEAD

1

Toward Granger Homestead, outside of Des Moines we now turn our steps. Here again we shall see a co-op community— but then should any community be anything but co-op, and should any proper co-op be less than a community? Here we shall see people who in the first place got together to make their plans, and then bought land together and built their houses together, and now have house near house and every family with its patch of land alongside the neighbor's land.

Of course these people have always lived as families and as communities and to some degree as persons. But that was only be- cause it is so natural to us and, one may say, so absolute with us to be persons. And it is so natural for us to have families and to build neighborhoods that, whatever the conditions and whatever the pressures on us, we will have families and build neighborhoods. Even so, sometimes persons and families and communities are con- stricted and cannot breathe and grow, and have only half a chance. The persons and families at Granger have in the past operated on the old plan for miners in Iowa and America generally, and till lately did not have an opportunity to be what God certainly in- tended them to be.

It is this old community now made new that we want to visit, and to see the persons as neighbors and as members of the com- munity. The trip is made by bus and train and trolley. Today under the hot sun at the end of June the Iowa corn is growing by leaps and bounds. As they say, "It grows while you sleep!" The alfalfa is ripe, much of it too ripe, for in some fields all is a delicate blue, the most tender baby blue. And how lovely is a level field of it stretched away from the sun and against the hills and woods, its blueness so light as to suggest purple and white. Along the roads and hanging into every ditch are pale wild roses, whitish pink with only one row of petals, and white morning-glories are beginning to run over the ground, ready to climb and suffocate the corn. Near the creeks the new corn, lately come through the ground, is still underwater, but on the higher ground the men are in the fields today and are cutting alfalfa and plowing corn.

At a little town as we pass I notice signs for two co-ops. These are the farmers' co-op elevator—an institution which I believe first proved itself in Iowa—and the farmers' co-op feed and lumber. Granting that these truly are co-op on the Rochdale plan and work toward remaking and toward keeping the families and the total community, still, even then, antico-op people appear, especially in the little towns. "It's never been done this way!" In an Iowa town a woman meant to slay the co-ops when she said, "They take the bread from my children's mouths." No doubt, the farmers, men, women and children, had been putting bread into her mouth and the children's mouths too, and possibly going without enough bread for their own families. Let me be bold and say: Iowa ought to go co-op. The Midwest ought to go co-op. And it is traditional and almost native for the landmen to be co-operators. A community, a lot of families each with its own land and house and perhaps livestock, but threshing their wheat together, and in the first place combining it together, marketing most of it together, but grinding a bit of it together, possibly together baking whole-wheat bread of it, and in that way really becoming a community at the same time that they save their economic hides—that is something of what a co-op, at Granger or elsewhere, can be. Hence the oddity and perversity of saying that it has no right to exist. It is like saying that the community has no right to exist.

As we worked toward Des Moines last night the rain was pouring again, and this time it came in volume through the sides of our car. A boy farmer-soldier, in high school last year, boarded our train almost carrying his satin fairy of a bride. A big rough, talkative man got off, and man said to man, "Horse buyer?" The reply came in one word, "Cattle."

In the morning the sun pours like rain out of the sky. On one square of the capital are the First National Bank, a bus station, the cathedral, and an extensive station for the Wacs. Profit-men signs are all over town. One of them shows three men each of whom looks as if he had been trained for the ring; the three are Fighter, Factory, and Farm, and what they say is, "With us it's Chesterfield." We might guess that the next ad is for Coca-Cola or Burma Shave, and its legend is "War or peace the same high standards." On one side of a main street are A & P Super-Market, Grovner's Super-Market, and Thrift Super-Market, and in a drugstore are a yellowish-looking Wac and Wave holding up an ad for cokes.

Surely here is no place for co-ops and for people with a Rochdale nonprofit principle, since Iowa, that is to say the land and business of Iowa, is largely held by profiteers and aliens.

2

It is here, nevertheless, in the heart of absentee landlordism that fifty families have set up the co-op Homestead we have mentioned, and this is learning now to go on all fours.

Granger is modest. Not the trunk of the tree, but the most insignificant bramble. Not the bellwether, but the least and gentlest little lamb. That is Granger in Iowa. It is not talk when I say that the people whose homes and families were to build the new community were unknown, uncounted, unimportant in the state, and in their own settlement not so much as received or wanted. They were coal miners in a place where, as I have known for forty years, coal mining is little respected. These mines do not rate with those of Pennsylvania and Ohio or even those of Illinois, and it is "bohunks, wops and niggers" that operate them. These nice names tell what we farmers, ourselves not Rockefellers and most of us candidates for American Gothic, think of the miners. They are low and trashy, and we do not mix with them. We don't want them at our dances or our churches, and all we ask of them is to keep to their pits and their shacks.

It is a matter of record that Iowa miners are insecure. In normal years they have worked about half time and been idle half time. It is in the winter that they usually have work, but in summer they may count on only a day or two a week. Insecure, semiemployed, and most of the time ready for and fit for the dole or relief that we have thought unfit for an Iowa farmer. Also, of course, unstable and in many cases going—as, in order to live, they must go—from

camp to camp; and never owning anything. I was in a county of
southern Iowa and with miners when in 1913 they were sinking
"18." Company houses appeared, and a company store, and a settlement. But "18" is gone, and so are "19" and "20," and though
some of the shacks were moved to the next camp most of them
were left behind. The people had no houses of their own, no land
or gardens, no store or bank of their own, no hospital, no school
that was properly theirs or amounted to anything, no coal mines.

They owned nothing. No wonder that we farmers who had land
or meant to get a claim on land thought so little of them. It is only
a slight exaggeration to say that they had no ownership, no stability,
no security, and no freedom. They did have the rags to their backs.
In a measure they were free to swear, to love and hate and marry,
and to move on to the next mine or to another job. The farmers
said that the miners were Socialists, and I recall that a miner named
Bleke read more books on socialism than all the farmers of the
county.

The lowest income group in Iowa. The least stable, the least
secure, and the least free group. Without land, in Iowa itself!

The company houses that presumably sheltered them were
shacks, squares of walls thrown together and roofed over, as cold
as barns in winter and like ovens in summer. That is the fact, and
it is not something of the past simply, since it remains true of
mining settlements in Kentucky, Illinois, Missouri, and Iowa.
They are hardly places for people to occupy. Health precarious,
moral life for children and adults precarious, religion precarious,
the schools no great honor to the community. In fact, the local
people at Granger ran along for twenty-five years before one of
their children, at last in the 1930's, managed to get through high
school. Wages for miners in Iowa in 1935 came to the handsome
average of $890.35, and out of that sum the big family must pay
for rent and fuel and light, pay the grocer and the butcher, get
its recreation, go to school, keep clothed and well and strong, and
build up what hopes it could for the future.

Not much chance for such people to be decent and free and
Christian. But what can they do? Can these pauperized people
lift themselves by their own bootstraps? Their condition is what we
commonly call proletarian: a people reduced to living wholly on

work and wages or on the chance of these, and in hard times and always in their old age State-dependent.

Suppose that in such a fix men should begin to want to be free and relatively independent of the State and the "operators," possessed at once of homes and land and health and food, and thus self-respecting, happy, content, self-secure—how could they do it? How on God's earth could they ever boost themselves out of the proletarian condition? How could they even be brought round to the stage where they would "want to come out of the doldrums"? That is really the first problem—that wanting to be free and secure. So says the man who more than any other moved the fifty families at Granger. "Mostly they don't rebel," he says. "But apathy is worse than rebellion. It was necessary to go to them one by one, family by family, and tell them they could be free. 'Don't you want a little bit of land, and your own home and your own food?' That is what had to be put to them."

That was part of the problem. Now, it happened that just at that time a sum of money was by statute "made available to the President, to be used by him through such agencies as he may establish and under such regulations as he may make, for making loans or otherwise aiding in the purchase of subsistence homesteads. The moneys shall constitute a revolving fund. . ." It is well known that most projects of this kind have failed. They are too artificial, too mechanical and paternalistic, and are managed or mismanaged from afar, by politicians, men without knowledge or love of the little community lost in Iowa or Alabama. Of course, they fail. But they can succeed, and if in time and by a struggle they get completely on their own feet they may be a triumph. To date the Granger Homestead shows wonderful vitality and promise.

The formal arrangement with the federal government is as follows: The people borrowed the money at 3 per cent and are to pay month by month over a period of thirty or forty years. In that way they were able to buy an excellent farm of 225 acres, and each family now has three or four acres. Does the government not in the long run simply give them the land? The government gives them nothing. The people borrow the needed funds, and anybody to stay on his land must make his payments. In the company houses, often unfit for habitation, never modern or with toilet or bath, they paid a rent of ten dollars a month, and had no land or gardens, and these wretched houses they would never own. Now they pay, in a typical case, $15.50 a month, and for this they have land and a modern house, both of which they are coming to own. Says the present manager, "The people are buying it on long lease running to forty years," if they wish. "Complete payment save the last payment can be made at any time." This last payment cannot be made within the first ten years, lest any homesteader should pay up and then sell out, turning himself in the act into a profit man. This is against the common agreement and consequent law. At first the proposal—and, I believe, the practice—was to have the Homestead owned by the government; but happily the people now are legally in control, and the management is local. Since the people have taken over, no problem of delinquent payment any longer exists. "At the present time [October 5, 1943] I don't believe we have a member a month behind. We have three who have paid out in full, and expect two more by the end of this month."

The family pays interest and insurance and amortization month by month, and also for management and maintenance and community facilities and contingency. A part exemption is allowed on taxes as soon as 10 per cent is paid, but of course nearly all have gone beyond this limit. For land and a home that are to belong to the family and even now have a warm and personal quality, the cost is $1,894. The monthly payment on this runs to $15.37, for the following items:

amortization and interest over 40 years	$ 6.78
management	1.70
insurance	1.22
taxes with exemption for 10% paid	.49
contingency	1.75
maintenance	2.50
community facilities	.93
total	$15.37

3

Do the people like these new places? Do they like them better than the old ones? Do they like the new community that already and against odds they have begun to build? This is like asking whether people like to be free and at least somewhat stable and secure and in command of their fortunes; whether they like to have families, to see to their children's health and training, to have good food raised by themselves and cooked at home, and whether they like to have neighbors and to be neighbors, and to own good land and a modern home. All in all, it is to ask whether man likes to be a person and a free man, and not a parasite or slave.

The houses are modern, are of four or five or six rooms with bath and cellar, electricity, heating, plumbing, and landscaping. They are built of wood, the ceilings are of celotex, and plywood is used instead of plaster. In the basement are a hot-air furnace, a hot-water heater with tank, and an automatic pressure tank that is hitched to the electric well pump. The houses are not scattered miles apart, but are arranged in a unit or group with the community center nicely located. In this way a neighborhood is at once suggested.

The land is the best, and the families have their own food, raised on their own plots by their own intelligence and labor. This makes food ever so much better, giving it a human vitamin that cannot be had in any other way. It is better food, and only such food can be had in plentiful amounts. We need not argue that poor people cannot have plentiful and good food unless they raise it. One might hope that the wars would help to jar or jolt that fact into our heads, and it is a fact that many co-operators, wishing to be free, need to learn. People fed from tin cans pay too much overhead and do not yet know freedom. Just the other day there came to my desk a pamphlet, "What Can the Co-op Mean to You?" Among its offerings was a page showing co-op tin cans, including canned tomatoes and tomato juice, asparagus, peas, cherries, and peaches. I am aware that in our times some canned living is necessary, but I am afraid that to the co-op label we need at times to attach the words "canned dependence."

The Granger homesteaders, who in a dozen important ways are co-operators, have, at least in their own case, declared for the freedom had in home-grown, home-packed, and home-cooked foods. That is, they raise their own, and pack it, cook it, and eat it. Wherever possible, this is the better economy. It means your own, from start to finish.

But in the sort of economy represented by Granger, the suburban, foot-on-land, foot-in-industry economy, it is not enough for persons

and families to produce their food. The families need to co-operate in order to get the most social good and economic good out of
the local possibilities. Neighbors need to work together in little
co-ops, and at Granger this is just what they do. They buy seed
together, together they own an all-purpose tractor with plow and
disk and harrow and mower attachments, and I am told that they
have never had trouble deciding whose turn it was to use the tractor.
To work in this way means a needed saving, and it is more neighborly and better.

The people at Granger are poor and will always continue to be
poor, with no stock-and-bond or other profit men among them. They
really need gardens and pigs and chickens and cows or goats to
make ends meet and to live a human life of their own and on their
own. As lately as 1938 the total annual wage for the fifty families
was as low as $49,000; some families drop as low now and then as
$600 a year, and seldom does any rise above twice that sum. Their
income depends on a wage, about forty of the families getting a
wage from the mines, and others as carpenters or mechanics or rail-
road men, and some cash income and a considerable noncash income arise now from the produce of the land. Their first year was
1936 when the crops suffered badly from drought and the families
were far from masters of the situation. But even then they "stored
away more than 15,000 quarts of canned vegetables and fruits,"
and it is estimated that the crop from their part-time farming was
worth $3,000. The next summer it jumped to eight, and the next
to thirteen. How far this serious bit of farming will carry a family
depends on management. The current authoritative statement says
that four or five of the units are able to make the land meet "all
the payment and complete care of the families, and one of these is
a large family with eight small children. . . I would also say that
the units' production would more than average the payments taking unit for unit. In other words, the produce raised will average
more than the payments."

4

It was on December 15, 1935, that the first family moved into
its new home, and many of us recall that from about that date
the winter was ferocious. Never was the like in Iowa, at least for

decades. Two of the women tell me now of the difference in the lives of the homesteaders and in what we may call their human attitude. It was at that time that these women, Mrs. Biondi and Mrs. Lammi, moved, "just when the worst winter was setting in. But we liked the Homestead right from the start, it was so much better than the poor houses and paying rent for what we'd never own. We never lived in a company house, either of us," says Mrs. Lammi. "But this—it was your own house." All of us are in the house of a homesteader as we talk, and it is a decent and proper place to be, for the woman of this house where she and her husband and ten children came to be masters, has died today and is being waked. It is their own home, their own place, shaped up into their own by themselves and the neighbors.

What the co-op life comes to in such a spot as Granger is this: the co-ops are economic tools, and also ever so much more than economic tools. With the help of them, the home, and the neighborhood, that have so commonly withered away, have the chance to be reborn. And we have, in estimating them, to keep in mind the pitiable flotsam that usually serves as home and neighborhood in an American mining camp.

Here at Granger they have a real and beautiful home life and neighborhood life. No wonder that in March, 1939, Pope Pius XI wrote to congratulate "this significant enterprise in social service." But it is more than "service"; it is enterprise, construction, creation, an effective declaration of freedom. President Roosevelt's greetings at their first Christmas and ten days after the first family occupied its new home, were closer in tone to the life at Granger. Said he, "Those of us who believe that the home is the cornerstone of society will rejoice with the Granger Homesteaders that they are realizing for themselves and their children that sense of comfort and peace and security which home ownership brings."

As stability goes among our people and especially among our miners, the men and women here are fairly contented and settled. Hardly were they in the new places when one woman said she would not stay, would not live outside a city. Well, they let her go. But thirty-five of the original homesteaders have not budged. Two or three houses have had a succession of occupants. Just this year one young man has gone into the perhaps greater stability of full-

time farming, and another into industry. Where do the young
people go when they marry? More land is needed, and perhaps the
people will in time provide it and thus allow the settlement to
propagate itself. We know that two couples of newlyweds have
taken homes left by others, and "in many cases the younger make
provision to take over the unit when the old folks pass on." All in
all, this is a problem that only experience and study will solve.
The high school is in important senses ready now to face it, with
boys learning for two hours on each of two afternoons a week
some of the arts needed by men with one foot on the land, and with
girls giving as much time to learning what it takes to manage a
home. No rural or suburban school in America but must consider
what is beginning to be done along these lines at Granger. "Charm
House" I hear advertised on the air: a person goes and sees the fur-
nishings ready-made at the store, and goes through the interesting
mechanical action of writing a check for them or taking them on
time. Canned goods again! But at Granger the boys and girls are
learning the first steps in making things. Planting, breeding, spraying, grafting, sewing, cooking—all the arts of free men and women
on the land. What one hundred thousand of these tiny Grangers
well worked out, in our rural and semirural areas, might do to
"national advertising" and—shall we say, incidentally?—for our
national being!

    "Life insurance . . . put aside some of today's earnings. . . The
Banner man in your community will be glad to help you plan."
Of course he would. And perhaps something may be said for our
letting him do it: whatever may be said for the little dictator. So,
too, would the national meat man and the ketchup man and the
bank man and an endless series of these good souls. But it is better
for people to get together and make their world. It is better for the
community to see to its own insurance, and dispense with the Banner man, better for the community to see to its own meat and credit
and burial. Can the people do all this? The Granger experiment
suggests that they can. Miners can have land and homes and security
and freedom. If people have the courage to plan and own and operate the communities, we see that they can do it, and it is clear
now that wherever we have people with the necessary intelligence
and courage we could assimilate another community on the Granger

model, the people with one foot on the land and the other, "the cash foot," in industry.

In 1938 I first visited the Homestead, and in my old notebook of that time and also in my new one I find this dictum, taken from the wall of the schoolhouse and attributed to St. Ignatius: "Preserve always your liberty of mind. See to it that you lose it not by any one's authority or any event whatsoever." This the people cannot do unless they have home ownership, and they cannot have such ownership now unless they plan and work and build together.

For our freedom then, for the rights of man—that is something of what such an experiment may look to and try to provide. But can it be done, and can we do it? These questions are answered perhaps by a set of questions that I copy from my old Granger notebook. "Have we not the resources? Have we not the intelligence? Have we not the good will? And 'we' equals the American people."

Resources, intelligence, good will—which of these do we lack? Of course we would dare anyone to say· we are short on any of these vital materials. And yet we have not the freedom for all our people, and are not likely soon to have it. Many of our people have been more and more enslaved to the few, and now it is almost as if they wanted to be enslaved to the State. What is worst is not necessarily the fact of enslavement, but the attitude of despair, the attitude that says: "The land—that's no good. Decentralized and co-op homesteads—they're no good. The community and neighborhood—they're no good and can save nobody." For these persons nothing but despair, and in their view man is doomed to be **owned** and enslaved. There is nothing people can do about it.

Possibly our small and homespun Granger with its community life, its co-operation among families as the elementary co-op units, begins, if not to answer that attitude, at least to challenge it and to tell men to look twice at our resources, our intelligence, and our good will. For even if Granger itself should fall tomorrow, what it has to date done stands, and is a challenge.

Ten

A CO-OP PARISH IN IOWA

1

At Westphalia, in Iowa, they have an interesting set of co-ops that will revive the faith of any believer in democracy. The community here is a parish, and we must say that any real parish is the most basic kind of co-op. People cannot believe together and worship together and hope together, without at the same time having and ever re-creating in themselves an elemental oneness. Everybody belongs, and just as if it were a sixth sense, everybody has in him a deep, unconscious sense of belonging. And it is not only that vital point, the point we have so often seen in the co-ops, of being with the community and at many turns for the community. It is more fundamental than that. It is indeed the community members among themselves who count, but much more the community with the one God the Father of all.

A religion always has this effect. It has to have it, since it supposes oneness in faith and hope and worship. Religion is the virtue that gives to God His due, and that is to say the virtue by which we worship God. This "we" properly and literally is everybody, for the reason that each person unavoidably pays the highest tribute to what he sees as the highest good. In that way the world of man makes up one vast "ecclesia," or body of worshipers. On the word of Christ, the Christian religion sees God as Our Father and all men as brothers. As Christian I may not do anything else. I may not hate man. I may not hate Jew or Gentile, yellow or white or red or black. I am actively to honor and love all. My nature, as well as St. Paul's word, says that I am to love that which is good, and this above all includes man.

Now, no one will ever understand Westphalia unless he sees the parish as a healthy little branch on the immense tree of the Christian Church. The co-op life here in its very soul and foundation is religious.

Believers are sometimes grouped against believers, but in the Catholic Church, and certainly among Protestants, we have had plenty of individualism, a contradiction that all have swallowed. Protestants went in for private judgment, every man for himself, and achieved an endless series of sects. Catholics have kept to a common doctrine and a common rule, but went in for private devotions, and while they have worshiped at the same time and in the same place, they have not always worshiped together and as one.

It is together and as one that the people of Westphalia worship God. By good fortune my coming to them is on the eve of Corpus Christi. The farmers are busy, but in the evening a few of them are talking and shopping together at their community store, and a few are together in the community center. The next morning every family is represented and many families have every member present for the Mass and the procession through the church grounds. And at the Mass, it is not simply private devotions that they have, every man by and for himself, but all the people singing and praying the Mass as one body. This means that the prayer is common, it is everybody's at once, and is surely "public," and it has the fully democratic and plebeian wording and sense and manner that come from its having been the central prayer of Christians since the days of Christ. A lot of people together in a church need not mean more than a lot of people together in a Chicago street. But a lot of people together in a church and together also in belief and hope and in one central act of worship, many words of it reaching back into our Christian and Hebrew past—that is democracy at worship. And that is what I am happy to see this morning at Westphalia.

The people have their own band. Of course, the people here and everywhere must have this, because they must more and more have their own entertainment, their own dances, their own games and their own shows. All these must in large part go co-op, if we are to have freedom and democracy, and not slave-minds and autocracy. Am I not more than delighted, then, to see that the boys and girls have brought their musical instruments this morning? Around the grounds, too, we go in our worship, and through the cemetery so that the open fields and even the dead are counted as within this democracy of prayer. Afterward the pastor, a big hearty man who writes songs and composes and plays music and has painted "The Spirit of Iowa," takes up the baton and away he and the boys and girls go playing patriotic airs. It is their music, their own entertainment made by the group and enjoyed by the group, some of it so native as to have been composed here. "As the caissons go rollin' along. Hi-lee, hi-lo . . . Shout out your numbers good and strong!" "Right makes might. None other can be, In the Land of the Free!" "When this great war is over!" The "Marine Hymn" goes well with these people as it does with everybody. Also, their own Westphalia's Pep Song:

> Be a booster! Be a booster!
> For only babies cry.

It is the complete life they aim at, and they have a theme song for it:

> You live among the birds and flowers,
> Mid lovely dells and woodland towers.
> The waves at shore all roll to greet you,
> The mighty trees all bowed to greet you.
> The stars on high are gleaming,
> And that something there just keeps on dreaming.
> To mountains' might we all surrender,
> To nature's God our praise we tender.

Company, attention! Forward! March! Well, indeed they do go now, because they know they are headed for the community center where each boy or girl is to have Seven-Up or a chocolate bar on the parish.

Lately they went the sixty or seventy miles to Council Bluffs and played there for the mothers of the boys who had made up the 168th Infantry Band. These boys lost their instruments on the way over, and then in the first awful days of battle in North Africa, so hard on Iowa men, every boy of them was killed. "Only the bandmaster survived, and remains on duty in Africa. In May he wrote, 'It's been plain Hell here since February.' How very proud the mothers are, and how happy they were to have our band come!"

2

Besides their music and the co-op they have with the common Father, the Westphalians have long had co-ops in the narrower sense. For over fifty years they have had their own insurance on livestock and on homes and farm buildings. What does this mean? For one thing, it is their own. It is insurance of each by all. "Each for all and all for each." That is what co-operation always supposes and demands. Why not, then, in the insurance line? Why should not the people out of their own resources and intelligence and good will create their own insurance? Why should each family be handing over to remote and semialien companies a few dollars a year? No company could ever give the people more in the way of service than they have had these fifty years: prompt and immediate payment on losses.

Their own, homespun from the resources, the brains, and the goodness of these people. No insurance company in Chicago or New York or Hartford ever would or could give them this element of a parish creation.

Is not the service of the big remote company, nevertheless, better? No, in the sense of a people's creation and the sense of democratic control, it is so far from being better that it is no good at all. It would pay, presumably, just the same amount. But would it not, after all, be safer and more economical? No, not any safer, since in fact all losses have been covered. And not more economical; on the contrary, it would have been much more costly. The people would have paid, over these fifty years, not less than $250,000 to absentee insurance companies for no value received. That is the economic saving effected by the co-op, though for each of 420 policies[1] the annual saving would have been little. Four hundred or so *times* fifty years *times* that little annual saving for each *equals* a quarter of a million dollars. That tiny amount turns out to be immense, and as we have seen at other centers, if it is put together with the savings effected at the store, at the gas station, and so on, it makes the difference in time between slaves and free men. That is properly the saving: in terms not of money, but of our freedom.

We all know that the farmers, as well as many others, need to learn the co-op formula. What they know well is poverty. I have seen people hungry on Iowa land in the twenties. For we had a de-

[1] The insurance co-op includes but is wider than the parish. I can get no official statement of savings, and have cut the unofficial statement by 50 per cent.

pression not merely from 1929 on, but as early as 1922, and this was not cured by the later one. In 1917-1918 men and women were lost to the land; so that we may say that for twenty years the farmers knew serious distress. The rich farming land around Westphalia was no exception to the law. But after two years of the industrial depression had been added to the other depression, the people "began conversations." In effect, these were and they continue to be study clubs. Man meets man and talks things over. The pastor especially had begun to get a vision or the promise of a vision that something might possibly be done. At least he had not ceased to hope. And it was he who most of all promoted these conversations. He would meet a farmer or two on the road and throw out some ideas. And anyone who knows farmers knows also that they like to mull over ideas, and to try them out with the next man they meet.

Ideas, as Father Tompkins of Nova Scotia is so fond of saying, have hands and feet. They go to work. That is what eventually happened here. But farmers are conservative, and take their time, a fact that holds good everywhere, even though it was almost at the door of Westphalia that at this period farmers took up pitchforks against an official who came to sell their land. At Westphalia they tried a different sort of action.

Their co-op achievements were in the following order. First the church, and long ago the effective insurance co-op. Then the clubhouse or social center. What is this for, especially in a country place? For the social life of the people. In the parish school is a hall where they have parish dances and play basketball and put on plays. Why, then, the clubhouse? For talk in little groups, for playing cards and billiards, for refreshments. And these people are Germans and are going to have beer. If not in the shadow of their own church, if not here at home in their community, then away from here and among strangers. Not only would they have to go out among strangers, but their money would be siphoned off. They have therefore seen to the matter: they serve beer here at home.

In the worst depression winter they took timber land in common, cut it in common, and brought it home for the common use of the parish. In the spring they always put their baseball park into shape, and they have played together so long that teams within range hardly dare to face Westphalia.

Still, too many things had passed out of their control. Worship and games and dances were at home, beer was at home, insurance was at home. But where did they "trade"? Progressively, in the surrounding towns. This was unhealthy, and would have to be stopped. They would get feed, groceries, meat, and oil and gas here at home. But to learn how to do this would take time. Farmers are never radical, or easily hurried, and are slow to get trapped into an outright losing of so much as ten dollars. Nevertheless, things were going right from under their noses, little by little. "Rapid transit and consolidation," says the priest, "took everything out of here. The gas we never had, or banking. And then the food and the wear, these were the last things on which we could be held up. There was hardly a dollar's worth of trade left in the town."

In 1934 came the great drought, and Iowa was parched and scorched. This good land returned hardly a thing, and the men had stock to try to bring through the winter. They bought grain together and thereby saved money, and then, just when conditions were the hardest, they made up their minds to "hold up the profit and throw it into a pool, in order to start the co-operative."

Then a dozen men got into cars and went to a Nebraska town to study the co-ops. What they saw did them good: a co-op store, a co-op elevator, "the co-op [feed] buying, the petroleum setup, and all the opposition." That night they were home with the story. They went again, and came home again with great talk, and one of the men said, "I recommend going to visit some place where there's a co-op wholesale." The wholesale in Kansas City, however, at once sent a man to them. Their constitution was made ready, directors were named from among themselves, education was provided for. Still, they had no money in hand.

Says a leader, "We worked at collecting. It was ten dollars a share, and we got up to five and six from some, but mostly we got promises, with one dollar down and nine promised. But that promise was and is good. The trouble was, people didn't know what to think. They talked about it, in every house and on the party lines, and some wouldn't join and some only brought up all the points they could against it. And they did have some good points! Would we get enough in subscriptions? See, there was only fifty or so subscribers, because some took two shares. And was there enough trade in Westphalia to justify a store? Besides, we had competition on every side, and opposition too."

The farmer who tells me these matters is a filled-out and solid man, his arms so strong that they seem packed into the sleeves. "Mike thinks things out and gets them straight." So a neighbor says of him. It is true, all the same, that Mike and a few others were caught by profit men who "sold them" on electricity. They gave a thousand apiece to have the "juice" brought seven miles to their farmhouses, and this price was so outrageous that after several fights they got a rebate of two hundred to the man. Farmer Mike says he still feels "a kinda burnin' from the skinnin' we got," and when the REA came to all the farmers he was incredulous and wondered whether it was not some sort of politico-financial deal, to be rewarded by a rake-off.

The store managed at last to exist. Says Farmer Mike, "Some think they'll reform things, but in office they get leveled off. They learn by doing. There's always danger of friction: men have been their own bosses. It does men lots of good to get on their feet before half a dozen: that is our study club."

In its first year, which was 1936, the store did something. It had a trade of twelve thousand, if my figures are correct, and under "a smart Irishman from Omaha," a gain of eighteen hundred. In 1942 it did a business running to $168,000: in the six years a trade increase of 1400 per cent; and in 1943, it went over two hundred thousand. Since the parish has only one hundred families, the present turnover seems impossible. But the land is extraordinarily good, and none of the farms small, and the store carries groceries, and gas which is at the door, and light hardware, and cold meats, and processed feeds.

It took from 1936 or so to 1940 for the people to become interested, get the store on its feet and make it go. Now it needs four full-time employees, besides some extra help, and in 1941 the people built a new store. That, then, is the co-op in its evident effects. And all this came to pass, "at an Iowa crossroads, where they said it couldn't be done. We are so proud of it!" Surely the effect it begins to have on the persons and the community is ever so much more important and vital. The reason is that such a venture, if well planned and well done, tends at any town to revive the common life, but here, relative to trade, it has created that life.

The venture at Westphalia is what we may call a total co-op. All the people down to the last family have come in, down to but not including that last family.

The difference in spirit is so great that a person is tempted to say it is everything. But it rests on a material base, and cannot be separated from this. The base, if a possible 6 per cent is made on the turnover, is incredible. Without interest it comes, in one hundred years, to just short of ten thousand dollars per family—enough to buy for each family a small farm of Iowa land.

On the material side that is what a well-managed country store can do. Just the somewhat inclusive store by itself.

Of course, the people have now started a little bank. Says the man in charge, "What do you people in colleges do about teaching on money? Won't some scholar be honest and put the thing simply, and so we all can understand it? Why the mystery?"

The priest is present and adds some questions. Young men and women, he says, are taught "advertising" and "insurance" and "selling": they go out "to sell people. Does your school or any school, little or big, anywhere, teach people to buy, and not get fleeced?"

They say the people's bank or credit union got started in 1939. Had it been going when the store was trying to be born, it would have been a great help. In its early stage, the pastor made this promise: "When it hits twenty-five thousand, I'll give a party," and was told, "It already is at thirty-two!" By 1942 it stood at forty thousand, and by the summer of 1943 at sixty thousand. But they hope to go up to one hundred. That would readily care for small loans. The people, however, see no vital need or good of it. True, it does protect the small borrower from the 42 per cent legally allowed in Iowa. But in normal times few small borrowers exist or are menaced in so rich a farming section. And until it is hitched up with others of its kind, say on a regional or state-wide basis, it remains too small to do much toward financing Iowa farms. The whole problem of manufacturing credit on a big scale—supposing this desirable—is only on its way to being fully worked out by co-operators.

3

Westphalia is intoxicated with the triumph of its store. The people in effect say, "Instead of trading at Harlan and Dunlap and other big towns around us, we have our own center, and what would be their profit comes back to us as an overcharge on ourselves." And, as we saw, they might go on to say that in a century each farm family would pour into those bigger towns an overcharge of ten thousand dollars. For what? For absolutely no value received. And worse than that: the people would have to spend time and gas and overhead to get to those towns; and this is estimated at fifty dollars annually per family. For what, again? For nothing, unless as a reward for stupidity. Well, Westphalia in this matter has become pretty smart.

In other matters, too, the parish has begun to think and is ready to act. Among the interesting plans are these: First, a feed mixer or processor. The people raise the grain. Why haul it off at a cost and pay for having it processed, and then haul it back? Second, a creamery. These farmers are mainly in corn and meat. But for safety they need to diversify, and in fact they have begun to do this. Why, then, pay a toll to outside creameries? Third, perhaps a small slaughterhouse, with a butcher from among themselves and a store-box electrically cooled, possibly saving the hundred families several thousand a year. These people produce the best meat in the world. Why not have some of it at the cost of production? Why the roundabout and costly method we have now for an Iowa farmer to get a bite of meat? The costs pile up, sometimes including all these items: the local dealer or rustler's toll, the toll for trucking to Omaha, toll for use of the yards, toll for selling in the yards, toll for slaughter, toll for storing and for reshipping, and toll for sale at last over the block to a man whom we may call the slaughtered farmer. Why not slaughter some of the meat, and store it in a co-op quick freezer? "You know what our present system is like?" said a Westphalia farmer. "It's like a fellow milking a cow and finding only a pint in the bucket—because fifty suckers were taking their toll."

Other plans are more tentative. These include a bit of study toward forming a burial co-op. As one hundred families cannot sup-

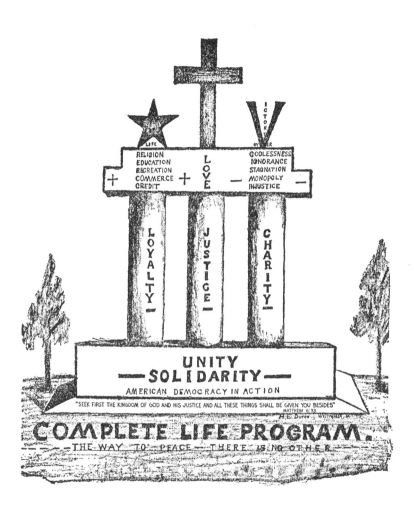

port an undertaker, the thought is to send a committee to some undertaker near by and tell him, "If you want the trade of these hundred families—" possibly excluding the one family which refuses to co-operate— "you can have it: on just these terms . . ." As it has done in insurance, possibly the parish can also someday tie up with neighbors and look to its own hospital and medical care.

What the people begin to aim at is the complete life, and on the lawn of the churchyard they have an immense board outlining their plan. It runs like this:

COMPLETE LIFE PROGRAM
"Seek ye first the kingdom of God"

institutions		negations
Religion	vs.	godlessness
Education	vs.	ignorance
Recreation	vs.	stagnation
Commerce	vs.	monopoly
Credit	vs.	injustice

LOYALTY JUSTICE CHARITY

UNITY AND SOLIDARITY

"Let's rebuild the small towns of America"

That undoubtedly is a big program, and will take time. The only possible question here or anywhere is whether we have or have not the resources, the intelligence, and the good will to undertake and to effect it. The constructive institutions rest on the three pillars of loyalty, justice, and charity, and everything is rooted in unity and solidarity. Says the pastor, "We've got to keep shooting at the skies, in the line of ideals. The material base, we are strong for it, but with this necessary start we aim to go on to the highest. Collectivism is everywhere the trend. But in the form of fascism it won't do, or of state socialism, or of communism. The result is that only co-operation is a feasible American procedure. If co-operation goes out, we can only get some unacceptable brand of collectivism."

And I see in the parish plenty of families and conditions ready to go for and with the social good. The people usually have ownership, and have never been the slaves of any man. Families in many cases live largely within their farms and within the community, and neither exploit nor are exploited. Such happiness and sanity in a home that has sent two boys overseas, that has two boys this morning in the corn—and looking over the fences at the neighbors' girls, too—that has daughters understanding the household and family life, girls who weed and cook and preserve, who worship and sing and dance. That is one sort of family here. Another kind is out for big money, and has gone commercial. This second type grabs up farms and looks less to the common good. It is one enemy of rural reconstruction. Another problem, if possibly not an enemy, is the big debts that are a hang-over from inflation at the end of World War I. A third problem, and the worst enemy, is absentee ownership. This leads again to commercialization and the lust of the profit man.

Here are some figures on the fact of absentee landlordism. Says a writer in the Des Moines *Sunday Register* for June 13, 1943:

Conservation and parity payments show that much of our land is under the control of insurance companies and other absentee landlords, and in many states the largest payments (by government on parity and conservation) went to landlords and banks and insurance companies, as follows:

State	Companies or persons	Amount
Ohio	Union Central Life Ins. Co., Cincinnati	$ 49,153
Wisconsin	Northwestern Mutual Ins. Co., Milwaukee	$ 47,517
Iowa	Equitable Life Ins. Co., Des Moines	$ 33,418
Missouri	General American Life Ins. Co., St. Louis	$ 52,170
Mississippi	British Owners of Delta & Pine Land Co.	
Nebraska	Federal Land Bank of Omaha	$ 77,605
Minnesota	Federal Land Bank of St. Paul	$ 75,761
New York	Metropolitan Life Ins. Co.	$101,863

That, of course, is an intolerable condition, and the co-operators at Westphalia and elsewhere must find out whether they can, even retroactively, do anything about it. Above all, they must know that they now have a proved technique which allows them effectively to say that not another foot of their land will go alien or absentee.

4

The temperature is at one hundred as we go on a rickety bus into Council Bluffs, and it is not any lower as we wait four hours in order to get started east at all. The people in these parts are native, of course, and vigorous and rawboned, and I have special reason to like them. But I am left wondering whether they unhappily lack some of the human resources needed to manage their world. The material resources are here, certainly, here or nowhere on God's earth. The good will is undoubtedly here, though it is badly dispersed and its owners are unaware of its strength. The intelligence also is present.

What, then, stands in the way of their social good? The same factors which I have several times said block the path to our freedom and development. These people have been nursed at the breast of individualism. This has been in our way, and now with the law of nature—the almost physical laws of economics and psychology —catching up on it, the old jungle practice is willy-nilly giving in to new collectivisms. These also will get and long keep in our way. We have the material resources, and on the other points, of our intelligence and good will, I don't want to yield, and no fact or law makes me yield; the truth is that we have these requirements. What we lack is co-ordination. We lack collaboration and co-operation among these elements. Intelligence must be used: it must be applied by these local people to the given situation. Things that look as simple and practical and automatic as a machine may demand concentrated and concerted study. Mere John-D-will-do-it-for-us or some Franklin-D-will-do-it-for-us is no good. Neither big business nor big politics can do what demands to be done.

That is strong talk on my part, especially in view of the high temperature. Most people take things quietly and as they come. But which things they will take as they come, which institutions and persons and movements they will accept at all—that is the real test.

Here, at any rate, are some of our people. Across the street to the bus station come two pedestrians on a lark. They mow down the traffic, cutting it crosswise, and as is the way with men between drunk and sober they escape injury: as people say, "A fool for luck!" At the station and outside against it are a few persons, all of them patient. One is a young woman with fiery red hair and a face that is the color of mottled blood in water. How sparingly she is dressed, in a white waist that lies flat to her bones, a wide, flowery skirt, and tennis shoes and red anklets. She is simple and unaware of her mannish stride and the posture that leaves her a trifle nude. If people are made in part of dust, her bit of clay must have been an uneven, brushy hill.

On the bus across Iowa in the middle of the night the people are chattering and friendly: poor people, good people who in the immense turnover of the past hundred years have not learned to apply their goodness and intelligence to saving their liberty and humanity. Things just happened, things just happen now and will just happen. That is something of people's attitude. But I am glad to say that in a hundred places we are beginning to learn, even if it takes depressions and imperialisms and dictatorships and wars to knock the beginning of wisdom into our souls.

"Get your hands up, Sally! Away above your head!" So a woman on the bus is saying to one of her four little ones, every one of them whooping. The little woman and her man are traveling by bus from San Diego, with the four, to Chicago. A woman is coming two days from Cheyenne to an Iowa town to get to her dying grandfather, and her daughter of four, his one great-grandchild, with her. The two are worn out, and at the last lap the child gets sick. Bus follows bus, and the drivers work together and keep track of each other's passengers and problems, and they know children by name and older people by the names of their towns: "Mickey . . . Dotty . . . San Diego . . . Cheyenne."

Through the open windows on this hot night sweet smells are coming to us from the great body of Iowa, from the live, green, unbruised trees and corn and the new growing oats, from the plowed earth, and the lush alfalfa that just this day was cut.

5

In October of 1944 I am again at Westphalia, with many others, to help celebrate the Rochdale centennial. The visitors include four bishops, persons from a dozen states and from Nova Scotia and Jamaica. Westphalia is called the Rochdale of America, and its achievement is referred to as democracy in action.

The songs for the events are created locally and sung by the local people. It is incredible that all the men and women and children should know every word of the lovely "Panis Angelicus," and as they together and as a recreational-devotional co-op sing the words "O res mirabilis," the words have a special local sense. We see a co-op movie, made here by these people. The commentator says, "A May wedding, the boy a great co-operator . . . Some of our little boys: the children in our school come from families that average seven children . . . That boy fell over Germany . . . That's our band . . . That whole family is an orchestra."

Farmers come on to the stage and tell us what a credit or a grocery co-op demands and what it produces. "Just know the man, if he's honest and a saver, and can be trusted. It takes good judgment and a little common sense." They say that the insurance for which the "best companies" charge four dollars they have for a dollar-fifty: a saving of over 60 per cent. The trading at the store went above two hundred thousand in 1943, and in 1944 will go higher. A few years ago the local trade amounted to almost nothing, "and we couldn't get the things we needed." Just suppose this local gain was multiplied by 37,000, the number of American towns as small as this one!

It is true that the co-operatives cannot by themselves effect the total redemption of man. The centennial co-op cake suggests what is basic: its layers from top to bottom are Justice, Loyalty, and Charity. But "every fellow boosting the other fellow," in matters of food and schooling and sales and trade and patriotism and worship, and this real community life resting on loyalty and love and fairness—such a union of Man and Faith and Nature has in fact done wonders. We must get this fuller meaning when the commentator says, "This is the shrine built with our own hands."

Westphalia has begun to furnish part of the pattern for freedom.

Eleven

WHAT LOCAL LEADERSHIP CAN DO

1

FOR fifteen years the people of Noble County in Indiana have had much of their business and much of their life on a co-op plan, and as a county this is one of the co-op models in America. The accomplishment is great, and the hopes are at once sane and real. Not many who have worked elsewhere with co-ops can easily believe that of the twenty-five hundred farm families in Noble County over two thousand are in one way or another in the co-ops, though at the end of May, 1943, the shareholders were short of fourteen hundred.

The first co-op was organized here in 1927, under the influence and impetus of the Farm Bureau, but for several years the local co-op has felt somewhat free of this. The county has two co-operative general stores, at least one co-op service station, the co-op handling of farm machinery, a co-op bulk plant for gas and oil that keeps seven truckers employed, a co-op elevator, co-op burial, co-op insurance, and co-op credit, and it has had and again will have co-op recreation, especially for its young people.

All of these, put together, do an immense lot of business, and much for the educational, social, and neighborhood life.

What has occurred in the new spirit and hope and "lift" to the people is more vital and important than the visible fruit. If dire things should come after the war, we may bet that the people of Noble County will be among the first to rediscover their way. The people here have had leadership of a native and homespun kind. When the rural depression had been going on about ten years, they brought a credit union or people's bank into existence. This was in the June of 1931, and "sixteen or eighteen fellows did it: they started it. There was a couple of fellows that didn't put in five dollars that night: they was a little scared of it." But some dared to put in ten. It was a bank with eighty-five dollars capital. By 1933 it had worked up to twelve thousand, and then in one year it jumped to thirty-two. This advance was due in large part to a co-op school that traveled from county to county and made ten one-week stops in Indiana. Said one of the visiting leaders, "We can co-operatize America in five years!"

The local people were interested in the week's schooling, but knew that such an estimate was optimistic. "Ya," they said. "That's all right. But it can't be done. Five generations would be nearer it."

Nevertheless, in spite of men's apathy and the farmer's fear of innovation and also his standpat individualism and our American belief in new frontiers that will make good times, the credit union grew and the co-ops in general grew. The sit-tights tried to discourage study and action on the part of the people. Their slogan was "Co-operation is Communistic!" Still, the people's bank has continued to grow, and by the June of 1943 its capital was just short of one hundred thousand. This bank or credit union is more supple than the usual run in our country. It keeps the rates down to one-half of 1 per cent a month, and as recently as May of this year it made loans of a kind that elsewhere have been carried by Farm Security; and I like to see this: not that these people are ready to get rid of Farm Security—a wonderfully beneficial and human setup—but that, if the local people, the smaller body, can do part or all of the work, it is better that they do it. Three-fourths of the financing on farm machinery in 1942 was done through the credit union. And this people's bank will go farther, in the aid of persons and families and of new and old co-op societies.

Take a case of its work. A family, sick and tired of looking for work, went on the land. This was with the help of Farm Security, and soon, also, of the credit union. Everything is on file with the co-op people. What the poor family bought was an eighty costing "about one hundred an acre, darn good land, but not improved." The man and woman and boy and girl—these eleven and twelve, and undersized—worked; "an' they've got a baby, too." The main crop to date is turkeys, "because she came from Michigan." Last year they raised nearly three thousand, besides five hundred chicks, and three or four hundred bushels of tomatoes. This and much more is on file: a note on the hogs, the ten or twelve milk cows, the five or six head of heifers, and the fact that all work is done by the family. "His stock and machinery is worth half the price of that farm. And he'll have it all paid for this year, if he has a good year."

It is not merely "he" that will pay for it, but she and the kiddies. She is short and fat and quick, and he lanky and stooped. In they come to the co-op to trade. Why to the co-op? The little girl—in tow to them now, she and the boy—lost chicks last season, but had great success when she tried co-op mash: so the family goes out of its way now to trade at the co-op. The father was sick, and the mother ran the tractor-plow on Saturday when the girl was at home to take "keer" of the baby. Then the next week the boy and girl stole off at schooltime to the field and plowed all day till time to be home from school. So people say. And it's probably true, for it is the little girl who says now, "Come on, daddy. We better be gittin' on home." The mammy with the papoose on her hip would have chosen to stay and talk awhile with neighbors in the store.

That is what co-ops are for: to help good people, over even so hard a road, to own some land and a home.

The custom and practice in Noble County favor the family farm. As everyone knows, the nonfamily farm is a big business, it is the commercial farm, and its aim is not the good and happiness of people, but the luscious business of making money. In short, its aim is profit, and for this reason I am surprised that people taking to co-ops could, in any of our states or in any country, support the sort of farm that we may term nonfamily and antifamily. In Noble County the co-op people go with the family and its enrichment and freedom.

That, no doubt, is why they so readily went with co-op recreation, a youth program, and dances and games for young and old. Just now, unhappily, they have let the program lapse, and it is out for the present. The people consciously, and in fact by vote, did this: at the very moment when, as events already prove, the growth of such a program was one of our greatest needs.

The people are especially proud of one consumer co-op, a healthy little store for a country town, and they certainly have no reason to be ashamed of the other. Most decisive in this line is not the stock or the turnover, but an understanding of the place proper to the consumer co-op. "Down in Indianapolis," says one of the co-op men at Albion in Noble County, "they don't know that the farmer and the laborer are consumers. What's the use of giving a workman a raise of ten cents an hour or the farmer half a cent extra on hogs, if they lose it again on the increased consumer prices?" It is true, of course, that no legitimate store can at present get everything it wants, and a woman says the co-op store "has to take and use some brands not under the co-op label." The store keeps Scott's hominy, and though it is unrationed in bulk, it sells fairly well in jars rationed at eleven points. Red beans, also rationed, do not sell: a profit store has them in unrationed bulk. "Beans are not hard to can, but corn and peas are." Jars are not rationed, nor cereals or spices or egg noodles.

The storekeeper says to a shopper, "How's your chickens doing?"

"All right. They're growing fast. It seems they've growed ever' time I look at them. They fly up and set on top of the brooder. Have to take them a bucket of water about ever' two hours. They drink more water!"

When she's gone with her hands full of groceries, a woman at the store says, "Three or maybe four children. Lots of work, in the house and out. She's a good manager, and she's a woman that likes work."

2

The plans are great, for new co-ops and the expansion of the old. Why cannot everyone have co-op insurance? The old-line is too costly, and people need protection. About six hundred in Noble County now have insurance for their cars with the co-ops, and over one hundred, "one-thirty-two, to be exact," have co-op life insurance. "And fifty in the new policy." This is written automatically for certain borrowers at the credit union, so that in the event of death "it is not necessary to go and collect from his people, and put that added burden on his family."[1] Another new form of insurance just this year is on accident and health, and "in case the general public would be injured by coming in contact with his machinery or stock."

---

[1] Many credit unions, such as Studebaker Credit Union, automatically and without charge give this insurance to all members. For instance, if a man dies owing $1,000, the debt is canceled.

The co-ops will develop each of these forms. The burial co-op is well on its way—the first in Indiana—and its own benefits will sell it.

Says one of the leaders, "We got to get co-op burial everywhere. Can't afford the undertaking business. Cost can be cut nearly in half, for the same service. It's too costly, that's all: practicing highway robbery on a man after he's dead! He's afraid to die, because he can't afford to be buried. We'll see about that. The difference might as well go to his family. Mr. X here the other day, he had a costly funeral: it run to eight or nine hundred dollars! For the same service, three or four of that, maybe four or five, could have gone to his widow, and she needs it."

Will the people stop with these few services? No, they say. They will not. "Medicine and a hospital," one of them says, "these we've got to have. Look at Dr. Shadid, in Elk City, Oklahoma: in one of the poorest counties, and all his doctors taken from him again. They did it before, you know that: the state medical men wouldn't let him have a hospital for the people; that is, if they could help it. The draft board can't take a doctor: they're sent by the doctor's association. And they sent all of Dr. Shadid's doctors! We've got to have medicine. It costs twenty-five dollars a year per family in western Oklahoma. It'd cost thirty-five here, including chronic diseases, broken bones, full clinical examination once or twice a year, all ordinary care. No law has a right to keep us without medicine."

Why could not Noble County become the Capital of Co-operation in rural America? This is not my question, but the local people's, and it is likely they will provide the reply to it.

At this moment they are getting ready, and will not hang back. Of course, we are deep into old ruts. We have a vague hope that everything will be all right, everything will take care of itself. Nevertheless, a few of these local people know how empty and fanciful is that hope. Hence they are busy with postwar plans. Last summer they bought a corner lot where a garage had burnt down. They will build, "after this war is over, and we get squared around. Right on the corner there, a filling station." Also, they will have the agency for a truck and a low-priced car, and for tractors and farm machinery. Then "the grocery store in a separate room. And a hatchery, bigger'n we got now. All of them right along," that is, all alongside one another. "But the grain end of it and the feed end in a separate building."

Is not all this "radical"? It certainly is! It looks to social reform and social reconstruction. It looks to the people's good, to their property and security and freedom. Nothing could well be more radical and dangerous.

Naturally, not everyone will take hold. As a matter of fact, few qualify. How many here would make the grade? Perhaps all could, but not many do. "In this county, lots are in the co-ops. But you can count just sixty-six that are natural co-operators, and that—if we say there's twenty-two hundred to go on—is just 3 per cent. That's how many are naturals, men that before they ever heard of this co-operation, wanted to help their neighbors, and as soon as a co-op project starts, they're for it."

"They're in on the ground floor," I say: a flat and inept reply.

"They're natural co-operators. They believe in co-operation. I guess they believe in the brotherhood of man."

They believe in neighboring, and in man, and not in their own dirty old pocketbook. Of such is the kingdom of co-operation, and the kingdom of man under God. Will enough of these men be found at Albion, and in many places, and in our whole country? Possibly so. But we must remember that the Indiana or other farmer has now, for nearly a hundred years, gone much his own way, and it is he who is the father of the small businessman and the insurance agent and the doctor and the priest and also of the contractor, the banker, and the manufacturer. Like father, like son—like him and, as the Latins say, more like him. What we must also remember is that at Albion and at other places where we have visited, is a handful of picked and sifted men, ready to and able to move the community. At Albion, it is not too much to say that they have already moved it.

3

It is a considerable jump from the drowned-out cornfields of Indiana to the great level plateaus of wheat in western Kansas where we conclude our review of rural co-ops. In a way, however, it is the same story, the story of American farmers working upward toward emancipation. On an immense board as one enters the town of Beloit far out in Kansas, is the literal sign, now peeling off under that hot sun: "The Townsend plan will save you." That may be true. But neither the Kansas nor the Indiana farmer believes it. He does not and constitutionally cannot believe that any nice plan coming down from the State can save men. His salvation does not lie in the lap of any State.

The people have a lead of their own. One might say, in spite of the State. By which I don't mean against the State, but certainly not by it.

Nor by corporation finance; not by any of the big companies featured in these arid little towns: not by J. C. Penney, or "Gamble Stores: official"; or Red and White Stores, or Clover Farm stores, all of them fighting for the bit of trade.

At a first glance this appears to be a dry land, a one-crop and burnt country. On the uplands the occasional cornfields are scorched, and show only some nubbins. The wheatfields are wide and open, and by this date—the end of August—have all been combined. The farms have cattle and pigs and horses and chickens, but are not alive with these as are the Iowa farms. The homesteads are far apart, and the farms are big.

But a first look can be deceptive. What one does notice at once, and never ceases to find among the people, is a wonderful friendliness and an openness that is as simple and frank as the plains. The attitude and manner of people are intimate and neighborly, as if everybody was supposed to know everybody.

The little buses are Santa Fe Trailways, and are good. On one of them a man is saying, "You one of the Sear's girls? . . . I thought so. But you're which one—what's your name, now? Is it Mrs. Amman?"

"No, that's m'sister."

The tone is broadened out in comparison with that in Iowa and Illinois, and not so flat and dull as that in Ohio. Here people say "yores" for "yours." "Didn't rain enough last night. No, it didn't. Tenth of a inch. Could stand more'n that. Wish it was three and a half!"

To an outsider, used all this summer to rain and green fields, it seems dry, and today's wind seems hot.

"You ought to been here last week!" says a native. Then they had hot winds, three days running. That's what fixed the corn. "Ya, good till last week." To the local folks things are right and fresh and even better than normal. It depends on what a person is used to. The dry spell came only at the end of the wheat harvest when of course the wheat was made. "Wheat is our major crop." The early corn was out of the way too, and the early gardens. It's a big crop, wheat averaging twenty-one bushels in Mitchell County where Beloit is, and in Cheyenne County, the farthest northwest in Kansas, it is said the average reached thirty-one bushels, possibly the highest ever for a whole county in this state.

It is these plainsmen, so happy this year about their crop, who have for a good while bought together and sold together. At least, some of them have begun to learn to go markedly co-op, and in this line Beloit and its county are not far from model. In terms of finance, what does this come to? The people have their own way of putting it. To keep the old method going a family has to hand over about one month's pay each year. Or on the co-op plan, it gets about one month of its purchases free. That is the immediate and obvious result.

The first co-op was organized here in 1911, "as just one union." This initial co-op unit was an elevator, and "by 1918 we had five elevators and one grocery in Mitchell County, and two of the men who were on the board of directors then are still on the board." But there was plenty of bad management: boys got jobs through nepotism. "That was bad: it was like me or you going to fight Joe Lewis. The boys couldn't do the work. In 1922 things started to change a little for them, and they started to get some crops." In 1930 the present manager came up from lower Kansas, and found a debt facing him. To make matters worse, "through three years, 1933-34-35, we had droughts. The next year we raised a fair crop. Still, since 1930 we paid back to our membership over half a million in patronage dividends. That's just in this county."

So much is of great human interest and importance. But what I'd like to know is whether the people are getting any better hold on the land, and are thus more secure and independent.

The manager is a firm, ready man, fit for and devoted to his work, and the matter of ownership for the people is not far from his heart. "They do," he says. "They get a sense and feeling of ownership. I certainly give Farm Security a lot of credit for that. For example, seven boys bought farms around here, and all seven have paid off the debt. If we hadn't this Farm Security, well, they wouldn't look so good. After all, our problem is to get away from tenant farming, and get farmers to own. The co-ops have helped, too. I'd say there's a gain in ownership of, oh, say about ten per cent in twelve or thirteen years. We notice it in grain delivery: some tenants paying checks to owners in Pennsylvania and New York, and we have one payee in Edinburgh, Scotland, a man that was here in 1920 and had money and bought land on the river bottom, good land, too. Absentee landlords are hard to deal with; they don't care for the land or community: they like a cash crop, all wheat."

The co-ops have done something real and decisive. They have returned a dividend of two cents a pound on cream, and although this is "not a dairy community," the refund in 1942 "for one family, south of town, milking fourteen topnotch cows, was ninety-eight dollars." The dividend was one cent a bushel on grain. The refund "regularly" on oil and gas is about 10 per cent. "Many men use two and three hundred dollars' worth of petroleum products a year, and one of the farmers said, 'I get just about one month of my gas and oil for nothing.' Standard and all of them went immediately to the ceiling [of seventeen cents], but we don't like to do that. We stay at fifteen and a half. At the ceiling we could refund probably 20 per cent. In 1942, we sold 39.6 per cent of the petroleum products in the county: according to state of Kansas figures. Stores, well, we have one good one, and two others; the dividend is about 6 per cent, but some years it's dropped to two and three."

In all this area, say from Canada south through St. Paul and Iowa and the Dakotas and Nebraska and Kansas and to the Gulf and west to the Pacific, the Farmers' Union is strong, and in important matters it appears to me sane and wise and human, with its belief in the family and in ownership. And everywhere the union has been for and with the co-ops and in the early days particularly with the co-op elevators. Mitchell County now has twenty elevators, and nine of the busiest are co-op; this condition brings the others into line. The co-ops handle 60 per cent or possibly 65 per cent of the wheat, and the 1942 crop, I believe, ran to 4,200,000 bushels. In the 1943 season the co-ops took care of 1,500,000 bushels in three weeks, one of their elevators managing to put away 400,000 bushels; a direct refund of about $15,000 went to the farmers.

Beginning in 1928 the people took over light and power as in effect a co-op. They almost had to do this, since the utility company "had got to where we couldn't afford to have sufficient street light." Enough is earned now on the plant to make the city of four or five thousand totally tax free. The REA co-op also is effective and reaches at least a fifth of the farmers, giving them power and convenience.

These are the co-ops, the people's business, in one county of Kansas. Each unit helps the others, but does not depend on them, because "each is set up on its own feet, and if one unit fails that is not going to affect the others."

4

At the end of August, Kansas wheat men are busy. As I talk to the manager, co-op truckers are making plans for day and night.

"We got to get that shorts over at Clyde today . . . and dump that load of corn. . . . It ain't fifty miles east of Concordia. . . . We can get that alfalfa deal . . . we're pulling about seventeen ton. . . . He can fag over there and get the corn in here. . . . No use starting out anywhere tonight."

"That's good corn," says the manager. It comes from Iowa and Nebraska and "is laid in here at a dollar-fifteen and a dollar-seventeen. Our ceiling is one-twenty-one." No refund on it, but people need corn at the most reasonable rate.

Of course, in or out of the co-ops "it all depends." If the co-op is not well handled, the people need not be any better off than under the profit regime. The manager puts this truth into a formula: "Anything can be badly managed. You know that."

While the manager is called away a moment, a trucker tells me about the co-ed who, he says, got a job at the fourth elevator. "A farmer asked for shorts. 'We got no shorts,' she said. 'You sure have,' he said. 'I want shorts for my cows.' 'Shorts for cows!' the girl said."

Over us on the wall is a starred and striped shield looking much like the front of Uncle Sam's vest, and above it the words, "Proud to be American."

As I leave town, the manager is telling me that the grocery stores are Rochdale and are on a cash basis. But "it's hard to operate oil and petroleum units strictly cash, because the farmer may be in the field when oil is delivered. Right now the farmer here is in the best condition I've ever known him."

Twelve

FACTORIES FREE OF CHARGE

1

With the exception of co-ops among miners at Dillonvale and Granger, our study so far has been mainly of co-ops among rural people. These co-ops can help families to own, and to be thereby secure and possibly to be free. We have said that, even if this declaration of freedom were feasible for farmers only, we'd nevertheless be 100 per cent for it. And a person might argue that to its fullest extent it is possible only for farmers. Yet this circumstance would not inhere in the nature of the co-ops, but in the nature of urban living. It may be that the mass of urban men and women cannot be so free, or readily be so free as rural people. In that case, we should not conclude that co-ops are therefore unadaptable. The truth is that, even after war and inflation and depression and war, the farmer may still have the better position. He is closer to ownership, less removed in attitude from ownership as possible and desirable. Besides, he can control the productive process on the farm much more readily than can the laborer have a say-so in the production of cars or stoves or guns.

As matters stand, laborers do not own or control the plant or the materials or the product. How, then, could they establish co-ops to produce what they need? It cannot easily be done. Can co-ops then mean anything visible to these people? I know they can, because in many places and many countries they do. And they had better! For unless laborers can control the cost of living, they are out of luck. This they must learn to do, at first through consumer co-operation. In the meantime they suffer: plant and materials and products beyond their power, cartels running wild at their expense, wars whipped up and prolonged over profit, and farmer and laborer in the end bearing the brunt of wars and their aftermaths; and the high cost of living and installment buying fit to lap up the gains that Labor pressure is able to make.

But laborers have begun to learn in our country, as they have learned in Sweden and in England. On the Swedish and English pattern and on the pattern worked out by our farmers and by Labor's own experimentation, the laborers of America will almost surely go forward, and faster than the farmers have gone, into consumer co-ops. That question we wish to take up later from the point of view of fact.

Suppose, however, that laborers and both urban and rural people could own factories! Suppose they could own a few Ford plants, and Carnegie mills, and Rockefeller wells and refineries! That may seem funny, especially in the light of the fact that the Rochdale pioneers failed as owners of factories. Yet the experience, in the last few years, of the people taking over factories of a dozen kinds suggests that the idea is not a dream.

The simplest type of this procedure is in the case of the flour mill. Usually we have been taught that flour milling is best and most cheaply done by the companies in the Twin Cities. We raise the wheat for hundreds or thousands of miles on all sides, then ship it in order to have it milled in a big way, and afterward it is proliferated back to us at a considerable cost: it is no longer a dollar or a dollar-ten a bushel. It is natural, nevertheless, for people to tinker with milling, and they have always done so. A dozen years ago an Indiana Farm Bureau co-op took to milling in a small way. In 1942 it milled ninety-two million pounds, not a large amount of flour, but enough—if my figures are just—to furnish flour for half a million people.[1] The man in charge says, "Unbleached flour is better. It has in it all the ingredients God put into food for us. But people have to be educated to eat it, because women still want snowy-white flour and bread." That is why all mills now "enrich" the flour; they put again into it just what they had taken out of it.

This is one of the co-op flour mills already in operation. Another is in Albany, a third in Buffalo, a fourth in Spokane, and a fifth and a sixth in Canada. The mill at Auburn, Indiana, is a factory, its grain traveling more than a mile up and down and shuttled back and forth in the milling and refining processes. It comes from a radius of a hundred miles by truck, and is trucked and shipped as far as New York, and to Kentucky in exchange for coal that goes

[1] Allowing each person 171 lbs. of flour annually.

to the Indiana co-ops. In ten states the co-ops have their own feed mills.

One of the triumphs for co-operators is the plant for manufacturing fertilizer. Ohio pioneered in this enterprise, and we already have thirteen plants in ten states, and each year we have more. The private manufacturers had acted as highwaymen; prices soared, and the buccaneers refused to deal with what they called the "scab farmers." These latter were the "folks" of the Ohio Farm Bureau. The result of this treatment was that the scab folks bought where they could, and at first had to take an inferior, lumpy grade and work on it with hammer and sledge, so that to do hard work now in Ohio is "to pound fertilizer." But the scab folks did more than coin a phrase. They knocked the pegs from under prices. "As a direct result, fertilizer prices in Ohio dropped four dollars per ton below 1929 prices. Everyone benefited whether he bought from the co-operatives or not." The way the scabs did this was by building their own plants, and for the past three or four years they have output enough to meet all their own needs. Neighboring states have followed suit.

2

In these instances, and others that we shall see, the challenging points are two. The less important is this: The people, as a Nova Scotia co-operator said to me, are no longer "oversoaked" on prices, and along with this goes the fact that the government therefore need not wear itself out trying to control business or to be a businessman. The second point is that the people own. Not an absentee owner or a cartel, but the people own the fertilizer plants. One result of this consumer ownership is that no profits are made.

How, then, are dividends actually distributed? Are not these profits? The fact is that the people have overcharged themselves. Why should they do this? Only in order that the business will have a safe margin of operation. At the end of the year or half year this overcharge goes back to the people in proportion to patronage. This is a Rochdale principle: distribution of the overcharge according to patronage and not according to stock.

Hence the nonsense of supposing the plant ought to be taxed on that refund. Take a simple case of overcharge. A profit man at a gas station happens to overcharge a man 35 cents, and runs after him and returns the money. Should the business be taxed on that 35 cents? Of course not. But the profit man, because he overcharges the consumer and keeps the difference, is in a different category. Of course, as we have co-op business on a large scale and will have it on a larger scale, the problem of readjusting methods of taxation will arise. That is a problem for governments to consider. But the need for taxes will be less, because with the profit system deflated, we will suffer less from cartels and wars and the costs of "patronage" and "bureaucracy."

These remarks on the overcharge and dividend are relevant to any and all co-ops: to the ordinary producing and marketing co-ops so common among farmers, and the consumer types proper to all men, and to co-op factories.

The co-ops begin to own factories in a dozen lines. "This is ours," they say in Ohio; and the people are proud to say it. We have paid for all the factories—we the people. "But these we own!" So we say in Indiana, as we name the plants that are ours.

Consider the list of factories, the length of it and the kinds, that we the people begin to own, and this is an incomplete and growing list. We have sawmills in at least four states and seed mills in Oregon and Minnesota and Indiana and Virginia and Pennsylvania and New York. These we own, and we no longer depend for lumber or for seed on the closed corporation. We have our own hatcheries that are state-wide in Indiana and in Ohio and Washington and county-wide in a score of places. We have immense feed mills from Carolina to New York and west to Minnesota. These we own. We have a cosmetics factory in Chicago, a serum factory and a grease factory and a fly-spray factory in Kansas City, an alfalfa dehydrator, a large cannery in Nebraska, one in Missouri and one in Pennsylvania. We have a coffee "roastery" in Wisconsin and one in New York City. We have a bakery of our own in New York City and one in Superior, Wisconsin, and the miners at Dillonvale plan to have their own. In four states are printing establishments that are ours. We have a factory for making tractors and other farm machinery, and this is to serve both the United States and Canada.

How are these owned? Who are "we the people" that own

them? In some instances the co-op units in a state such as Indiana own a particular factory. Again, units in two or three states own together, or co-op ownership may be regional or international. Where does the money come from? As little as possible from commercial banks and commercial loan companies and insurance companies. Private persons of a co-op mind are welcome to invest in stock and get a limited rate of interest, and an increasing number of persons tend to do this. At the great center in Kansas City they show me letters they have today received from strangers in Illinois and in Massachusetts taking stock in expanding co-op enterprise. One hundred dollars someone sends, and another sends four hundred. An eastern woman, otherwise unknown here, has added bit to bit till she has eleven thousand in the co-ops. One correspondent says he does this because he wants to go with the people.

All these persons help. Man speaks to man, and the gospel of co-operation spreads. Besides, the co-op journals let more and more people know.

But the best and most common working is through the co-op units. Suppose a local in Nebraska or Pennsylvania had an overcharge of ten thousand last year, in addition to a safe reserve. The directors may turn the last dollar of this back to the members, and are bound to do so, one way or another, but they are also free to invest part of it, to store part of it away for a time, in some co-op project. Of course, the members have chosen these directors, and if they wish they can soon eject them and choose others. I have known no case, however, of the members' complaining when the directors put part of the overcharge into co-op stock. The finance man in Kansas City explains these matters, and says, "We want co-op financing of the co-ops. And we increasingly get it. Just this morning, one thousand dollars came in from a local. This is invested by that local in preferred stock at four per cent interest."

Everywhere it is the same story. The co-ops are determined to own the co-ops, and their principle is sound. The principle, says an Indiana leader, is this: "A business is pretty largely controlled by whoever owns the money in it." We should own our co-op institutions. The credit unions take care of some local needs, but not all even of these. For wider purposes, we shall have to get a considerable union among these, or set up large co-op banks, as is done in England. "We must manufacture our own credit." This we are doing in the ways mentioned; and we have set up banks. In Indiana, for instance, the state unit of the co-ops and some locals—"wherever it could find locals willing to go along—" some years ago bought the controlling interest in a bank, and now have made it totally their own. It has sixty stockholders, most of them local co-ops and local credit unions and in 1943 it sold an additional hundred thousand of stock.

The people as consumers of goods and services and credit are ultimately the men who pay for every factory, no matter what its products are. Why should they not manufacture their own credit? And why not own banks and factories? "Factories are free!" This co-op dictum means that factories commonly pay for themselves in a year or two. Strange indeed, then, that we who pay for them should never own them.

Open membership! That is a fundamental Rochdale principle, and it applies to co-op banks and factories as well as to co-op trucking groups and co-op stores and bakeries. All it means is that anyone may join unless his aim is to wreck the co-op. Limited interest on capital! That, too, is basic Rochdale law, and it holds for co-op banks and factories. So also of the patronage refund or dividend.

3

Now and then a Rochdale principle is by-passed by American co-ops. Such procedure is rarely if ever advisable. For instance, some midwestern co-ops will allow membership and dividends only to members of the Farm Bureau or Grange or Farmers' Union, and some allow sales "on time." And, though it is Rochdale law to trade at the going rates, the insurance co-ops commonly find that they cannot take these rates and not feel like robbers—even though the people who foot the bill get the overcharge back! These co-ops force the rate down, and more sharply down than was the case in the fertilizer industry.

In co-op factories the usual thing is to pay for the plant, to expand and to return a dividend. I do not say, "if possible to return a dividend." For in all instances to date it is possible. The fertilizer plants in Ohio cut the price of fertilizer four dollars a ton and yet soon paid for themselves and also made a refund to the user. So of many other plants. And if plants owned by farmers do this, why should not plants owned by Labor or by farmer and laborer and professional man and white-collar worker?

At Waukesha in Wisconsin the co-op people from many places in the nation have taken over a small factory. The town, naturally, is a profit town, and one gets to the new co-op factory by way of the Stop and Shop Market: the Best for Less, and by way of the Adele Beauty Shop where the stalls or stanchions for women's heads look like dairy equipment. In one of these a woman's head is fixed, we might say caught by a topknot of wool so that it has a new fixedness and limitation; the woman appears impatient but resigned, as if she had got up her courage to face this ordeal and whatever the cost she would go through with it. In another stall is a little girl's head, her face the picture of joy and contentment.

At the new co-op factory they are making milking machines, and one hundred and twenty persons are at work. Why take over such a plant on the co-op plan? It is for the following purpose: so that those why buy and pay for milking machines may in the long run have them at cost. It is so that all those who buy and set up the cash for these machines may own the milking machine plant. They did pay for the plant every single year that it existed as a profit plant, and yet it was not theirs! In other words, it is so that any overcharge may go to the consumer.

But can people possibly run the factory? They are doing it! In fact this plant promises to be a great success. I visited it when it was an eight months' old co-op baby, and a healthy and happy baby it was. Just before the co-op people took charge of its diet the plant looked like a decrepit old fellow. The co-op people took over in January, 1943, found some materials ready to melt, and soon the plant had new life and hope. They looked for sales of over a million the first year, and to have enough earnings in the twelve months to meet the operating expenses, to have a reserve, and to pay for the plant. Have not the old "operators" therefore given the factory away? It is true that conditions forced their hand a bit. But it is also true that wherever the co-operators have bought or built a plant, they have almost invariably been able to pay quickly for it; often in one year, almost always inside twenty-four months. How do they do it? For one thing, salesmen and competitive advertising eat up business gains. As a co-op the Universal Milking Machine, having in advance its own market among its owners, no longer has any salesmen or "runners" on the road, and the manager says this annulment is the chief reason for a drop of $106,000 in operating expenses for the first nine months. No radio ads—think of it! No pressure men out to "sell" people. Just a quiet statement of fact, information that could guide in a decent way those who may need machines.

4

The people produce, the people, if need be, ship and process, the people distribute, and the people consume. Who better than the people to own? But to own what—merely a house, or a claim on it? Merely a piece of land, or a claim on it?

Indiana co-operators among others have an answer to these questions. Families and persons should have private property, such as homes and land and stock in the co-ops or the people's business. But on the old dog-eat-dog procedure we know that few get a chance to own our oil, our shipping, our processing, and our re-shipment. All these I have called "ours," and ours the Indiana co-operators have begun to make them. It will be well therefore to suggest the interlocked list of goods and processes—not an exhaustive or final list—taken care of by the Indiana people for the Indiana people.

Over many years the people asked government to save them from trusts. The government did not do it, and in many matters perhaps could not. For instance, the grain trade, the oil business, and the fertilizer industry were almost beyond control. But the people now find that they can manage these matters. Farmers used to pay a heavy toll for using the Indianapolis terminal grain elevator: in seven years, "200 per cent of the value of the structure." No longer do they suffer this toll, however, or the problem of begging legislators to do something about it. The reason is that they own the terminal and another one in Louisville. So of petroleum and its products. "Not again shall we, like children, beg the petroleum industry for fair play as we buy our gasoline." Why not? It is our industry! This is now matter of fact. The first step was for the people to set up a bulk plant which made its way so well that now they have eighty of them "all over Indiana." Next, they went into compounding and into manufacturing fuels and lubricants. Then they set up a truck transport system, and a refinery for processing the crude oil, and "finally"—so they said not long ago—a pipe line to bring the oil to the refinery. Even that was not final, and now they have acquired a dozen oil wells and a barge and towboat for use on the Ohio, so that the co-operators control from the deposit in the rock to the farmers' car and tractor, and it is reliably estimated that 35 to 40 per cent of the petroleum products delivered to Indiana farms come via the co-ops. In grain shipping and in oil they had been paying for something they didn't get: for the plant, for the transport system, for the oil wells and the refinery, and for the refund. In the fertilizer industry the co-operators have the same sort of story. They could not get a square deal, as is shown by the fact that in Indiana the state-wide savings to all farmers using fertilizer now probably run close to an annual million dollars. Besides, the people own the business.

In each industry, grain handling, and oil, and fertilizer, the people were paying for what they did not get. For fertilizer they were signing over an annual million for no value received. So in oil and grain.

Better therefore set up our own shipping units, our own refineries, and our own factories. That is the human and democratic way. The thing does not automatically get itself done; and the State, trying to bear all burdens, cannot do it: so our interminable struggle with the problem of trusts would suggest. But an intelligent people in Indiana and elsewhere can do what needs to be done. They do this as an autonomous group within the State, and in doing it they shake off economic serfdom.

The three units cited represent only a fraction of what is now done in Indiana. The people also have a bank and an endless lot of credit unions. They have a serum factory, and go with the national machinery co-ops and in a big way with the rural electric co-ops. Insurance also, on cars and on human life; and Dunne's Report for 1943 assigns to Hoosier Farm Bureau Life "our highest rating of A+ (Excellent)," with tops in assets, management, and claims, and "a remarkable gain" of 68 per cent for the year. The people have the marketing of livestock and of wool and dairy products. A printing plant, too, and a coal mine in Kentucky and co-op sawmills in Arkansas where Indianans can get lumber "on the stump" and at rates that will allow them to build houses. A ten-ton soybean processing plant, too, opened in 1943.

As important as any other, perhaps, is the co-op unit we have in the line of "feeds." This is an eye opener, not primarily in cash but in quality. And, one may say, in honesty. "Our interest is in producing good goods. We have no wish at all to hedge or hide. The reason is that the goods are produced by the people using them. Or, if you like, they are used by the people producing them." What silly goose would want to trick himself out of time or money or quality? The Indiana co-operators use the Open Formula. "You know there are a lot of by-products in the feed line, and a feed is made, say, of ground corn and an oat by-product. But what is this 'oat by-product'? Is it nothing but oat hulls? So our feed department said the user has the right to know how much of this and how much of that, and we write an Open Formula and tell him."

The co-op people also do experimental work. This is done in view of costs and of quality, and is done on feeds and on chemicals for pest control and on paints and oils. The findings to date are a revelation. "We tried to get ourselves a law to check on the usefulness of chemicals sold for pest control. But no go! The reason was that an insecticide industry had grown up. We set up a plant of our own, here, to mix the chemicals, and our department goes on and works with Purdue University as to formulas and mixing as it should be done."

All these state-wide co-ops may be added to our local co-ops: to co-op creameries, and local gas and oil bulk plants, to buying co-ops and co-op stores, to our beginning of co-op burial and co-op hospitalization; and also to our sharing in regional and in national co-ops, such as a paint factory and a tool factory. All these give the Indiana farmer some control over business, not just over his own productive and distributive units, but over others checked and brought into line by these. In Indiana we continue to do our biggest co-op business in petroleum, and we control this right back to the pocket of rock where man first found it. Next in volume come feeds, and then fertilizer. That is, "as a rule; and then on, the goods and services are hard to classify." For instance, the central co-op elevator service on soybeans ran to thirteen thousand in 1942. But what good, all in all, does it do us? Take a typical county or two. County X had sales in 1942 of $254,000 and earnings of 6.3 per cent, or $16,151.67. County Y is much stronger than typical, because it has "a good manager and one of the best boards of directors in the state: they go right along with him, studying the problems." This county did a business of $604,000, and had $35,000 in what we may call immediate earnings and $8,806.53 in "other income," making the total come to 7.3 per cent. This other income arises from the county's sharing in the wider co-ops, such as the chemical plant, the feed testing, and the central co-op elevators. In 1944, the statewide earnings of nearly one million, in addition to the forcing of old prices downward to a fair level, were as follows:

DISTRIBUTION OF EARNINGS FOR YEAR 1944

DEPARTMENT	39% General Patron's Equity	61% Cash Refund
Seed	$ 9,996.81	$ 15,636.03
Printing	1,810.71	2,832.13
Implement	3,208.15	5,017.88
Poultry	16,163.65	25,281.61
Petroleum (All)	146,732.44	229,504.62
Feed	21,058.63	32,937.85
Farm Building Maintenance	49,303.27	77,115.36
Farm Home Modernization	15,569.58	24,352.42
Fertilizer	91,766.16	143,531.68
TOTALS	$355,609.40	$556,209.58

That begins to be something of the complete picture, but only something of it and only for a fraction of the farmers in the state. These now have some co-op shipping, some co-op manufacturing and banking, some co-op stores. The picture remains incomplete in terms of goods and services, and in terms of the population.

These things a few farmers in Indiana have begun to do. Why cannot the townspeople do many of them? Why cannot the people of Indianapolis and Chicago own and control the sources of the lumber for their houses, of the oil and coal they burn, of the gas that makes their cars go, the factories that make their furniture, their stoves, their cars and radios? Are they not smart enough or free enough?

Thirteen

SIPHONING OFF OIL PROFITS

A FEW families can start a co-op housing project, a dozen families man a buying club, and a hundred start a good store. As we saw, four hundred can get along in insurance of certain kinds, and four hundred could launch a respectable bank, to say nothing of a credit union. But when we talk of a people's hookup—and for freedom we will and must talk of it—we shall need families by the thousand, and hundreds of locals joining hands in the regionals, and these again in a national group: a co-op of co-ops. Even now in National Cooperatives made of fourteen wholesales in the country and two in Canada, we begin to get such an effective unification.

The hint of bigness frightens some who believe in decentralization and who in spite of the times grow in numbers and conviction. With *Free America* they believe that "freedom can exist only in societies in which the great majority are the effective owners of tangible and productive property and in which group action is democratic. In order to achieve such a society, ownership, production, population, and government must be decentralized."

So far as possible, better have home production and community production. Yet we do want trucks and stoves and cars, and not every small town can be efficient in making them. We want oil, and not every householder can have an oil well and refinery. Centralized productive power is needed, and through the co-operatives this can be had along with decentralized ownership. Bigness is not bad, but only the principle "The bigger the better." Besides, we have got to thinking that not the people but only some Carnegie or Ford can own and operate a factory. We have seen, however, that the people can have co-op units for making milking machines and tractors. Can they not have others for making cars? They have some coal mines. Will they not have more, and also some iron mines? Who says they will not take more steps in banking, and now that they have tasted the sweets of co-op insurance they may in time eat the whole pie. They are in lumbering and canning and milling, and will do more of them. Sugar refining, steel mills, plants for planes—all these will be the people's. At least so it will be if freedom and private ownership are to remain, and if American co-operators keep to the direction they have taken for a decade.

Suppose some Carnegie or Ford or Gary or Van Sweringen to have been from the start with the people, a man knowing business and also knowing and loving the people. Suppose some Mellon who should have been of the house of mankind. Suppose the man gifted with power should be the prophet and apostle of a new economy. Suppose the schools and churches should teach youth that the first claimant on one's power is not one's own gain, but human good.

2

We shall now recount the astounding story of the people's beginning to own oil wells and refineries. For a long time the oil people siphoned off from every little community ten thousand a year. Then the thought came to some men that the people could own the oil business. Little by little they have moved that way, and now they do own nine oil refineries, several hundred miles of oil pipe lines, and some fields of oil wells. "*All yours, and you can thank yourself.*" "All these we own: a business system growing from 'the grass roots.'" So say the co-operators whose wholesale is in Kansas City where paints are compounded, grease is manufactured, research is done and more will be done, and whence has come the vision and courage to go in a modest way into oil for the people. This wholesale has tied up with four other large units to purchase the Globe Oil Refinery at McPherson in Kansas, and the co-operators now own 296 oil wells in Texas, Oklahoma, Illinois, and Kansas, and each unit tends to pay in short order for itself.

In Kansas City's great railway station I see many well-fed persons and also the most charming little family of lost Oklahomans, father in wide hat, mother with a racy accent, and two worn-out tots of girls. Out of there it is a long trip to Phillipsburg, lying far west and all the way north in the state, a small town high on the plains. Here they have the first co-op oil refinery in the United States.

At Phillipsburg, at 6:06 on New Year's morning, 1940, the first gasoline produced in one of our refineries " 'came over' from the topping plant."

So I read now, and no doubt heard two or three times while I was at Phillipsburg. Even that sentence has technical words in it, and the language does not get easier as a person goes through the refinery. A layman hears talk of "the crude," the raw oil ready to be broken into all kinds of fuels serviceable in cars and tractors and stoves. A technician tells me, "We get the crude, and then remove the straight-run products." He means that they take from the crude oil such products as gasoline, tractor fuel, kerosene, and distillate. "The balance of the heavy residue we crack under heat and pressure, to produce cracked gasoline and cracked tractor fuel. Codimer, too, a small amount of it, and this is shipped to California where hydrogen is added, and the resultant product is used as a component of aviation gasoline; for example, alkelate."

That is what the uninitiate gets from the story so quickly told him, with so much taken for granted. The machinery itself, of course, is formidable, and is immensely expensive. Great tanks or containers—well, one can understand their purpose, which is simply to hold the crude or the refined oil. A series of great steel pipes or stacks going to various distances toward the sky, some of these narrow-gauge, and some of them amounting to towers. Through these runs the oil at this or that moment of the refining process, and now at one temperature and pressure and again at another. This is only to say that the chemistry and the physics are complex, and to suggest that delicate research has been done and the recipe worked out with care.

The cooking, if we may call it that, is now done on the line. The heat must be just so much, say 1400°F., but the maintenance of this, once the requirement is known, is a minor problem; the tenders keep records telling of "furnace and tower temperature," and "still and tower pressure," and "tank gauges," and the "polymerization section." The furnace and tower temperature in the "cracking unit" is put under such headings as furnace, furnace gas, oil .inlet, flash chamber, and fractionator. Space is allowed, too, for

Operator's Remarks, and this is what he says: "Cut crude charge to 65 G.P.M. (gallons per minute) 600° F. on Furnace." All this is in outline, straight up and down, on a chart, and naturally it is read at a glance by the proper persons. Sometimes the remark is "clear" or "cloudy," or "wouldn't settle out." For the most part, however, the working is recorded hour by hour, not by men but by the machines.

The crude carries salt, and this has to be removed by electricity; otherwise it will plug the tubes; in a thousand barrels of crude there might be sixty to eighty pounds of salt, and at certain seasons it might run to two hundred. For power and pumping, a temperature of 1400°F. is maintained, and this keeps the steam at 150 pounds, at which level it is called open, or live, steam. A variety of materials has to be purchased and used, such as caustic soda, lead oxide, copper chloride, Fuller's earth (brought from Florida), lime for combating erosion in the process, soda ash, and chemicals for fighting fire; dyes, too, to color the gases; for example, in Nebraska the law requires that tractor fuel be blue; and expensive leads, and salt for dehydration, and oxygen used in the process, and tools, and valve fittings, and electrical supplies.

To the people working among all these things, the materials fall into their places as do things at home in the kitchen, and besides the steady technical language I hear man speak to man, about the machinery and the product, in human terms. Says one, "That baby there . . ." and I notice they refer to gasolines as sweet and sour. "It's not determined by tasting!" says someone. "Look: the sweet is copper-colored, and the sour is olive."

Forty-five persons work in the plant, and a fleet of trucks is kept going. Because the work is dangerous, the place is fenced with wire and with danger signs, and a certain Mr. Churchill, an important person who is a cross between an old-time plantation man and a cowboy, stands guard at the gate. An ethyl fluid is got from Baton Rouge at fifty thousand a tank, and is unloaded by vacuum, because it is deadly poison. "One of our worst enemies is static electricity. This builds up through truck and tires, and even by feet shuffling. That is why every truck has to drag chains behind: to ground the electricity." An absolute order says: "Ground truck before loading."

By eleven o'clock two girls are testing the quality of the morning's products, and marking the specific gravity on samples stored in jars or bottles. "Cracked gas," says one of the men, "is not straight-run, and is colored." All now, he evidently thinks, will be simple to the stranger. What cracked gas means, I believe, is this: the particles or atoms of the crude have as a matter of fact been smashed under pressure, and several distinct and relatively new products have been freed.

3

A map of Kansas made in 1940 and "quite obsolete now" shows that oil fields and gas fields were known and developed then in the middle of the state and straight east, too, from the middle to the east border and south along that border to the confines of Kansas, and gas fields were being worked in the southwestern part. McPherson is in the heart of that biggest east and south and middle area, and it is at McPherson that the co-operators at the end of 1943 took over Globe Oil Refinery, and Phillipsburg is north and west of the middle. In the past few years development has gone in that northwest direction. Refineries in Kansas are—if I may trust an outline on the walls of the local refinery—twenty in number, and the capacity in crude is 172,000 barrels daily and in cracking it is 93,000. In each of these the Phillipsburg plant does 2 per cent of the state total. The refined product is shipped in co-op trucks to Kansas, Colorado, Nebraska, and South Dakota. Of course, the co-ops have other refineries throughout the country.

How are they paid for? Just as are other large co-op enterprises—by the people. Most of these people are members of local co-ops, and it is the local that subscribes the money. The local or person buys stock at a limited rate of interest, and this procedure is the effecting of a Rochdale principle. But what about "profits"? Literally, no profits accrue. What happens is that the people who use gas and oil are subject to an overcharge, which in the case of the profit system goes to the capitalist, but which in the co-op system goes back pro rata to the consumers. On inquiry this is what I learn:

"You're correct—the earnings of the co-op refineries and the co-op oil wells go to the purchasers of the product. The purchasers are technically co-operative oil associations who purchase through C.C.A.[1] Now, it so happens that part of C.C.A.'s members get their refined fuels from refineries that we ourselves own and a little of that oil that is refined there at our own refineries comes from our own oil wells. However, the savings made on the oil that comes from our own oil wells and is refined in our own refineries are very much greater than the savings made from gasoline which we have refined for us in someone else's refinery. But we have to do this in order to have enough for all our members.

"We have therefore felt that the savings made in our refineries and from our oil wells and pipe lines should be pooled with the savings made in our wholesaling operations and then all the savings divided equally among the co-operative associations, depending upon patronage of the wholesale."

Thus it is not altogether a question of whether the local co-op oil station was or was not able to get oil that came from the co-op oil establishments.

C.C.A. owns all voting shares in the refineries and also the oil wells, and the control is vested in a board of directors that represents all the co-op associations. Once the limited interest is paid to nonvoting persons who have money in the venture, the rest of the savings is part of the total savings made by the wholesale and goes along with the latter to the locals and through them to the members.

How much does it really come to? That depends on several matters: on the savings made in the co-op wells, pipe lines and refineries, on the volume of refined fuels bought by the local from these co-op setups and from other sources via the wholesale, and most of all on the efficient management of the local. For bad management here at the end could wipe out everything. We know in fact that in 1942 the savings made by C.C.A. were as follows:

SAVINGS PER BARREL OF CRUDE

production	pipe line	refining	wholesale	TOTAL
.77	.03	.23	.07	$1.10 per barrel

SAVINGS PER GALLON OF GASOLINE

production	pipe line	refining	wholesale	TOTAL
1.84	.07	.60	.25	2.76¢ per gallon

[1] C.C.A. stands for Consumers Co-operative Association, Kansas City, Mo.

"2.76¢ per gal.×50,000,000 gal.=$13,000,000." That is estimated to be the savings directly possible annually on gas through the American co-op wholesales, if these wholesales owned their own wells and pipe lines and refineries.

These we own. We the people have paid for all. But only these we own: a business system growing from the grass roots—and from beneath them! The C.C.A. earnings on petroleum products go back now to 135,000 personal members.

It is no wonder that the co-op people can so soon pay for the plant and return a dividend. "Factories are free." That is to say, we pay no more for gas or tractors or fertilizer, and the first thing we know we own the factories and are actually being paid for owning them. When C.C.A. with four other large units paid $100,000 down "to bind the deal," and then on July 26, 1943, wrote a check for $3,400,000 to the Globe Oil Refining Company, no seasoned co-operator trembled at the bigness of the figures. For he knew that following the usual experience, this co-op enterprise should in a reasonable time pay for itself.

The co-op refinery at Phillipsburg soon paid for itself. It cost $572,000,[2] and "net savings from refining operations alone in the 12 months ending July 31, 1941, were $204,314." So, too, of the refinery purchased at Scottsbluff, Nebraska. This was taken over from an old company, at a cost of three hundred thousand, and when I visited the plant the manager was confident on its record and prospects that at the end of twenty months it would have paid the total bill. Of course, this payment is in addition to the cost of operation and maintenance.

Factories are free. Oil refineries are free. When people do not own them, or when people own them though at a cost, they are cheated. The people should have them free of charge.

The same is true of oil wells and oil pipe lines. These are by right the people's, that is to say the consumers'. It is we the people who pay for them when someone else has them, and the incredible thing is that when we pay nothing for them we have them. They really are free. They are ours for the taking. Think, besides, of the troubles we are relieved of when the people own the people's oil

---

[2] The refinery plus the pipe line ran over $800,000, and with the crude oil to start operations the cost approached a million.

wells. The trouble of trying to keep track of, to control, check in terms of human welfare—all this trouble on the part of government evaporates. All the hatreds, suspicions, fears, all the monopoly and cartel troubles, the millions a year tribute for no value received, and all the national and international war troubles—all these are gone.

That is the significance of co-op oil, whether in wells or refineries. It looks toward human good, toward ownership and freedom. This it does by two means. First, it shows that the people can own the people's business. What the people have paid for they can have. Next, a new heaven is not thereby born, and yet with the people in possession, the government of Kansas and of the United States can be unburdened, and a major cause of modern wars removed from the face of the earth.

"Good will among men. Its Name is Brotherhood, its Method Co-operation." So says a sign on the walls of the Phillipsburg refinery. Deliver us from evil, says another, and a third is the co-op slogan: "Neighbors built America. Today neighbors are building co-ops."

The digging of oil wells or their purchase from others, the piping and refining of oil, and then its repiping or trucking—doubtless all this is a complicated and costly people's business. But to date we do not see any other way to own and operate in oil. For it is oil that perhaps above all other commodities lends itself to money and machinery and a few technicians. Here money and machinery and the expert talk. Here the "rationalization" of industry is at its peak. What this means is that everything is done in a big way, and the whole industry can well be a sort of mechanized unit, from the boring of wells to the consumer's purchase of gas or oil. It is not easy to humanize and personalize this process. But it is something, surely, if the people own and control it from start to finish.

While I am visiting in Kansas they take me to see their first oil wells, a group of seven called the Laton field, or pool. This field of eighty acres they bought, I believe, with one well already operating, and then they sank the others. Several hundred thousand barrels have been pumped from the field, and now most of the wells— each pump automatically clocked to work so many hours or minutes a day—are merely stripping. The co-ops have therefore acquired new wells, and we go to see a prospective new well. This is down now to 3,100 feet, and in another five or six hundred it should strike pay dirt. That is, if this is not a dry well. The cost of putting down a well, dry or productive, is immense, and though the co-operators have sunk only a few dry holes, the average strike is about one in twenty. Then the well, at last hit, may be worth pumping only a few hours a day.

One old driller, forty-five years at it in Ohio, Indiana, Illinois, and Kansas, cups his big, rough and rusty hands as he says the pool is a rock pocket "where the oil is trapped." It is really a cup or pocket or valley; the geologist can tell just where there are "highs," or underground hills, and the driller hopes that he will find in any underground valley a lake of oil.

Once oil is struck the problem is to get it to refineries. This is done by way of pipe laid in trenches dug by machines, and digging and piping run into money. The maintenance of the line also is costly. Yet the cost of transportation of oil in pipe lines is as nothing to the cost by truck or train.

The men who grabbed oil were undoubtedly smart business-men, efficient men who recognized a good thing. The question is not about their good or bad qualities. The system, judged by its results, is in fact not too good. Negatively the results are these. The people do not own, and by this method cannot own. The people, we know now, do not get a fair and square deal on prices. Wars are promoted, abetted, or encouraged. Government is left with needless and intolerable burdens.

Suppose any of these evils mitigated by co-ops going, in their roundabout way, into the oil business. Then government might be freer. People might be more in possession. Wars might be fewer, less vicious and effective. Co-operation—"a system of trade that makes for peace among nations." The co-op people have such a good start, in C.C.A. territory covering nine states, and in Minnesota and Ohio and Indiana and throughout our country, and also abroad, that they cannot easily be licked. And they cannot permanently be kept down. Their steady and rather sure slow growth really talks.

On the wall of the office at Phillipsburg is the fisherman's prayer asking the Lord not to let the fisherman down. The co-operators might adapt the prayer. "O Lord, don't let monopolists rob us. Don't let them alone own and control oil and grain and homes and shops and factories. Don't let the people be stripped dry. Don't let them be keener for their wallets than we are for human good." A second plaque on that wall reads: "Warning—Sabotage." This consists in interfering with war effort or making in a defective way any war materials or any materials used in making war materials. This warning too might be adopted and adapted by the co-operators. Warning—sabotage: which consists in overriding the people's good, their chance to own and be free and secure. What the people have done in the nonco-op way is to have dug down and down, and at immense cost. They have broken their augers and got new costly ones from the profit man, and when at last they should be reaching pay dirt they find that the oil man has tapped the pocket and left to them nothing but the dry hole.

The third saying on that wall is from Woodrow Wilson, and the co-operators may take it as it stands: "The whole purpose of democracy is that we may hold counsel with one another, so as not to depend upon the understanding of any one man, but to depend upon the counsel of all." We need common counsel looking to common understanding, and also to common action. This is true in politics, and for a large part of industry and economics it certainly is not less true.

Fourteen

LABOR AND THE CO-OPS

1

DURING the past three hundred years, Democracy in its modern form has come to be, both as a struggle and as a qualified achievement, and Capitalism also, the economic system that mans an age whose dynamic is ever renewed profit made with the help of theoretically free Labor, arose and came to its height and has been challenged, and modern Science has developed in those same three hundred years. And over the past two hundred years there has arisen the proletarian body. This has arisen within Democracy, and with Science in the sense of mechanics as a condition, and as an inevitable result of Capitalism. In our time, it is the chief social and human event.

Briefly, it means this. People live by wages. It would be odd if all people lived by wages, everyone taking in a neighbor's wash and sending out his own. What happens is that most people work for a relatively few. Most people are minus productive property. The few with money control production in some cases, and in almost all cases control processing and distribution; they hire people who have not got property or control. These, then, live by wages; in the circumstances that is all they can do. Dependent totally on wages— that is what is meant by "proletarian." Most people now belong to this group, and with some justification are called "wage slaves."

Can anything be done about that condition? The negative reply is: "No, let man stay in that fix. Nothing can be done that would be worth the cost. Just don't let men unite, or get to thinking too much or hoping to get free. The status quo! Business as usual!" That is the conservative speaking, the man who likes what he has and is willing to get more.

Government can protect man in that status, pass laws in his favor; it can soak the rich, and can go into business. It levies high taxes on high incomes, tries its hand at business, and passes laws to see, after all, to the security of the wage slave. It would try cradle-to-grave security, much as has been tried in Germany. In the Beveridge way, the State would furnish the plan and pass laws to see that the State plan is carried out; the people would pay part, and the wealthy owners pay part.

To the propertyless and proletarian fix the second reply may be put in words I have used elsewhere: "Let the State, as well as it can, keep picking up the pieces, the broken bits of humanity. Let the State also, by way of special taxes, keep checking, as well as it can, the economic and political dominance of the wealthy few." The basic problem, man's proletarian condition, remains.

The third reply is simpler. Let all institutions be wrecked, because all are associated with rich men. What, then, becomes of the proletarian mass? Everyone is proletarianized, the wage slave of the totalitarian State.

In theory and fact, this method is dictatorship, and the second leads to dictatorship. Three would get rid of the wealthy few; Two would perhaps give security; none of them would allow man economic freedom or effective political freedom. But Two and Three, bad as they are, at least admit that people haven't property and therefore haven't security or freedom.

Man is not supposed to be propertyless and master of nothing. He is supposed to be man, that is to say, master, on his own and with those near to him—master of his work, his time, his home, his children, his churches, his schools, his lodges and unions, his banking, his insurance, his professional and agricultural and industrial processes and products. Why not this freedom? Why not this control, this expression of manhood?

In a machine age, a man by himself cannot do anything like all this; not on his own. It is only with the collaboration of his fellows, hundreds of them, thousands or on occasion perhaps millions of them, that he can do this. In other words, with them and only with them can he be master and truly man. Therefore unions and co-ops, and community schools, and parishes and community worship, and townships and local government, and lodges or clubs, and regional art, and societies to promote science and art. Without these man cannot be free and master and truly man. This is the positive reply: man can free himself. The negative one is this: neither an economic dictator nor a politico-economico-cultural dictator can free man. But the lone man cannot do it, the lone man going on an individualistic tilt against the machine and big finance and the trend toward the swollen State, cannot do it. Men studying together and working and playing and worshiping together and acting together by the score or the hundreds or thousands, can do it. Not at all easily, and never once for all. Freedom demands persistence and sacrifice and intelligence. The wish or word keeps no society sailing the high seas of freedom.

In short, in the capitalistic era men had jobs—at best had jobs— but only if and when the jobs were profitable to capitalists. Therefore, as this is a bad condition, let the State do it. Now my reply is, the State cannot do "it," since the State does not and never can provide man's freedom. The best we get under the several proposals is this: First, jobs when profitable, but without security, ownership or freedom; second, security without freedom. Neither way is satisfactory, and that is why it is a healthy sign when for a hundred years men have kicked against the first, and when they have always kicked against the second.

2

Poor and unknown as the co-ops are, I'd like to get some hint of what in such circumstances is the possible good in them. Not that the task of emancipation is easy. Not that it has ever been done. Not that the not-free man has been less than a constant on the face of the earth. But if in these matters the co-ops hold out the hope of action in a truly human way, surely they are worth a glance.

The problem is the emancipation of man, and in our time the emancipation of Labor. What have the co-ops to say in this vital connection? Happily, it is here that they are proud to speak up. For one thing, it was weavers who formed the early model cooperative. The men of Rochdale were not farmers, but poor laborers. It was the seven laws or principles written by these persons, and written intelligently on the solid stones of their wills, that were to remain forever the basis of co-operation.

That is what Labor can do in the co-ops; namely, set the pace, draw the permanent blueprint.

In Great Britain to this day one might think that only Labor could co-operate, because Labor is so heavily in the co-ops and does such a voluminous co-op business. Just look at the figures. The total membership in Great Britain for 1943 was estimated at above nine millions; the retail business turnover in 1942 reached toward a billion and a quarter, and in 1943 went to a billion and a third. Was it Labor that did all this? Very much of it, certainly, though the co-ops and the trade unions are separate bodies. "While the co-operatives have been built up as separate organizations with no organic connection with the trade unions, *the success of the co-operatives has been almost wholly due to the initiative, leadership and support of members of organized labor and the working class.*" Everywhere the retails exist with their many locals, 12,000 of these latter in England, Scotland and Wales; and the two big wholesales, the Co-op Wholesale and the Scottish Co-op Wholesale; and then the next regular step, the factories, 230 of these processing or making almost every kind of product in the line of food, clothing, metal goods, leather goods, glass, tobacco, and tea. The list is endless, and though I think our own co-ops have a better social or community effect, still the production of co-op articles by English laborers is a main economic phenomenon of the past century. It shows something of what laborers can do to control production, processing, distribution, and both wholesaling and retailing. Laborers can own factories, and get them free of charge. Laborers can own retail plants, and get them free of charge. All it takes is intelligence, initiative and patience, and the will to be economically free.

"What an amazing story it is! And last year the cooperatives of Great Britain returned to their members in patronage dividends an estimated one hundred and fifty million dollars, which otherwise would have gone in profits to private owners! Who says that labor acting as consumers can't run a business? They can do so, when the business is organized and operated strictly on the principles of consumer cooperation!"

That strong statement, from *Labor and Co-ops* by James Myers, is not so strong as the following, from the Senate Small Business Committee: "The British co-ops have grown more and more in popularity during the war: These distributive units are comparable to the variety chain stores with respect to their vitality and power of survival. They continually extended the ambit of their activities in the pre-war period and sold in the aggregate as much as 7% of the total sales of clothing, 9% of the total sales of footwear, 3% of the total sales of furniture and hardware and 25% of the total food sales. An estimate made in 1938 that 12% of the total retail sales belonged to the cooperatives, would now be too low."

In England we have had the greatest development of co-ops among laborers. On the Continent, the growth is at once among laborers, farmers and professional men, yet in many countries organized Labor has been active in building consumer co-operatives and in pushing the co-ops into factory production. Especially is this the case in the northern lands: Finland, Sweden and Norway, Holland and Denmark. And wherever unionists have given a hand to the co-ops, "the employees of co-operatives enjoy better wages, hours and working conditions than they do in general in private industry."

One thing is important here. Labor that is mere labor and is without organization is helpless. The union gives it part of the control it needs, a reasonable and due control over hours and wages and conditions of work. But that is not enough. Labor needs control over the prices it pays for oil, for shoes, for coal, for meat and coffee. And if the laborer has only his union, it is likely that what he gains with his right hand he gives over with his left. He needs the co-op. This is a new type of union, operating on consumer problems, on production and processing, and even on sources.

3

With the union and the co-op, Labor can begin to have the freedom it ought to have. Fortunately, our own unionists are rapidly learning this fact. The co-ops are just beginning to get a hold of American Labor, and the well-grounded promise is that tomorrow we shall see the Automobile Workers and possibly all the workers swept into the co-op movement. In several centers the growth has been healthy, and it will not likely yield to mere difficulty; co-operators are like unionists, a determined lot of people.

One of these is Racine, a city of sixty thousand located between Chicago and Milwaukee. We are hardly out of the Loop going toward it on the "Four Hundred" when we pass a few blocks of slum houses. But the man in the seat with me, a squat fellow, tanned and square-faced, routs me with his complacent "What'd-you-expect?" A husky woman in a flat straw with green ribbons on it, is pommeling her mild companion: "Let's see if we can see Nell's house in Wilmette. . . Here it is! Don't she live in convenient . . . Cases of polio in Chicago, the paper says here; seventeen new cases."

In Racine I am welcomed by Big Ed's on this side of the street and by Little Nick's on the other. Also by Matranga and Son Super Market, and by Church of God in Christ: Everybody Welcome. A monument, surrounded by cannon, was erected by the citizens in 1884 "in memory of Racine's Loyal and Noble Sons, who enlisted to defend and perpetuate these United States." I see ads and signs for Miller's High Life, the First National Bank and Trust Co., Kroger's Self-service, Hughes Store, and L. Wiemann's 5¢ to $1. I don't know when I saw in one street so many people not made right. Maybe it is just their day out!

In this busy city of profit people the co-ops have taken a firm hold. In 1934 five local men signed a paper before a notary, as required by Wisconsin law, and got a license to start a co-op; and I read their names, put down boldly: one an editor, and the others laborers. What they and their friends started was nothing more than a gas station. Some of them had stopped one day at a farmers' co-op station, and on inquiry and reading and further visits they concluded that they could keep up to Wisconsin farmers. Early in 1935, after great effort, they had collected $1,500, and opened their first station. In nine months it did a business of $38,447.

That was the spark that set Racine on fire for co-ops. So one might imagine. But the matter has not been so simple. It is true that the co-ops have advanced in this city. When I visit the co-operators, they have six gas stations, two of them, because of rationing, able to operate only in the red, but the six taken globally keeping in the black; and they have plans to buy spaces for two or three more. Also, they have two food stores, one of them a big one including a meat market. They have insurance on a co-op basis with two companies in Milwaukee and one in Minneapolis, an eminently respectable credit union with a capital of sixty thousand, a central coalyard that does a lot of business, and a recreation hall which (I understand) is not simply a union hall.

Says an official, "It is mostly a Labor setup, but with teachers, and doctors, and lawyers, and post-office employees, and a few farmers, and several policemen as members or patrons. Over three thousand patrons, though not all of them are members." On a wall of the main office is a map of the city made by a member working evening by evening at it. "He came to the office and worked it out." This map shows where the three thousand family patrons, probably making fifteen thousand people, reside; a section heavily dotted means that it has a live co-op promoter.

Shopping in the store across the street is a teacher of economics. "All my life, I have attended to the study of economics, and have to look fairly and squarely at the merits and demerits of capitalism and the proposed substitutes. What we can only expect is a mixed economy. It is the only thing practicable. It is not all or nothing. That is the extremist's point of view. If co-operators had fifteen per cent of the trade in Racine, we would never have needed any ceiling prices, as the co-operatives could have controlled. What a difference that would make: all that bureaucracy would be unnecessary!" Some of that tremendous cost of being ruled in a capitalistic world eliminated.

Here is the story of E. Hormberg, a man who was in the Kaiser's army back as far as 1896. He was told what to believe and do, even in the most sacred relations. "If I tell you to shoot your father and mother, you must shoot them!" Says he, "I did not believe that or accept that. And when orders came from the Kaiser to destroy all Socialist literature the army had, I wanted to know what socialism was. For if the Kaiser was against it, I was for it.

"Now the co-op. It's a nice, clean, peaceful way of liquidating Capitalism. If we all get our gas at co-op stations, Rockefeller goes out of business. If we all get our groceries at the co-op, the A & P, that skins us, goes out of business. And so on, on down the line. If we own, they don't. If they own, we don't. If we sell to ourselves everything that we buy, we won't ever have to complain about prices."

At the Laborer's Hall, many groups are represented. The painters and decorators, the Lithographers Local #54, the carpenters and joiners, the journeymen barbers, the molders, the stage employees, the united garment workers, and the metal polishers and buffers. Many busy offices are in this building, and among them is an office where I find an ardent co-op man, Walt Meihofer, who tells me about the origin and problems of the local co-ops.

"It was in 1934 and the depression, and I had no job, and all I had to do was think. And I began to think about this co-operation. It could do something, and I said that, but most of the fellows, they didn't do anything or say much. Four or five were ready to try anything we could do, and we collected $35: only one fellow could pay a full share, we were so poor. And we started a gasoline station.

"But the whole business, it moves slow. A few keep joining themselves, and a few dropping out, but it keeps going. Our educational program—what could we do? We printed a folder, and sent it out, in plain figures of what was done among Labor in England and Sweden, to show its advantages. But how we reach the nonco-operators? A good speech like Andy Marske gives won't do it, because only co-operators come, and a dance or a picnic, it's the same thing. A slow growth, but maybe that's better. We grow too fast, maybe that's not good. The best way is mouth to mouth, that's education and the best speech. You believe someone if it's a man that works by you."

It is slow and hard, and is made harder by some few dishonest or ignorant persons. "They say everything they can against us, true and false.

"They say we don't pay taxes." But they better be careful! "I say, 'You better find out what you're sayin'! We pay taxes on property and income, but none on profits, because we don't make any profits. Why should we pay taxes on the overcharge what we give back to the people?'

"One fellow, he says, 'It's against the spirit of enterprise and it's not American.' And I say, 'Capitalism the spirit of enterprise! What enterprise *you* got in system of Capitalism? What *you* start? This is the spirit that is American: the people want to control their business and not leave it to some crooked rich guys.'

"And one of them, he says, 'You pay refunds and no profits— how can you keep up business?' And I say, 'It's because you think we don't provide everything. We do! We allow for depreciation, and a reserve fund for emergency, just like any business. But look, if wages is paid and insurance and reserve fund, and four thousand is left over, what's that for?' 'For profits,' he says. 'Nonsense,' I say. 'Profits! It's for the people to pay back to themselves what they overcharged themselves when they bought things in their own store.'

"And fellows, they say to me, 'Businessmen built up the trade and they got a right to keep it.' And I say, 'Let them keep it, if they can. Businessmen are corporations, and now we got our own business. Which is better?' "

He says co-op education must begin in a man's own home. "It's the principle and the quality. My wife—women are bargain hunt-ers—she said she could get fruit two cents cheaper at the other store. And I said to bring home a can from the co-op and compare the two: that's the way to tell. Co-ops go for quality and honesty, and they label their goods. We got to educate our wives, and get them sold on co-ops, and if the others would undersell the same quality goods, we would not buy from them. It's the principle; it's loyalty, and building up our own stores."

Walt Meihofer is 100 per cent sound in his doctrine on co-ops. He says the co-op is not a union setup, but for all the people. Walt is broad across the face and arms and body, with a thick lisp in his talk, and he is in the act of going to work as he says: "Men working in meat markets can't buy their meat at the co-op. It's just like some men say to me: they don't dare. And the same for grocery men. But all the factory men, there's nothing to stop them. But unions can't join in a block, because then they think they'll control the co-op. And we have to tell them that's not the way the co-op works. It has to be open for everybody."

4

To date in Racine we have Labor beginning to control, or mak-ing some bid for control. Of course, it does not go far, but it is started in the right direction, and it includes farmers or primary producers as members of its co-ops. What we would want would be a union or co-op working both ways. We would want the farmer to own his land and home, and everywhere to have a co-op with his fellow farmers. This would be a marketing co-op. The urban laborer would have his co-op or body of co-ops, and here the co-op would be of the "consumer" type. The farmer as consumer would likewise need this type of co-op. Along with this we would want some kind of union between the marketing and consumer co-ops, something like a co-op of co-ops. This is no mere fancy, for it is said that the urban people in Waukegan, Illinois, form an immense co-op that is organically linked with the farmers' marketing co-op. The latter furnishes milk to the urban co-ops, and I am told that an arrangement is worked out whereby farmers and urbanites sit together as directors, and the refund is divided in a prorata way between the marketing and the consumer co-ops. Sometimes one of these types evolves so as to include the other. This is a common experience in dairy co-ops, set up as strictly marketing co-ops, but very soon buying feed and machinery and gas for the farm.

In South Bend we have what is in many ways the most interesting promise of co-op development. A few years ago six men pooled $25 and bought some nonperishable groceries. This is the ordinary way to start a buying club. These goods they sold and with the proceeds bought more goods.

"I suppose you started in a basement," I said to one of the founders.

"Not even that," he said, "but in an attic!" Soon they had moved into a basement, and were able to nurse their co-op along till it is now a vigorous first-floor shop. It is well kept by a woman who knows co-operation, and from many points of view, though it is yet small, it is a model.

It has grown in the slow, steady co-op fashion. But more important is its tie-up with Labor and the largest credit union in the city and also with the county Farm Bureau and thereby to some extent with farmers. Its founders were laborers, and its location is in the hall of Studebaker Local #5. Across the corridor is the credit union, which on New Year's Eve, 1945, had capital just short of a million. The arrangement is healthy, since the store and credit union naturally work together. The manager of the credit union is a co-operator, and the manager of the store believes in the people's own bank: "organized by themselves" (to use language given me by a credit union man), "managed by themselves, run in every way by themselves, and entirely for the people's welfare." Any refund at the bank could be used to help pay the grocery bill, and any refund at the store could be banked across the corridor. Upstairs is the Union Hall. Of course, it is not exclusively Labor that may or does trade and bank here. Any member may get his coal the co-op way through the Farm Bureau co-op, and in the winter of 1944-45 Labor and the farmers organized combined study clubs.

But if Labor had its consumer co-ops developed and if—as is unlikely—it were commonly to tie up with farmers' co-ops, Labor would not yet have gone so far in the co-op way as it ought to go and as it will go. The natural movement, once consumer co-ops are established, is into co-op wholesaling, first on a regional basis and then on a national basis. But as the farmers have learned, that is not enough. The next natural step is to set up co-op factories. The farmers have in many instances gone through this evolution and Labor or Labor with the farmers will do the same. In that way ownership will begin to be the people's. Banks will be the people's, as in many places they now are, and stores and gas stations will be the people's as they now often are, and refineries and oil wells and factories will be the people's. All that Labor needs for this consolidation and progress is patience and diffused education, and we have good reason to believe that both the CIO and the AFL will go all the way.

"In the oil industry, consumers have moved from retailing back to ownership of refineries, pipe-lines, and even oil wells. Manufacturing may be engaged in by local, regional, or national units. In all cases, earnings become savings, flow back step by step to the consumer." With patience and persistent education the laborer can reach this height. Think of the ways in which his achievement of this almost inevitable goal would be good; good for him as a person and a member of a family and neighborhood and nation, and good also for the family unit and the neighborhood and the nation. In all countries its coming is the natural, inevitable working of the co-ops: from the consumer co-op to the wholesale and at last to the factory.

The people ought to own some factories, and at present they do own 113 of them, and in these and their wholesaling and retailing they employ over 16,000 persons. They will own more, as they "drive back into the economy, particularly in industrial production."

That Labor should have a say about wages and conditions is good, but it does not let them love their work and its product, and is not good enough. To achieve ownership and copartnership with Capital is better. But it is best for co-operators, rural and urban, to buy some going factories after consideration and study, and to operate them with the aid of experienced businessmen and engineers who at the same time are co-operators. Even then great inhumanities might remain, such as greed and war, depersonalization, loss of independence, of neighborhood life, of conversation, of hospitality, and a kind of progressive helplessness with its consequent demand for statism. These have everywhere gone with highly industrialized life, and possibly are inherent in it. Co-ops can at least mitigate these evils, and allow men's lives to be more free and fully human and self-possessed.

ᶘifteen

DOCTORS AND CO-OPERATIVE MEDICINE

1

Iᴛ ᴡᴏᴜʟᴅ be great if through private, individual housing and co-op housing we could have our own houses. Then we would not depend on owners, nor on possible monopolistic corporations. By the same stroke, the housing and the people would be protected from government invasion, and in this matter could remain free and creative and possessed of property in so vital a line, and personal members of communities. Undoubtedly we could do it.

It would be great if we would work out our own banking system and credit, and were independent at once. It would be great if we worked out an insurance that would be our own democratic and neighborhood insurance: life insurance, property insurance, health and accident insurance, and old-age insurance. The man willing to have his parents on the county or the state, and willing to look forward to going on county or state, is not much of a believer in freedom. Just to have insurance given is mechanical and depersonalized and not the condition of free men.

I do not say that government ought never to take over, even pro tem, any such utility as railroads or telegraph or coal or iron mines, or that there should not be a lot of private ownership. What I do say is that ownership should neither be left open to monopoly nor be hogged up by the government. To keep a mid-position between these extremes we must, in our times, develop co-operatives.

It would be great if we would work out co-op medicine and co-op hospitalization for one-fifth or possibly one-third of our people in every city and every county. For several reasons it would be "great."

First, and most evidently: Millions now have no adequate medical or surgical or hospital care. "In the United States today 40,000,000 persons—one-third of the population—live in families with incomes under $800 a year. Studies of current living costs make clear that when the average family of four is supported by this sum, life is lived at an emergency level. If sickness strikes, doctor bills, and medicines mean 'cutting down' on food, clothing, or shelter."[1] That is the fact.

Second: The old method, though good and on many occasions benevolent and beneficent, will not and conceivably cannot work out adequate care for those millions. The fact in that case will remain.

Third: With the general movement toward statism, the State will continue to move into every business and service, including the care of health: giving the State more control over human lives, and with more to do, an ever bigger unnatural load to bear, and bureaucracy without end. In our country this movement proceeds independently of party turnover. It's the custom, it's in the air; that's the way things are going. When we see abuses or inadequacies in medicine, in banking, in insurance, we think the government ought to do something about it.

"Socialized" medicine, as we know it or envision it, is State medicine, and many things said against this by the American Medical Association are justified. Such medicine has come in part, especially because in our hearts we have accepted it, and more of it will come. It is as if we loved statism. So simple a matter does it seem: the State investigating education, and medicine, and banking and insurance, and then supervising and controlling, and at last without apology operating; and man is made subordinate in almost all that he has and all that he is to the political community.

Fourth: It is always a great thing if people in smaller and autonomous bodies do tasks that need to be done, and perilous to invite leviathan to take control. That is just what has happened, no matter by what methods, in every collectivistic nation. The dictators gobbled up power, got control of goods and services: of education, the radio and the press and communications, medicine and hospitals, insurance, banking, manufacturing, farming, and labor. At the critical and decisive moment the man lusting for power appears, and all he has to do is to pull the string. He has an impotent people in the bag.

From every human point of view, it would be good for people

[1] *Who Can Afford Health?* Public Affairs Committee, New York, 1939; prewar figures.

to own and manage as many services as people can manage. Private persons owning and managing whatever they can, within the limits of human good, and autonomous groups smaller than the State controlling for the common good "functions which can be performed efficiently by smaller and lower bodies." Among these groups must surely be Labor and the co-ops.

In the line of medicine it would be great, but perhaps it will not be done, and I want to suggest why not. First, the movement toward statism has been formidable, and we shall see more of it before we see less. State control of men and operations is now the rule, and equipped with secret police and concentration camps it can hardly be questioned. Second, people mostly are conservative and let things go. Third, the co-ops for their part develop slowly, and in order to be the people's and at the same time be sanely and safely grounded they have to come along only at what is relatively a snail's pace. Fourth, the medical men, allying themselves on occasion with politicians, withstand co-op medicine precisely as they withstand State medicine, and they do it so effectively that State medicine is sure to be precipitated.

2

Theoretically the case for co-op medicine, though likely to be naïve, is powerful. Take South Bend with 100,000 people and with another 150,000 inside a radius of thirty miles, 250,000 people representing 50,000 families. Suppose these families contributed as neighborhood groups to a central clinical and medical fund. An annual $50 per family would run into the sum of $2,500,000.

I find no special fault with our local doctors or hospitals, but am youthful enough to conjecture that even if, because of poverty and ignorance, one-third of the suggested total could not be collected, still we would have a sum that could afford us:

First, a clinic where every person could have medical and dental examination once a year, thus getting ahead of such diseases as incipient cancer and tuberculosis. As matters now are, the poor avoid doctors and wait till disease has progressed to a hopeless stage, and then are likely to spend ten times as much as precautionary steps would have cost.

Second, at least one expert for every major human ailment. This can be afforded by any center of a quarter million, and would be an improvement over the present condition. Think of the good and comfort that the people could get out of that. A few can now go to experts at Mayo's and elsewhere, but 90 per cent of us get the ordinary care, though on occasion many need more.

Third, medical and surgical and dental care for all. Probably 40 per cent of us are now without adequate care.

Fourth, hospitalization as needed for everyone. This would entail the building of hospitals, a matter that in fifty years would be possible.

Fifth, adequate pay for medical men and hospitals, and this might be on the average more and would undoubtedly be surer than they now receive.

Sixth, encouragement, not often had now, for study and research.

That is a rosy and simple picture, with its suggestion of a nearly total co-operation on the part of the people and the doctors. The scheme is too big, too complicated, too good. But suppose that in one such center we went at it and by the date of the second Rochdale centenary had made a start toward accomplishing it. Naturally, there would be struggle and name-calling and hair-pulling all the way, but at the end we should have adequate medical care for all, and the people should have provided it.

Still, the picture is not mere theory, since we have in the United States some developments of co-op medicine and co-op hospitalization, and we got in 1943 a court provision allowing us to continue to have these. This was the decision of the Supreme Court convicting the American Medical Association and its District of Columbia chapter for violation of the Sherman Antitrust Law in obstructing the Group Health Association of Washington, D.C. From the first this association had been molested by the profession: far from being helped, it was perpetually harassed; and after a four-year battle the decision went against the obstructionists. In three ways, said the decision written by Justice Roberts, the societies tried to nullify the health group: ". . . to impose restraints on physicians affiliated with Group Health by threats of expulsion or actual expulsion from the societies; . . . to deny them the essential professional contact with other physicians; . . . to use the coercive power of the societies to deprive them of hospital facilities for their patients."

3

That is a considerable victory for the co-ops, since they have for years suffered running fire from men whom they call "medical politicians." The most severe case of this and also the most astounding success in American co-op medicine to date has been in western Oklahoma. On the struggle and achievement we have the founder's own story.

The struggle of Dr. Michael Shadid and the people to set up a people's hospital is the liveliest fight in American co-op history. And it is truly co-op: it is for the people and by the people and their loyal leader, Dr. Shadid. This tireless and invincible man was born a Syrian; hence the nice name "rug peddler" applied to him by those who will not go with the people. As a young doctor in western Oklahoma he built up a practice and income and the respect of people and doctors. And yet he suffered; he felt that it is not the business of a doctor merely to build up respect and income. He suffered because the people suffered. Is it not the doctor's business at all costs to look to the good of bodies just as it is the priest's business to look to the good of souls? Dr. Shadid could hardly ask the question, since to him the matter is evident. The doctor is the priest of health. And have we not in our nation enough intelligence and good will and money and medical men and science to see that no one shall be needlessly a cripple or blind or an invalid? Yet the fact is that we have forty million without adequate medical care.

In Oklahoma, Dr. Shadid saw plenty of disease, broken bones that never mended, and broken bodies. He saw faithful doctors, and doctors who were good men, but lacked science. He also saw quacks and racketeers who posed as doctors.

Says Dr. Shadid: "I have never been satisfied with existing conditions in my field of study and have always wanted to change them to something I considered better . . . my income rose, in 1928 and 1929, to its highest level. I still looked about me and saw great need and many abuses in the practice of medicine. From the first days of my career in Maxville, Missouri, I have encountered doctors who were incompetent, or unscrupulous, or both . . . suffering resulting from their mistakes, their neglect, and their grasping for money."

Mistakes, neglect, grasping for money; the people suffering. That is the massive, inhuman fact that moved Dr. Shadid.

Men who claimed to have secret formulas, to be specialists in goiter or cancer. Men who took out a man's appendix and took his mules and cows also, and managed to get a mortgage on the patient's farm and then to get the farm. In a small town a man "who performed seventeen appendectomies in one week during an epidemic of gastroenteritis." Men who in city or country performed needless Caesarian operations.

But quacks and racketeers aside, the people cannot afford adequate medical care. In the city the specialist's fee is too high, and in the country we have to date no way of getting the specialist's service. Under existing conditions the doctor cannot look to the good of bodies.

The first thing, said Dr. Shadid, was better training of doctors and an effort to get rid of the incompetents. But even with that done, we have to find a way of handling the economics of medicine, a way to free us of the individualistic scramble for money and bring adequate medical service within the reach of all. To do this we must have equipment, science, and experts available not only in cities but in the country, and not only for the rich but for all. The neglect of preventive medicine leaves good doctors trying to cure diseases that people need never have had.

Adequate medical attention for all—that is the ideal. But the question remains whether the ideal is impossibly high.

The government could conceivably come and do it. That is the top-down method worked out by Beveridge, for instance, and in national socialism and every form of collectivism. Will the doctors themselves therefore do it, for the good of the people and to keep us on this side of statism? On the old individualistic plan they cannot do it. They cannot assemble the equipment and experts everywhere, and we need them everywhere, and the people cannot pay even for adequate nonexpert care. Either, therefore, the State and a step toward Hitlerism, or the old inadequate care, or the people must have co-op hospitals and co-op medicine. *The State, or inadequacy, or the co-ops.*

The doctors have never yet faced this simple set of alternatives.

In his own town of Elk City and all around him Dr. Shadid saw co-ops succeed and do things the people could not otherwise do. The people in his town had a co-op cotton gin, and in the next county they had a co-op that bought lumber and coal and ran an elevator. Could the people have medical care and a hospital on something of the same plan?

Dr. Shadid saw that they could. But this was yet a vision, and he had many battles before he made it into a reality. His plan at first, as he says in his wonderful book *A Doctor for the People*,[2] was like this: let each of two thousand families subscribe fifty dollars toward building the hospital and getting membership in the co-op. Let a discount of 50 per cent be given on all services, and the maximum for an operation be fifty dollars. "But all the doctors rejected the plan, mainly because they were convinced that it would mean a reduction in their individual incomes." He says that from that time he knew he could count on opposition. He took the plan to the people, and though some families had a hard time finding fifty dollars or even ten dollars, the people were far from rejecting the plan. With two thousand members, these country people could have a chief surgeon, a chief physician, a urologist, a specialist for eye, ear, nose and throat, a hospital physician, two general practitioners, a technician for X-ray and laboratory, two dentists, and a druggist—and all of them guaranteed a salary!

During the first round the doctors of the region paid little attention, for no such plan is likely to succeed. But when the people started building, the doctors published a manifesto against the project.

The founder got a series of bad names. These charges were unfair, untrue and unethical, but are not the worst that could be made against a doctor. The doctors said that this doctor was "unethical." Naturally, then, they could not in justice keep such a man in their medical associations, and out he went. Out, too, went any doctor who dared to tie up with him in operating the people's

[2] New York, Vanguard Press, 1939. It is a delightful book, with great conflict and villains and martyrs. See also J. T. Ratcliff in *Collier's*, July, 1943.

hospital. Any new doctor therefore soon departed, and a rumor spread that it was hard to get along with Dr. Shadid. How could any doctor stay, with his license revoked and himself in a bad light with his profession?

Only a small percentage of the people stayed through these circumstances, but enough of them still understood that this was the best deal they had ever known in medicine. And the Farmers' Union, always democratic and human, stayed, and Alfalfa Bill Murray stayed too, and said that the people have "the legal constitutional right" to have a hospital and "will be protected to the limit by the Governor of Oklahoma."

To a young doctor's inquiry the president of the County Association wrote: ". . . I might say as a matter of justice that the head of the institution is a fair doctor, but it is the unfair and shady practices that we all object to." That is the perpetual refrain. Unethical. Shady practices.

How is a medical co-op unethical? So far as I can make out, the having of a people's hospital is allegedly unethical because it makes the involved doctors guilty of steering patronage toward themselves. They are charged in such a case with "steerage." On the other hand, the people's having a hospital and adequate medical service enslaves the people. The people are not free; they have paid by the year for hospital and medical care, and they do get these, but are not free to go to other doctors.

No doubt the charges could be differently preferred. It could be said that the doctors serving the co-op association were hired by the people and given a set salary and an annual vacation, and had for the first time a chance to study and to learn from professional contacts. It could be said that for the first time the people had confidence in their doctors, adequate medical care, and in spite of their known poverty the ability to pay the bill.

Thus one should exercise care before making up his mind whether it was a high professional ideal and the people's freedom and their genuine service that the county medical men and the state men and the A.M.A. were so zealous to protect.

The people's freedom, their adequate medical care, and a lofty professional standard—who is it that in fact is best promoting these?

The people now have the fullest and best medical and surgical care ever offered in that part of Oklahoma. A woman can give birth to her child in a hospital with proper attendants, and not be worried to death over the bill, and cancer and t.b. can be headed off in time. In short, all needed medical attention can be had without fear of exorbitant costs. If, then, we are to use the nice word "unethical," to whom ought we to apply it? To the people, or the new doctors, or possibly some sprinkling of the old ones?

A discount on all bills did not prove satisfactory, and it proved better to use a prepayment plan. On this "dues plan" an individual pays twelve dollars a year for "complete medical care by our doctors," two persons forming a family pay eighteen dollars, three pay twenty-four, and four or more in the same family pay "a maximum of twenty-five dollars." That, then, is the rate: "Medical care: $25 per family per year." That can be paid by all but the poorest or most improvident families, and it gives the people adequate care. This prepayment entitles persons and families to the doctors' attention without charge, and includes "examination, treatment, surgical operations, X-ray, and extraction of teeth." Hospital care is an additional two dollars a day, the anesthetic and room fee for a major operation twenty dollars, and for child delivery and a minor operation ten dollars each. "Thus the cost of a case of pneumonia, for example, would be but a small fraction of the two or three hundred dollars charged under private practice. A major surgical operation under ordinary conditions could, and frequently did, cost a thousand dollars, but under the dues-paying system a patient, staying in the hospital ten days, would pay twenty dollars for room and meals and twenty dollars anesthetic fee, a total of forty dollars."

By the time (1939) his book appeared, Dr. Shadid thought his troubles were past. I fear he was too optimistic, and has probably found that co-op medicine will for a long time have growing pains. A man who likes a fight and thrives on it, as long as he lives he will have to keep his fists up; but he says that never again do we need to hear from worried patients the pitiful question "How much, doctor?" "I dreamed about helping people, of relieving their suffering, and that dream has become a reality." The freedom that he has helped to effect is the freedom of the forty million medically undernourished to have adequate care, and the freedom of medical men, with the help of the people, to furnish that care. Freedom from fear and worry, freedom from disease, freedom from debt. That is what his shady and unethical practice has given the people. The Syrian rug peddler has laid a lovely carpet in which the hopelessly sick can see pictures of a Christlike charity, and down which his other patients can walk again in the blazing Oklahoma sun. Perhaps he has furnished us a pattern that may be used by every common man in America.

4

In a dozen places a hundred thousand people have been trying co-op medicine and in sixty or more cities nearly two millions have hospitalization that either is co-operative or approaches co-operative ideals. Because of legal restrictions, the name may be "health insurance," but that is a small matter. In Washington, the three thousand member-families must be allowed freedom to get medical care, and the doctors the freedom to give it. We have reason to think that this Group Health Association, set up primarily to serve government employees, reaches almost forty thousand persons. The attack on it by the American Medical Association and its local chapter suggests how serious is the problem of the people's medical care. The court decision was given in January, 1943, and government statisticians show that, even allowing for the relative youth of the members and their relatively high wages, the health record of the group for 1943 was well above the average. The association had net savings of $10,330 for the year, though its fees were among the few costs in Washington that did not rise.

Everywhere groups begin to work out adequate care. At the end of four years Group Health Cooperative in New York City had ten thousand members who might choose among 2,500 physicians. Its method is to take group membership, such as employees of the Book-of-the-Month, or *Parent's Magazine*, this or that labor union or co-op. The Health Cooperative of Greenbelt in Maryland has a clinic and serves most of Greenbelt. In December, 1944, the Farm Bureau of Ohio reported 38,207 "protected by group hospitalization insurance," though in Ohio "our Farm Bureau groups are only a small percentage of our total number of group policies in force." According to deKruif's *Kaiser Wakes the Doctors*, the Kaiser plan, in notable part co-op, provides medical and hospital care for almost a hundred thousand. Also within recent months co-op hospitals, inspired by the success at Elk City, were opened at Hardtner, Kansas, Moreland, Oklahoma, and Amherst, Texas. Other units are near to co-op ideas and practices; for instance, the Civic Health Center in Chicago, the Trinity Hospitals in Little Rock, and the Ross Loos Clinic in Los Angeles. The need is greater in towns and country places, but here is a service of the people and by the people that, like co-op stores and bakeries and credit unions, can be worked out more readily in the great centers of population.

The only health insurance or health co-op that I have seen at close range is Group Health Mutual, with offices in St. Paul. Its membership comes to about nine thousand. After studying this health co-op, Dr. H. E. Sigerist of Johns Hopkins said: "So far it offers only hospital and surgical benefits, but it does it under an arrangement which is controlled not by the hospitals, but by the consumers of hospital care. What seems even more important to me is that Group Health has established a state-wide machinery which makes it possible for employed persons to develop gradually the health services they need."[3] It takes groups having like interests and occupations, for instance, members of the Cloquet Co-op, and a teachers' club, and the meat cutters, and workers on the Soo Line, and a trucking group. In two cases, it has in its membership the entire body of workers at a plant, and its members run now to over nine thousand. It builds no hospitals, but uses existing hospitals and clinics. What it does is to provide "full preventive and curative medical care, 24 hours a day, in the home, hospital, and doctors' offices, on a prepayment plan."

[3] In *PM*, Sept. 16, 1940. For full information write Group Health, 2635 University Ave., St. Paul, Minn.

ADULT EDUCATION IN OHIO

1

In Nova Scotia both the people and the leaders have said that the co-op movement in that province is first and foremost an educational movement. And after seeing something of the results, I am ready to accept that statement. The logic of the procedure is like this:

1. Do you or do you not want to be free?

2. You cannot be free unless you are economically free. Any alleged political freedom without economic freedom is hardly better than a blind.

3. You cannot be economically free unless you free yourself. The State cannot possibly do it, and Ford and Carnegie, for all their beneficence, cannot possibly do it.

4. Going it alone you cannot free yourself, "you" here meaning, not just some wizard of finance, but all the people. You can do it only by going about the problem with your neighbors.

5. But the first step is an educational one: you and the neighbors must find out the economic possibilities in your situation. And you and they studying together must find out how we got into our present fix, what the fix is, and how we might reasonably hope to get out of it. "We need the co-operation of all men of good will to get us out of this mess," says Father Jimmy Tompkins, and he knows that this co-operation must begin not as a buying club or a credit club, but as a study club. And since we never have things once and for all under control, we shall always have to study.

For freedom then. For economic freedom. For the freedom of us all. That is the end. By study of the situation with the neighbors. That is the method.

Now, if a well-groomed Nova Scotia co-op man were to criticize our midwestern co-ops, he would in most areas single out our lack of study, and he might go further and single out our lack of faith in study. We are for action and quick returns, but are impatient with the discipline that democracy and freedom demand. Our schools are democratic in the senses that everybody goes to them and is exposed to a hurried program of studies. Yet it is easy to doubt that their rapid-fire results are in all ways the best. From kindergarten up, the schools are like mechanized units into which we throw our children at a certain age. In these units they get much good training, especially now in play and in music. What one may be slow to say, however, is that the schools always afford either a good theoretic or an effective knowledge of man and his place in society, or that they certainly light the way to freedom.

Do the co-ops simply by-pass the general drift toward the loss of freedom? The co-ops help people to help themselves and in theory and effect urge them not to surrender to dictatorships. But the co-operators are people and modern western people, and therefore have a weakness for expecting the old individualism or some nice new collectivism to come and save them. Precisely this weakness is what the co-op techniques, if first understood and then followed through, would ideally rid us of, and in many instances we have seen in them a promise to do this.

Possibly a school should be human, near to home, coming from the families in the neighborhood. Possibly, parents even in Chicago and Detroit should be slow to give up the school to officials whom they don't know and the schooling to teachers whom neither the officials nor the parents know. This is to say that schooling, so far as it is not done in the home, ought to be done through an autonomous co-op. It is a neighborhood job; it is done by the neighborhood, and it does much, in that case, to tie the people together and to re-create the neighborhood.

That is what they say the Nova Scotia co-op essentially is: a spontaneous schooling of adults in the neighborhood by those adults, and in vital relation to local and real problems. Denmark has something added to that, since among the Danes co-op education is also for youth, and is embodied in a religious and cultural tradition.

I am glad to say that among vast numbers of Ohio co-operators the education of the people by the people and with their eyes on real local problems has in recent years made an impressive start.

We saw the Finnish co-operators in Minnesota busy at some truly educational work, and noted that farmers and miners and others carry on in an informal way some co-op education. Almost everywhere I went, too, I found co-op literature, often not more than a few pamphlets at the store, but once in a while eight or ten or forty good books.

But it is in Ohio that the most concerted effort toward co-op education is under way. It is on the adult level and has come to pass independently of any state action and of any existing schools, public or private, in the state. At this writing, it has slightly over a thousand units, each of them a homespun body made up of neighbors who want to get together and see whether they cannot by study and action do something about their problems. The unit is designedly small, from twelve to twenty-four persons, and probably all of them together number from eighteen to twenty thousand. Hardly a unit has fallen by the wayside and, as the movement is spreading fast, we must say that this Ohio co-op education of adults by adults is in these times one of the major educational developments in America.

To date nearly all these Ohio "folks" are farmers, and in fact the movement was prompted by the Ohio Farm Bureau, and if one must say that the Farm Bureau in some places is not high in its ideals or blest in its leadership, in Ohio and, I may add, in Indiana and Pennsylvania it is admirable. One must note, too, that the Farm Bureau in some of its effects has invaded and will further invade the towns and cities of Ohio.

The bureau here is about twenty-five years old and has progressively had co-ops since 1926. Though the bureau everywhere has other than co-op functions, the movement into co-ops has been fast. The making of fertilizer—"this Red Steer stuff"—is a co-op achievement; the price is cut by four dollars a ton, and the pace is set for anyone who wants to deal in fertilizers. Insurance has gone at an incredible speed into the hands of the people in Ohio, and their brand of insurance, at the big reductions they have made, has now gone into eleven states and the District of Columbia. "We've cut the insurance rate one-third, and other companies have cut in Ohio: they have to." So claims a co-op man. The co-op control over the quality and price of feeds is also a fact, and to some important though minor extent the co-op control of credit. Some hospital-ization is co-op, and much of the rural electrification is handled through the co-ops.

"In short," says an Ohio co-operator, "we first get our Red Steer co-operatively, and then grind our feed co-operatively, and at last we begin to care co-operatively for the health of our bodies."

As a matter of fact, the first co-operative undertaking was the establishment of the Farm Bureau Auto Insurance Company in 1926, with a capital of $10,000. By 1944 the assets of the Insurance Co-operatives and allied enterprises had reached $33 million, the offices in Columbus employed over nine hundred persons, and membership in the co-op insurance companies totalled over 500,000 policyholders. The state-wide wholesale business of the Ohio Farm Bureau in 1943 was over $19 million. The commodities handled include petroleum products, household appliances, farm supplies and tires. The state association owns four fertilizer plants, an oil refinery, several feed mills, a chick hatchery, has part interest in National Co-operatives which operates a factory for making milking machines and a chemical laboratory in Chicago, and part interest in the National Farm Machinery Co-operative.

This is an inadequate preview of the things the co-ops do in Ohio. But it is not any or all of these, but their educational work that now begins to be characteristic of Ohio co-ops. For this reason we wish to go to a few educational sessions and see the people face their problems and also enjoy themselves as they do it.

2

It was ten or eleven years ago that an Ohio leader first made the pilgrimage to the Nova Scotia co-ops. Others went the next year, and when I went in 1939 I met eight Ohioans going over the same ground. They saw something in Nova Scotia, and began to think that what they saw could be transplanted. What they liked was the technique, the educational process by which adults in small groups study their problems. Is Nova Scotia the only place this can be done? Is it the only place where men are smart enough to get together and dare to think of solving problems with their bare minds and the local resources? The Ohioans also looked once or twice at the Danish folk schools, and thought these could add immeasurably to the undoubted good sense of the Nova Scotia co-ops.

The earliest venture of this kind, then, in Ohio came in a way from abroad and from the vision of a local man or two who believed profoundly in the people. The way an "advisory council" begins to operate in a community is for someone to go to two or three families and say, "How would you like to get a few of your neighbor-friends together and begin to talk over your common problems?" A likely person, of course, is selected at the start, and he takes the next step, and then he and his neighbors are responsible for nearly all subsequent steps. The persons are Farm Bureau members, and probably have already had some action in common, and in any case they are farm neighbors. The first four groups were all in a particular county, and set out with simple but not irrelevant questions, such as "What is the Farm Bureau?" and "What are our biggest problems?" Obvious as this second question is, it certainly would raise a considerable dust of controversy. Then: How would they like to continue to meet, say once a month, all winter and perhaps ten or more months a year?

"Don't they have a leader? And don't they have something to talk about and discuss?"

These are the inquiries made by a national co-op figure. They most certainly do have a leader and a problem. But the leader is not an imported one. He is a man chosen by themselves and from their group. Success depends on their landing a good man and of course does not always follow. Outsiders may visit the unit at any session; for example, one of the four or five fieldmen in the state may drop in at any meeting. But the unit makes its own way, under the guidance of its own "discussion leader." For convenience, it has a chairman and a secretary. The minutes are kept, usually by a note or two as the session proceeds, but in one place that I visited entirely from memory.

Let us meet with some of these people as they study their problems. This May evening the men are busy in the fields, and are late in assembling; the fieldman and I arrive at nine o'clock, and the first farmer and his wife arrive just as we do. Soon we have a dozen couples, besides a few children left to their tumbling on the kitchen floor.

This is an exceedingly democratic group, and the chairman allows the people their own way, with the result that they feel free to broach several topics. Last time they discussed what they could do to help save gas, and decided to take turns going to town. They touched on a farm budget, and decided against it, but for a farm account. They also considered the problem of group hospitalization. So the matter was recorded. And then—no doubt an assigned subject—they came to the problem of farm help. "Running a binder," they said, "is out for a green hand, or a mower. Operating a milking machine could be learned by any youth in a few days' time, largely up to the boy. Cleaning the barn is something any strong youth can do. Sticking wire into a hay bailer is something any youth can do and usually they like that work, though it is fairly hard. Dovetailing in with these jobs are small chores. The pay would be small compared with industrial wages, but the experience will be of considerable value in later years."

Next after reading the minutes tonight comes the unfinished business. The question here is about the "picnic." When are we to have it, and where, and how provide rationed food? Evidently what need not be discussed is whether we will have it. Better have it on a Sunday: we'd never get in from work and get the cows milked. Better, says a man with a comfortable look, better have it in fried-chicken time. In June, then? No, July is much better—on July 10. "Well, what do you say: twelve fast time, or twelve slow time? We made it on slow time last year, and we'd like to never got home."

Business, the minutes, and the discussion proper are all interspersed and I would say naturally interspersed, with talk of bus schedules, and the perennial problem in Ohio over fast time, slow time. "Changing back again next Monday," says a man. "That'll be a mess."

"Aw!" says his neighbor. "Things all balled up!"

In this and every advisory council the vote is heavily in favor of "having our time zone changed." Says one council in its minutes: "Our stock don't get up until daylight and there is no sense in going out into the dark and arousing them. It don't save light, it increases electric bills, and the children go off in the dark to school. Our crops have to wait for the sun."

In the local group we get down now to the discussion. "It's this inflation," says the leader. "The Farm Bureau sends out this little pamphlet here. They'd like us to say what farmers can do to stop inflation. That's the subject. What happens, if I get this right, is money buys less, and is worth less, even if we do get more for our stuff. And it'll get worse that way. Now, what can farmers do to stop that?"

Says a woman, "We shouldn't pay more'n thing's worth, regardless."

"That's right."

The woman pursues: "To plant potatoes, people'll pay almost any price, regardless."

"Why wait so long to put on a ceiling?" asks someone.

"To help the producer, I suppose."

"It don't help anyone."

"It couldn't help but help people that's got them to sell."

The woman is relentless. "It's people that's got them stored. The people that produced them in Idaho and these places around like that, they got very little a bushel for them."

Says a man, "You can get chicken fence and stuff like that. But if you want hog-tight fence that you really need, you can't get it. You go back that fur [to 1931-1933] on other stuff [than potatoes, which have "gone up three times"]: has everything gone up according? Hogs were down to $2.85 about 1923. But your farm machinery, she never went down like that."

"The farmer's not organized," says a lean black man. "As long as the farmer takes the dirty end of it, that's what he'll get. The bigger part of us renters is so heavy mortgaged we can't hold stuff off the market."

"If they had a co-op packing plant," dares someone.

"I don't think that's the answer."

"If they all stuck together and held stuff off the market."

"*If* they did. But some won't stick and hang together."

"If you had control of your own distribution and processing, you could get the markets, and the people to eat it. If they organize, that's the solution and go down the road together. That'd mean something."

A short, heavy farmer has been sitting with eyes and mouth open, and now he says, "The farmer *is* a-making some money. But he's not a-making it in proportion. There's the trouble. I'm not opposed to Labor; don't think that. If they wasn't organized, they'd get kicked down to where they couldn't live. Are the milk producers organized enough to assert themselves? Could they refuse to ship, and pour it out? Then something will begin to happen!"

The comfortable-looking man says, "People just farm, doggone it, because they ain't smart enough to do anything else!"

One man says that he does not clearly see that co-ops would fill the bill. "What does it come to? Just a few dollars for each of us. That's all. Got to hire a man to run the store; and men's scarce. Ain't it all the same cost? I ain't completely sold on it. I get sold on it once in a while and then I get unsold on it. This store here in town, what does it do?"

In this group, which is not up to par, the leader gives members a lot of leeway, and discussion is not especially effective. But something may be said for freedom, and in any case we are not to expect each of a thousand councils to be perfect and smooth in every respect.

After cake and coffee the talk peps up, but the central discussion is over. One woman helps the woman of the house, and the others are entertained. A boy of twelve is asleep across the arm of a chair; the men are grouped on their side of the room, and though they were up at five this morning and must be up at five tomorrow they would talk till two. The women want to get to the games, or "recreation." This is good; it is ultrasimple, takes no equipment or make-up, and compensates for the lack, at this session, of effective discussion.

Recreation is fun, and the people have been dying for it as surely as for political or economic freedom, or participation in international affairs. And it is strange that they have let this freedom, also, to make and play their own games, slip from them. Men and women in towns and on farms can work and get pay, and then give part of the pay to people who will play games for them: play comes in tin cans.

Not for these Ohio farmers. The most fun-play they've had in years can be cooked up here by the group and without benefit of a wire, a knife, a string or a hat. They play such a simple and silly game as "Seven." This is how it goes. The crowd is roughly in a circle. The first person begins to count: "One," and the next says, "Two," and on they go. But the seventh must say, "Eight," since seven and its multiples must be skipped, and anyone who makes a mistake is out. These people are not particularly dull, but it is re-remarkable how quickly they fall. Then they play "Rhythm." Everyone goes pat, pat on his knees, and then claps his hands together. Then the first person says "S" or any letter. "Pat, pat," they all go again on the knees and "clap, clap" with the hands. Just as this is concluded, the next person must at once spell a word beginning with "s." But he must do it at the right moment and without hesitation. Then after the regular round of "pat, pat" and "clap, clap," the next person has only, though at the proper moment, to name any letter. And so on. But a hundred errors are made. That is the fun of it.

The game is childish, and yet everybody stumbles and falls, and soon everybody is aching with laughter. How incredible and funny it is to be so incompetent. How good and healthy it is to be laughed at, and, after the first round, to enjoy being laughed at. Perhaps that is the chief good in this sort of game: seeing how ridiculous on occasion is a grown person, especially grown person Number One.

3

The study-action approach in Ohio is put in this formula: Get together, Plan together, Work together. A state leader says, "It is a plan for national unity through citizen participation in neighborhood action. In what kind of neighborhood do you live? That is what I have asked people. And I get answers like this: 'We live in a terrible neighborhood.' 'We have no neighborhood; all strangers to one another.' What help did they expect from the Farm Bureau in solving their problems? They didn't know! Helpless people! They don't do anything together; with the car to take them to movies, they lose sense of how to entertain themselves, and with the church less frequented, and the lodge faded out, they hardly are neighbors any more."

Now they begin to come together, and to think a bit together, and play together. And together they have done many neighborly acts: they have put names on their mailboxes, mended what are properly their common fences, improved the telephone service, managed to secure local electrification, and begun to think of group hospitalization, and already thousands of them have this. Work, play, worship together; all this is healthy human procedure. Where feasible, buy and sell together, get insurance and medicine as a group. All this they need, and it is ever so good for them as a neighborhood. To feel and think and act with the neighbors—this is human and decent. This is man's love in an undemonstrative way for man, and presumably, too, his real love for God. It would be a shame if the best we could do would be to lose all this, and once in a while turn semisavage and fight together against the rest of the world.

Little study-action groups make profound sense, therefore: little bodies of neighbors together on their own, to study and play and act.

"Mingling and neighboring, that's what it is," said a Michigan farmer. And an Illinois woman said, "Mingling, you know, breaks a lot of ice." The Ohio folks now mingle, and that is a necessary first step, and even by itself it is immense. They have fun, and the other three advisory councils which I visit are much better study groups than the one featured above. They are in the thick of problems such as interest on mortgages, car upkeep, gas and oil, co-op insurance, group medicine, and co-op buying clubs, problems that they understand. "Suppose we give car insurance to an old man and he has an accident, and we have to pay twenty-five thousand. What will that do to our business? Can we safely insure such a man? And suppose we refuse, what then?" These are questions not too remote from the people. "Do we have to take these old men, or create a feeling in the neighborhood?"

While these questions are asked, we are not in a public hall, but in someone's house, at home with the neighbors. A couple of babies are squawking, and a woman is knitting faster and faster on a green handbag.

On insurance, the decision is to send the question out to all the councils in this county, and then send the global decision to the central office of the Farm Bureau: "because it reaches the heart of things down there."

Here is another question. A local young man wants to go co-op;

his father, who is a merchant, says, "No. The co-ops mean to put us out of business." What are the co-op people to reply? The leader says, "If that was put to you—I don't care what line of business he's in—what would you say? We'll go right around the room. Here, Darlene, what's the answer?"

The girl is a co-operator, and is quick to give part of the Rochdale reply. "If he says we're underselling, that's not true."

"All right. Next."

Number Seven can't wait for his turn, and it is good method to let him speak at once. Says he, "He's not following good business principles or something; maybe too high on margins or something; and co-operators, as I understand it, don't mean to take all business; just a regulating share."

Others say that the co-op people would need someone to run their store, and "it only means we have to have a percentage of drugstores and mortuary parlors, not all of them. Thirty-seven fertilizer factories in Ohio, and we have four or five, and we control prices. I'd say twenty per cent of a business, and we'd have a lever of control. It's how far one system or the other helps or hurts the people—that's the question, and that's all we want to know."

The next problem is this: How are we going to get rid of monopoly-controlled business? The answer finally is: Through the co-operative movement—as we're doing, and as we've done, in the fertilizer and insurance lines.

In someone's home this session proceeds, and the next will be in some other home. No hired agitators, and no aliens. The lunch is made in the kitchen and served and eaten by the people. Babies go to sleep where they are, and one of them goes to the loft, with a woman at the head of the basket and a woman at its foot.

During the next day I visit the co-op insurance man, and am told that last year the dividend on car insurance was just short of 10 per cent and could have run ever so much higher. What did the directors do with the rest? It is used to expand co-op insurance into new territory, and in the meantime the rate is forced sharply down in Ohio. A neighboring county has 776 Farm Bureau members, and about one-third of these belong to advisory councils. At the evening session, I heard someone make this declaration of independence: "Education is education, and means us studying together. It is not just a handy instrument when the central body wants something done." At the meeting last month the members "expressed their general dislike of subsidies . . . Inflation and subsidy; and the second is the worse of the two. Rather general opinion that we did not like crop insurance." The question for tonight is "ceiling prices on farm land." The people want land and their own land, just as or more than a man wants his own shoe: "Well, I don't like to see those fellows come out from town and buy these farms, just because they have a better show than we have. We got to avoid and keep down speculation, or a generation of farmers is washed out."

At last the secretary says, "You'd say, then, first, modified ceiling prices, and, second, good dirt appraisers?"

All night a man has been the wit of the crowd, and a kind of nuisance too, in the discussion. Now he says, "Write it down, Madam Secretary, to the best of your ability, and we'll approve it." The list of subjects taken up continues: "Olemargarine, I never tasted it." Fluid milk, and dried milk. "The government, I suppose, makes mistakes, like all of us, only they're bigger and make bigger mistakes." "Whenever you get government aid, the government comes right back with authority." And at last: Are taxes to be federal sales taxes, or merely on luxuries, or simply income taxes? On these subjects they know some of the data; and all in all they are a keen and ready lot of men and women.

What an outsider might be tempted to guess is that the councils flit too much from topic to topic even at any one session and certainly from session to session. He might think more time is needed on any problem: the people throughout Ohio, might work, as on occasion they have done, in a concerted way all winter at a problem that is close to them, that really needs to be solved, and the solution of which is to some degree within their power. From experience they know something of subsidies and also of price fixing and crop insurance, but one might wonder whether they know much about ceilings on farm land or the question of inflation. Does not an intelligent statement on ceilings assume expert surveys on such questions as these: Who is buying up land? For what—to avoid income taxes? to plant some big inflated income? Are native farmers being pushed out? What, in fact, went on during the War One?

At this convenient point I insist on the oddity of people giving opinions on something they know little about, and I insist that far from Ohio but among co-operators I saw people doing it. A co-op crowd, many of them hardly more than children, was seated in a circle. Said the leader, "Where do we go from here? All right! Who's next?" He was a vigorous person, and it was as if he'd take them by force and make them see and solve problems.

Someone dared, "We spent the whole period yesterday, and got to no conclusions, did we?"

"*Can* you?" Bang!

Leader No. 2: "*Do* you?"

No. 1: "Can you arrive at conclusions? I'd say, 'Yes. In this sense: you explore, and act on the best evidence, but always ready to change my conclusion.' Okay, okay! Come on!" said he, beckoning to all and daring each and all.

The somewhat inclusive problem in hand was "what the war is doing to change our economy," and among twenty-eight minor problems to be taken care of by these people were "inflation, world understanding, feed the world, alien population, race problem, breakdown of home, higher development of the machine." Possibly no one of these people had any of the much special knowledge that would be needed even to see any of these problems, let alone to solve it.

I mention this real case for several reasons. First, it left me furious. Second, the Ohio method probably lets itself loose on too many problems and on some that presuppose expert knowledge. Third, this Ohio method, nevertheless, for the most part shows common sense. Last, it does over the short time of its existence show excellent results. It was from the first a plan for unity through sharing in neighborhood action. Unity, then, at least on a small scale; unity and the neighborhood: a bit of social feeling and understanding, and much enjoyment thrown in. That is score number one. And possibly a looking toward wider unity. The seeing that, at least as consumers, the farm people have a basic common interest with Labor and with all urbanites. Then it is true, says a leader, that the study groups have "vitalized the Ohio Farm Bureau," and I would add that they have done much to humanize it and thus to redeem it. Suggestions are always coming from the central body to the groups, and always going from the groups to the central body. Each side is supposed to help the other.

"In our co-op setup" the groups "are gradually taking a more significant place, as we discover their potency in getting people to think intelligently and to act collectively in their own behalf." They explore new lines of co-op development. They "studied and urged for a year or two" the development of group hospitalization. They took up the question, Do we want an oil refinery, and if so, how could we finance it? Some of their buying clubs have gone over into stores, and others will do this.

The people can see how to finance oil wells and refineries, and they can finance them. This means that they can work out a way to own, and can own. They can see how to establish insurance, and they can establish it. So of hospitals and surgery and medicine. So, no doubt, in time, of the land, of houses, of the schools, of drugs, of factories, of banking, and of recreation and entertainment. And so throughout the list of goods and services. All of them can—I say *can* by hard and persistent study and work—be the people's product and the people's possession. One hundred years of effort and intelligent loyalty have done much, and a few years of schooling and labor in Ohio have surely begun to show returns. For at least one hundred years we have had, and for a long time we will have, a war between the two capitalisms: the old individualistic capitalism and the new collectivistic, political capitalisms. And each of them, as well as the war between them, has been severe and ruinous on people. If the Ohio study co-ops have learned to stand between those fires, and to keep dampening the wood of each, they are a great event in our national and modern life. And I think that in effect they have learned to do something of this kind. Or they give us some promise of learning to do it, and some prospect of how we might begin to learn to do it. That is their significance, not simply for Ohio, but for the nation and for modern times. What this slow but vital method suggests is that the road to freedom can be kept open.

Seventeen

PEOPLE LEARNING TO PLAY

1

FREEDOM consists largely in the people's keeping a lot of functions in their hands. Food, drink, play, work, home, worship, finance, learning and arts and sciences may in large part be left to person and family and neighborhood. When the State must perpetually nose into such matters, freedom has evaporated.

It is pleasant to see the ways we have of spontaneous and creative play. Boys need hardly more than a string and a stick to have a good time; they make a little world, and run it. A few dirty old cards, and people can make their own fun. A bit of food and drink, and a nimble tongue or two, and five, ten, twenty people have the time of their lives. We re-create ourselves, as the saying is. It is true that tremendous crowds go to look at ball games, but on every street boys play ball and never care whether anyone stops to look at them.

The best developments we have lately had in recreations and games have been in two or three lines. The little theater lets a lot of the people in any town play, and pays sparing tribute to "stars." Even better, from the point of view of getting many people to participate, has been the recent development of music in our high schools, a growth at once in numbers and in excellence. School bands and orchestras have been reaching a peak which a generation ago we wouldn't have dreamed of; and this in a matter that demands discipline and persistent striving for perfection. The choral achievement of one school in South Bend is incredible. Third, I mention the now somewhat abortive start made a few years ago toward getting everybody interested, and so many in an active way, in softball games. It is a shame that for profit reasons the game was taken from the people, and given to the experts.

It is estimated that we spend eight billions a year on recreation. How much of this is, from a truly human point of view, thrown away is hard to tell. Unfortunately, much of it is spent in a passive way. People in that case are not like children making up and play-ing games, not taking each other's hands to dance together, not singing together in family or neighborhood. We let ourselves be crowded into the movies; by the millions we submit every day to this mechanical entertainment, and hardly one of us is able to take up the show, make it over, react fully as a person to it, and create a free, human world as the movie proceeds. The movie crowd is a great mass together, but it is not a community of people working or playing or worshiping or ruling together. Hard as the word is, in the movie crowd we are something like a herd.

One may wonder whether a people that is movie mad, or at least movie captivated, is fit for freedom. When we make this surrender to the dime-novel effect of the movie, are we really ready for free-dom and actively asserting our right to it?

This giving up of our leisure and our possible creative recreational life is one illustration of a general condition. What I speak of is our collectivized and mechanized work and culture. We have all kinds of things done for us and to us, whereas we might well and better do many of these for ourselves.

Ownership is something that is done for people: by wealthy men, by the State, and by corporations. The idea that property is, first of all, to be humanized and personalized, that it is an extension of the person, of one's personal and familial and communal life—this grand, ennobling idea tends to be lost. Finance is not one's financing of his life, but it is an external and mysterious something to which one must submit. Industry is there, it is given as the weather is given; and one may hope for a job in industry. But there is little that one can do about it. This means that a man is not a free man, not an initiator, not a director or dispenser in the matter of his daily work.

I believe that the co-operators as a body are the group most effectively back of our will to freedom. They take no official sides on politics, but they stand as a man against the State-down pro-cedure. In theory and practice they are for houses and land and fac-tories and timber and ore and oil going into the people's control; this we saw in many places and in eight or nine states. They can-not "abide" absenteeism. They want neighborhood medicine, neighborhood insurance, neighborhood housing; in a word, they want the neighborhood to exist and to have a certain autonomy. Freedom begins at home. We have seen that the co-operators want education, at least for adults, to be a neighborhood event. And in this chapter we come to their saying—even against the lords of Hollywood—that games and dancing and most of our recreation ought to go small-town, ought on occasion to go countryfied and homespun, ought generally to be made up by us and for us. In Ohio we saw that twenty thousand persons are compounding most of their own fun out of a few simple games. These are adults, and Ohio has, besides, a state-wide youth program which consists mostly of games and dancing. The people at Dillonvale have their own band, and the people in a hundred little centers among the Minnesota Finns have their own dancing and singing and theaters.

This, then, is the sanity and simplicity and neighborhood sociability that, all put together, helps to make for balance and goodness and health and happiness. A little game—a little game in memory and a little game in view—keeps the doctors and psychologists and police away. Good, sane people dance and sing. They must do this. To be good and sane and happy they must break out and dance and sing. Play is as spontaneous and natural and almost as good and elemental as love.

Not to have fun and recreation at all would be bad, but to have only the store kinds, put up in tin cans for us, is not good. We want handfuls of people getting together and making fun, dancing and singing and joking. That is the best way.

2

The co-operators are not the discoverers of play, nor are they about to make the world over with a few old-fashioned games. But many of them do find, at least for themselves, that play is spontaneous and free, that it is a lot of fun, that it knocks something out of people and something into people, and above all that it brings people together in a simple way that is ever so beneficent. For one thing, the co-operators sing. What they sing are all the commoner ditties:

> Take me out to the ball game,
> Take me out to the park!

They can all do that. And so of many others, such as "Hail, Hail! The gang's all here!" and "Oh, Susannah!" "When Irish eyes are smiling" goes with a crowd, and also "Old Kentucky Home" and "East Side, West Side," and

> Home, home on the range
> Where the deer and the antelope play,

and

> I've been workin' on the railroad
> All the livelong day.

On all of these the people can let themselves go, for a moment just cut loose and be part of this decent quiet crowd. It is not easy to sing with a neighbor and at the same time not to begin to like him or at least to have a tolerant feeling toward him. Nonsense takes especially well in these folk songs. Everybody can swing into

> Old MacDonald had a farm,
> E-i, e-i-o!
> And on that farm he had some ducks,
> E-i, e-i-o!

This goes on as pure nonsense, and with a sweep that makes it good to sing, though not much good to hear. Anyway, it is good for the people to do some singing, and not just to listen. People long to participate, to get in on it; that is why the simple song is so good. Perhaps it will not be impossible, next, with the help of a leader or two, to try

> Came a riding by one day,
> Zum-ta-dy-ja-dy-ja,
> A suitor jaunty, bold and gay,
> Zum-ta-dy-ja-dy-ja!

Of course, this kind of thing is hard, with the odd form of that second line, and with this repeated over and over. But I have noticed that people take to it, and want to keep up with the quick turns of the music.

What the people might happily come to is singing any or all of these, not because some co-op recreational leader wants them to, or is getting them to, but because the song is in their hearts and comes to their lips. I am sorry that not one of the four socioeducational groups I met with in Ohio seemed ready to or tempted to break out into song. They played games and had a good time, but sang no songs and danced no jigs. I was thinking, "What a wonderful thing it would be if they would fold up the kitchen table, get down a fiddle, and everybody begin to sing and clap his hands as they danced!" The social effect in the Ohio groups is already good, and it can readily be better.

The co-op people have recreational leaders and these conduct "national co-operative recreation schools." Sometimes I wish they weren't quite so serious. The dancing at these schools is beautiful, and it must be wonderful for those few who can do it. But an uninitiated person might wonder whether it is really for the people or ever by the people, and for that reason ask whether it may truly be called co-operative. I insist that it is lovely, but a bit expertized and special. At least, that is the way with some of it, hardly something for the people in every little neighborhood in Chicago and in Missouri and Virginia to love and to do. As a spectacle, yes; as a grand specialty, yes; but as co-operative fun in which the people can have an active part, not all of it so readily qualifies. It is true, of course, that the people can easily learn to sing and dance much better·than they now do, and can enjoy the better quality. And for the most part, this better homespun play is what the co-operative schools aim to teach.

Lately I have seen co-operators dancing in half a dozen places. They do the old dances and, as everyone knows, some of these are not much more than feats of strength or of speed. A main trouble is that some persons regard even the best "changes" as a sort of stunt, and tend to look with condescension on what they should take to as a duck takes to water. In many cases, the music is tame and incompetent. What we want is a musician who has dance time in his toes, and at every moment as he plays is anxious to abandon his instrument and get up and shake his feet. And the man who leads or calls must have a special gift. He must work with the musician and the dancers, and manage to be the unobtrusive soul of the entire event. What a strong man it takes, what a live man, what a dancer and singer and entertainer, what art and intuition. He must know when and how to help, and when to keep out of the way. He must have the sense to know that few if any of these American folk dances are immortal works of art. They are games for boys and girls and men and women, and he accepts them for not more or other than they are. Notice this one:

> All join hands and circle left,
>   To the left you circle one and all,
> Now right back home and swing your own,
>   Oh swing your true and careless love.

No great music goes with this simple directive thought, but when the words go with the music, and feet and bodies with the two of them, a bit of folk play easily results. In no time, everybody is singing and clapping with the music and dance. Everybody takes part, and not a soul is left as a wallflower.

That is the way that our country dances are justified, as acts in the simplest kind of play or game. They are for young and old. They allow for the light foot and can assimilate the heavy foot. It is "the dance of the people. . . . Its free style of spontaneous active fun sets up situations that allow young people to become thoroughly absorbed with their fellows in play." Young people, and old people. Why not active fun for both?

The lack of this social spirit is the chief fault with our more recent dancing as a type: it does not let people play as a community or neighborhood, and is in effect unsocial. Almost any play or game includes the notion of co-op; play is for a lot of people, and it is best, other things being equal, when it is by and for everybody. "Co-op play" is redundant. Of course, play is co-op, and even a nice dancing that is merely by doubletons is almost as undemocratic and unsocial as would be a dancing by singletons. Everybody in! That is the co-op way, and the democratic way, and it is naturally the method of play. A co-op dance is a dangerous place for an antidancer to be. I have seen a few of these persons, aloof, standing against the door, no doubt just dying to get to a movie.

3

Far better, then, a few of our old games and dances, and communal songs too, so long as they leave us well on this side of the Old Maids' Village Choir. And in many places I see healthy signs, among co-operators and others. To be frank, I was not too keen to accept an invitation to meet with a students' recreation co-op at Ohio State University. Yet this blind date that seemed to promise so little turned out happily. Boys and girls had got together, first of all, to provide their own recreation, and this play co-op had not only succeeded in its own line, but became the nucleus of one housing co-op for girls and two for boys. In fact, I had been at the university a couple of years earlier and had asked a professor why the students had taken to old-fashioned dances. He said they were cheaper: ten cents a person, and also they allowed everybody to get together and make a social event of it. Now, I thought, enough of them will be smart about it, and turn the co-op dance into a sophisticated stunt. However, that was far from the minds of the fifty boys and girls who met. They came to dance, and that is just what they did. The dancing was something to do and to like.

A fragile girl is dancing with a lithe boy, a girl too thin and weak to be a good dancer. It's nothing to him; he carries her and goes almost as if alone, throwing himself forward and then catching himself.

A heavy Scot girl with a thick leg and the black straight hair of a squaw pushed up a bit, is in every dance from early to late, even though she can't pick up her feet. She knows the techniques or mechanics, and I understate matters when I suggest that she likes to dance. "I love it," she says, with her eyes out before her and in a tone that says it is the relish of her life.

They do a Swedish dance in honor of King Adolphus, and Danish dances, and the difficult French reel, and many American folk dances. They do dances that require a clapping of the hands, and a dance that if well-timed can be very nice: with each one clapping or slapping his neighbor's palms and exactly with the pulse of the music. The best are the singing dances, especially when everybody knows the words and music. The effect is to get everybody in important senses into the dance. And the best instance of this tonight, I'd say, is "The Red River Valley." It is called or sung by a little short girl with a knife at her belt who so likes to dance and to help people to dance. She stands on a chair for the great occasion, and hauls the "mike" up to her. Twice she makes false starts, but is not exactly with the music. Then she is off properly, the music in her toes and in her mind and body.

"This *is* education," said a man to me at the co-op center down-town in Columbus. I don't believe it, unless we take education in a somewhat restricted sense. But it is good and sane normal fun. It is "mingling and neighboring." It is a learning to play, or a not forgetting to play, and we may safely bet that the folks from any hold-back groups will practice in secret before the next dance and will come prepared to do "Old Dan Tucker" and "The Little Yaller Girl." It is better than cards or movies or golf or liquor parties. It is "better," that is to say, it is more neighborly and social; it is more a throwing the people together, bringing them out of their private selves or dual co-ops; it is a letting fifty or sixty boys and girls— and with some graybeards thrown in—meet informally on one floor, in one central party arranged and run by themselves. "All Join Hands" is the name of one dance-and-game booklet. That is what this evening's simple party is: a little democratic fun, a little shuffling of the feet to patterns made sacred by Danes and Negroes and French and Irish and Swedes. A simple sense of belonging is what it gives above everything else.

If the co-ops will help to maintain and to build and rebuild com-munities, then good for them. If co-op dances and co-op play, and any dances and play for that matter, will help in this vital adventure, then by all means good for them. Believe it or not, there is a New York City Play Co-op. Think of the possibilities of balance here, of simple joy and sanity, of homelike entertainment, of neighbor-hood resurrection. In Chicago one autumn they had a harvest festival, and in the evenings they danced on the grass in Soldier's Field, hundreds of couples, and I must say that not all of them were dashing young people. Hundreds of people were beaming from the sidelines on the dancers. All the silly, or at least ultra-simple, old calls and changes: "Do-si-do! Hurry up, folks, and don't be laggin'! Same old tack! Meet your honey and a-promenade back!" While this was going on, I saw a good buxom woman trying to push her own girl or grandchild and another girl out to dance. The two girls were anxious to try and afraid to try. They giggled and went out part way till the managers shoved them off: "If you're not going to dance, keep out of the road!" But the mother kept after them with her bill or beak, like the mother bird dumping the fledglings out and making them fly.

In my own tiny community in Iowa we have always kept playing and dancing in this neighborhood way. Any dance is a parish dance, young and old on the floor together, each chaperoning the other. Women can't very well miss the dance, or leave the babies at home; so they bring them and put them to sleep rolled in blankets on a table. It is almost an all-Irish place, yet for the dances the Hoosiers or gentiles come too, and a young Hoosier mother says, "I don't think it's wrong to dance, do you?" Well, if it is, she is committing a gluttonous sin, she and her husband, he stripped to the galluses. The next morning an Irishman who used to shake a wicked foot asks who was there. "Vic and Louise." "You don't tell me Vic and Louise were there? What were they doing there—those old grandparents?" Dancing, that's what and that's all they were doing, they and their children and grandchildren. I noticed more than one case of three generations on the floor at once, the niftier little fellows jitterbugging a bit on the corners. And I cannot help thinking that it is a kind of sacred enterprise for a community to get to the floor and dance together once in a while. They do it, of course, because they are a community, and by doing it they remain a community.

$\mathcal{E}$ighteen

CHICAGO COMMUNITIES PULLING TOGETHER

1

MEN must have ownership and security. When the next depression comes the farmers may be in a position to ride it out. But only the unions and the co-ops can afford to the masses of city people the security and the stake in America that will prevent a proletarian revolution.

If the persons could own the materials, plan and run the work, if they could own the product and dispose of it as they liked, if it was their own bank, blueprinted by them and operated by directors of their choice, that had set up the cash, then the proletarian and "capital and labor" problem, so crucial in Western nations, would have some of the teeth pulled out of it. And in the co-op world we have reason to believe that the people can do all this, because they have on occasion done it.

We saw that in the several centers mentioned, the people have begun to do much of this. It occurs among the farmers of Ohio and Indiana, for example, and among miners at the village of Granger and in Dillonvale, at Cloquet and other Finnish towns, and in the considerable industrial cities of Racine, Waukegan, and South Bend. It shows promise, and for that matter achievement, in Detroit, the capital of the industrial world, where fourteen co-operative stores already function, where the people also have some co-op housing and some co-op dairy services. In part, our cities have been built on a hit-and-miss plan or on no plan at all except that of possibly making profits, and not step by step on a truly human and familial and communitarian basis. This is the matter that our co-ops must at least help to remedy: they must work to humanize and personalize urban life, as well as to make it fairly secure. The people, in cities as well as on the land, are to own, to have families and homes, to plan and to love their work and lavish themselves on it, to talk and pray and play with the neighbors. All this, or our struggles for human good are from the beginning largely defeated. The human life, the human family, the human community—that is what we postulate and must postulate. If the co-ops can take us some way along that road, we ought to cherish them, and I claim they make such a promise, and it would be delightful to detail their growth in many cities, such as Boston, New York, Washington, Philadelphia, Cleveland, Minneapolis and St. Paul, St. Louis, Berkeley, Oakland, and Los Angeles. Boston has at least a dozen healthy co-ops, the Philadelphia area has twice as many, and metropolitan New York has eighty, with a remarkable development in a chain of co-operative cafeterias.

I want now to look briefly at some typical co-ops that the people have begun to build for themselves in Chicago. This city has a good score of co-ops, and its Central States Co-operatives, like the Eastern Co-operative Wholesale located in New York, does a big business, mostly in the large cities; the former's business running now to more than an annual half million, and the latter's to nearly four million. The co-ops which we shall presently see are far from the best established within Chicago, but perhaps it is well to view them in the struggling and formative stage. For a co-op starts up and in time perhaps folds up, overawed and overpowered by custom and the dead weight of apathy.

Ten years ago they started a buying club in Hyde Park, and this has kept on its feet and is now the Hyde Park self-serve co-op store, a busy place on the Saturday morning I see it. A man who turns out to be educational director is at the door all day, handing out an occasional pamphlet, spotting and talking to persons who evidently are newcomers, often acting, as he says, in the capacity of father confessor. For it is true that most people in Chicago are somewhat at sea: without neighbors, almost without homes and families and bosom friends. Somebody must make up in part for all this loss. So they bring personal problems to this benevolent man who wants to sell them, above everything else, the rebirth of the community.

I ask a young woman shopper how she got interested in the co-op store. That is exactly her story: it gives her a real claim on the neighborhood life. And she had need of this. She says she "came up" from a small coal-mining town in Illinois "where you could phone to the butcher or grocer, and depend on him. But here! And that's the way the co-operative is: you can depend on it just as if it were your own." This is an intelligent girl who for a while was at the University of Chicago. "I'm a social worker; that's my line of work. A student of sociology was greatly interested in the co-operatives, and he was my friend." People do not at once build up neighborhoods or communities in Chicago, not easily if at all. Says the young woman, "I was sick in bed two months, and the woman in the next apartment never came in, and probably never knew. And then afterwards we found out she was from the same kind of background, and was just as lost as I was."

The store or buying club started as in part a sort of high-brow event. A few professors took to it as if in answer to some kind of mystical urge. But it has turned out to be democratic and generally human, and in time was able to assimilate or eliminate the elite. The bylaws retain to some degree the marks of the professor's mind. For instance, it is said that this society shall, among other things, promote "the participation of all members in the continuous development, by research and experimental trial, of the science of applied cooperation." Even so, the purpose is at the outset more simply stated: "to promote the economic and social welfare of its members." And the high proportion of "not less" than 10 per cent shall be set aside from the savings for educational purposes.

The store now appears healthy, in both the economic and the social sense. For May of 1943 its sales ran to $23,512.75, with net earnings of 3.04 per cent. It gets part of its goods through the co-op wholesale known as Central States Co-operatives, located in Chicago, and receives a refund on its patronage. In the general report for the six months ending March, 1943, we read that gains have been made in moving to a new location and in modernizing. At the main store "the problems faced have been reasonable, help has been adequate, our manager has been extremely competent, progress has been steady, and complication at a minimum." Inventory technique has been perfected, so that the staff and the time for this function were cut about 50 per cent; spice racks were made to keep small tins from falling; floor waxing improved, shelving altered and signs made to answer customers' questions. "On January 11, the butchers were raised to the new union scale," and pension and hospital plans have been studied. "There is a noticeably better spirit and a greater evidence of satisfaction on the part of many of the employees." Projects for the future include pensions and hospitalization for all employees, and the setting up of buying clubs "in this area" with these passing into stores; also self-service in meats, and expansion "into cleaning and laundry, a service station, a cooperative eating enterprise."

One may hardly pretend that this or any of our co-op stores is a considerable historic event. The Hyde Park store is new, and trying to feel its way along, and with careful management it will survive. It can effect a saving, and above all it can help to create community life. At this moment, people are coming and going, looking once or twice at things. "Fresh shipment of Jones Dairy Farm Sausage in today." "Brown meat points accepted today." Shoppers run little wagons from counter to counter, and a man shopper, meditating on the meats, rests against his wagon. "Please do not put children on top of the meat counter." So says a sign, and a boy clerk tells me, "Sometimes they put the children in the baskets [on the wagons]; we warn them against that." Boneless stewing beef is 38 cents a pound, asparagus cut and tips 34 cents and cauliflower 38 cents.

A big sign says, "During October, national co-op month, learn more about co-operation, America's training ground for democracy."

I do not see why the co-op store should not talk a lot about its ability to work toward the neighborhood life. The one at Hyde Park makes it clear that the co-op, even in so big a city as Chicago, can do something in this vital line. That is what the members already feel and believe and begin to see. Their tiny newssheet, the *Evergreen Weekly*, in its present issue says that the members who "attended the semi-annual meeting last week" thought that "orchids to ourselves" would not be totally unjustified. Someone reviewed the first ten years of this co-op's life, and the manager "complimented all staff members on their good work." The treasurer said the sales had gone up in the past year "with total patronage running to $311,073.75, an increase of $110,000 over the amount sold during the year ending July, 1942. . . . It's gratifying to know that we are looked to by other societies as a model. . . . Second call for turkeys," continues the newssheet, "Hurry, hurry, hurry! . . . Lamb shoulder roast a good buy this week (3 pts.) lb. 34¢. May we request our patrons to return all bottles, especially the pint cream bottles."

By way of the ordinary commodities sold in a store, such as lamb and cream and potatoes, there can come to the people a sense of belonging, the sense of and the fact of being neighbors, the sense of the people creating, family by family, some local composite good. This is something to be proud of, to have a claim on, and at least in some measure to rally around. "It's ours! We belong to it!" More important than the feeling expressed in these words is the conviction, and fact too, which may be put in this way, "We belong together and are together."

Any institution which helps decently in this direction is good. The store does it, and so, to some extent, does the credit union, and the co-op dairy, the co-op slaughter-house, the co-op refinery, and in varying degrees, every co-op unit. That is, if it is really co-op: of and by and for the people here in the neighborhood.

2

The good of co-ops is an economic good and a more general social good, two distinct though not separate goods. They occur at once, and in the same place, and to the same person or persons. In some sections of our population we evidently need the economic good more than the other, but in such an area as Hyde Park it is clear that the social or communal good is more demanded by circumstances.

It is otherwise with our Negroes in Chicago and in general. They have an admirable social life, making it sufficiently clear that such a life can be had without "means." For our Negroes own almost nothing at all. This status I want presently to make more concrete. But just now our old proposition: if the co-ops could do anything to correct this evil, then good for them. Can they do it? That is a question at this point, and probably for some years it must remain so. It will require everything the co-ops have and everything we all have, in the way of good will, courage, good sense, resourcefulness, and prolonged hard labor. This is not because the Negro is dispossessed. It is because, among other considerations, he has never had property and the freedom that can be had only with property. The theory is all right: the Negro is a person and ought to be allowed the rights of a person, and elemental among these is the right to ownership. But historically and factually something else has been the case.

This work of emancipation can be done. The Negro can best do it, and on the co-op plan only the Negro can do it. Hard as it is for him, a man without a bank, a house or a store or a foot of earth, it is he who can do it: not today or tomorrow, but in some years or, better, in some generations he can have begun to do it.

Chicago has a Black Lands of its own, an immense section where most of its Negroes live. I ask my intelligent Negro guide whether there are fifty thousand people here. "Two hundred and fifty thousand," he says; "and maybe three hundred thousand." In this place a few daring and enterprising Negroes have started a co-op. Just think of that: something that would be the Negroes'! But keep in mind both words, "think" and "would be." For in spite of good will and intelligent and magnificent efforts, from the nature of the case—from the way the Negro is "fixed"—People's Consumer Co-operative Society, Chicago, is tentative. It is an effort, it is on trial. But there are handicaps. The traditional, historical, factual setup, with the Negro not owning, but exploited, impoverished and victimized. Surely, however, wholesalers will sell to him when he appears with cash in hand, won't they? That question is not answered positively by the mere fact of cash in hand. No doubt, there is some sharpness in my mention of the matter. But the fact is that it was like pulling teeth to get one big meat company, to cite a single example, to trade directly with the Negroes.

They are exploitable. They are easily exploitable. They have always been exploited. Therefore the status quo is the most advantageous. That is at once the logic and the history of the matter.

At People's they conceive that they can change history. Some important conditions have certainly been in their favor. My hurried notes say: "About 450 tenant families—cf. poor white sharecroppers—across the street in such and such apartments—during the depression formed the Tenants' Association." What was or is this for? "To take care of grievances." Did the owner of the apartment house object? Happily he did not, and this democratic sprout was encouraged to live.

We are at People's and looking across the street to those apartments while I learn these things. Then, say my guide and three or four of the founders of People's, "then one of our men went to the co-operative school downtown and reported back enthusiastically. Then a few of us got together, maybe eight or ten or twelve, and what ones of us stuck used the contact we had in the community in order to build up the idea."

Negroes are inconceivably poor. The problem was, not to start a buying club: that would be easy; but to raise the money to start it. Twelve men gave three dollars apiece, and with this the club bought at wholesale rates some nonperishable stuff, and "the manager of the apartments donated a small locker in the basement to store things in." From these twelve apostles they jumped in ten months to 140 members, and from the $36 to $1,300 in share capital. Now they have 500 members and are doing about $5,000 worth of business a month. Though this is tiny where the people are hundreds of thousands, we have good ground for hoping that it is the germ of great things.

To make matters look worse, over these earliest years a large deficit was run. The Negroes tell me, "due to big overhead, in rent and salaries." That statement is true, but it has omitted something the Negro does not like to mention or to confess even to himself. This store is discriminated against, not just because it is co-op or has that fine name "People's," but because wholesalers do not propose to do business with Negro retailers. That is hard; it will leave certain shelves at times somewhat bare, and it is the way our mind works that if we do not find a complete stock of goods in one store we will do all our trading at another. "Especially the meat," says one of the founders. "Where the women get their meat, they want to get their groceries." It is particularly in meats that they have had trouble; at best, they have had to buy through middlemen, and to get meat they have practically been forced at times to trade with black markets where of course there is no guarantee of quality and no comeback. This meant that they were beaten on all sides: on honor, on price, on quality and guarantee, and also on the co-op practice, which now tends almost to become a retroactive Rochdale principle, the practice of labeling the quality of all commodities.

Fortunately, this problem seems now to be solved, through the persistence of the people and through the efforts of Central States Co-operatives. And the business is "in the black now." Such condition, of course, must be reached, but cannot always be reached in the first months or years of an enterprise. And in the case of a business to be owned and run by Negroes the problem is not any easier. "Now," says one of the men, "we are over the hump." Negroes are generous, unsuspecting men, and great optimists. After all their troubles, this man still does not say or think, "We hope we are beginning to succeed." For him the project is now a success. And he who speaks is one of those fifty or more lordly souls who, without a dollar in their pockets, have kept making up the deficit, and who over the last few years raised for this purpose from fifty to about one hundred eighty dollars apiece.

Praise evidently goes first to those men. And praise also to the manager or owner of the apartments across the street. "He allows us to use all their facilities free. We use the mimeograph machine, and the meeting room whenever we want."

The Negro is a great singer in the sense that he likes to sing and also in the sense that he sings well. He can talk too, and I'd love to have a command of his language. "For us to subsidize," says one of the founders, one of those who till lately had subsidized People's, and I wish I could suggest the gentle but sure way he accents "us," and his soft rendering of "subsidize" with a slight lingering on *b* and on *d*. "For us to subsidize, it would be nearly as bad—not so bad as for the government to subsidize. But it's bad."

That is why, $2,500 is wanted in new stock, at $25 a share. "Just a hundred new families. We like to keep that spread," which is elongated like "s-p-r-e-a-d." "A spread is always better: a lot of people belonging. Otherwise it's too much a strain on us. And that's democracy, to get a maximum of participation."

It is not easy to get the people to come and join. They are not used to this new way. "We got to educate them up. The most we ever got to a meeting was twenty, or maybe twenty-two, per cent of the members. We tried putting on a fun-fest with dancing and games. They liked that, but didn't know it was part of the co-op!"

Why do people trade here at all? It is not cheaper, it had not till lately a steady supply of the staple commodities, and it is in no condition to go pouring refunds into the shopper's pockets.

One woman says, "It's handy, and jes' as good. And, besides, it's our store." She says this with energy, and means it.

Another says, "My husband's a member, and one of the first. But we're too far away, and it's only because I had to take the streetcar anyway that I came today."

Number Three has with her own eyes seen People's rise up as a miracle. There was nothing at all, and now there's People's Store. She is a slight person with an outer refined bearing that can come only from an inner dignity. She is in a brown coat and brown skirt and a green beret, and her hands and face are like walnut stain. To ask her "why belong" to the co-op is almost to insult her; it is almost to desecrate the lovely and divine work done here by her people. Why does she belong? Let her reply. "Because I saw it. I saw something come from nothing. The men, they started with nothing, and now we have all this store!"

They have started a credit union, too, and I believe almost simultaneously with the store. One of its founders says, "It's done a great deal of service, and was a nucleus for building the co-op. It was in June-July, 1937, and twelve of us put in five dollars apiece, and started loaning it out." The capital now is about $18,000, and in all $65,000 has been lent. Says the treasurer, "Have yet to write out a bad loan. Haven't had to go to court, in any one case. We used to pay up to 6 per cent, but are down to four per cent, the least we ever paid: to keep in the spirit of the war effort." They have insurance also, risk insurance and thrift insurance: "through Cuna Mutual, the Edward Filene: through the Chicago office, to Madison, Wisconsin."

These and all Negroes will continue to have many problems, race problems and labor problems and educational and social problems. My guide Chester and I go through the rain to lunch, and have not bad food that is well cooked and superbly served. As we go again into the rain I dare to ask Chester the question that had kept coming to me and which nevertheless it seemed indelicate to ask. For several hours we have moved among these black men, women and children who, rain or shine, are a great deal in the street, and it is as if I had never seen any other than black men in my life. My question is this, "How much of all these things—stores, and houses, and apartments, and theaters, and cafés—do the people own?"

Chester is a proper gentleman anxious for his people's good, and he is not at all surprised or embarrassed at my question. He has thought often about this problem, and knows precisely about it. "Nothing," he says, with human hunger and desperation packed into that word. "They own nothing."

Nothing but People's, so far as they do own that? Not a house? Not a drugstore? Or a clothing store for men or for women? Not a café, or a movie house? Not a restaurant?

Chester's first reply was an exaggeration, though a slight and defensible one. "They do own, just very little. Not any of these apartments, or stores, no, sir!" They work in the stores and buy their things in them, but never own them. A Negro in Chicago hardly ever owns a house, though he may have a kind of claim to a shack. "But that restaurant where we ate," Chester says, "that belongs to Negroes. Besides that, I can't name any legitimate business they do own."

"Not any drugstores, or movie houses?" I ask.

"No," says Chester with not too pained a laugh, for he is a man cut and raked to his very soul by this condition. He tells me to which chain the movie house belongs.

That, then, is the condition that I decry, and that, as a man and a believer in man and in God and in Christ, and as a priest, I must decry. These people, no doubt full of faults, but full too of laughter, so ready with fun and jokes, so fond of worshiping God and in our time, alone among us, creating new and lovely songs for the worship of God—it is these merryhearted brothers of ours who do not own.

3

The Ida B. Wells Foundation is a lot of buildings able to house sixteen hundred families. The units form apartments, but from the start they give the sense and feeling of houses and even of homes, and all of the people in them are in truth a kind of colony. I need not say that with better houses, and with this sense both of

oneness and of importance, we have a happier and better community. The shortcoming in this method, as I see it, is that the
cash has come in the first place from the government, and also that
the people are never to own.

Suppose, however, that the Negro should own his schools, his
churches, his home, his stores, his movies, and factories, and banks!
That is the idyllic hope that the democrat and Christian and co-
operator will not surrender. And the men and women in the Ida
B. Wells have at least started a store of their own in a basement.
It is a little store that at first was a buying club and that, with an
inventory of not over $1,300, did a business of $670 last week.
Says the woman manager, "Possibly it can reach a thousand a week,
but the strain would be terrific." People really haven't room to turn
around, and every nook is packed full. A few started the club on
a prepayment plan, accepting orders for goods, but only if the
orders were accompanied by cash. The first order "totaled eleven
dollars, I believe. That was in August, 'forty-one, and in the first
half of 'forty-three we did over five thousand."

Can they collect their bills? They by-pass this problem, because
they proceed on Rochdale principles. "No credit. We never have
given any, and so we have no trouble keeping it that way."

Undoubtedly the store, this infant, one-small-room store, is well
managed, and at the rate it is going it may in a few years directly
claim the sixteen hundred family units and have a dozen branches
in the large colored district.

4

If the Negroes are hardly ready to launch their own housing
projects, that is not at all surprising, since few housing co-ops are
yet well begun in the Midwest. Nevertheless, we have some notable
ones, and I want to mention a recent small development just outside Chicago.

Often our social-minded people are made unhappy because men
and women in the biggest cities are not well housed, because in
fact they are hard put to it to find shelter at all. With the co-
operators I am looking for something closer to us and more a part
of ourselves than a roof and four walls. I want people to own
houses, and I know it is better for them if they plan the houses,

and select the materials, and go as far as may in reason be toward building the houses. And then it is still better if neighbors do all this in groups. What is meant by "better"? Just what the voice of the people means by it. No doubt, it is good for people to have a shelter at all. But it is better, because more human and personal, more in line with what we are as persons and as brothers in Christ, for us to own houses, and ourselves to plan and to build those houses. And it is still better if neighbors get together to do a lot of the planning of houses and the buying of land and materials.

Now, that is something of what the Chicago group mentioned has managed to do. They bought together, and I have a statement on the savings from a member of the co-op project. "We saved at least half in the cost of the land . . . We saved in the initial fee of the architect and the contractor . . . We saved by doing much of our own work in decorating, landscaping, roadmaking. . . We own some of our yard tools together and freely exchange every other tool." Also, those who have trees share them, and the people manage some joint use of cars.

The saving is something, but the gain in more human terms is a bigger and finer thing. The people appear to have found, even at an early date, what it means to help build a neighborhood and live in that neighborhood. Says the scribe, "Meeting together, deciding together, planning together, buying together, studying together, sharing together, working together, eating together, playing together"—all this has meant for us the discovery of "a new neighborliness . . . We seem to be touching the hem of a garment radiant with potential spiritual satisfactions."

In the Chicago housing co-op we have the following: People at the edge of a city, not in cliff dwellers' cells, but in houses, and these houses brushed by shrubs and trees, and the trees alive not only with their own souls, but with the souls of animals and birds; houses, as it happens, of redwood, unpainted of course, but the wood preserved with creosote; lovely, charming houses, and not just a few houses that by hit and miss and one by one or individualistically are beautiful, but the lot or group itself beautiful; and above all, built together in such a way as to invite and encourage the people's living together. Planned too by these people, and the acreage bought by them so that each family has a plot and a place for its house, and with the help of the people and the architect made into a beautiful and organic whole. Never yet, Frank Lloyd Wright says, has an architecture reflected the freedom expressed by Christ and been based on an economic order that would make that freedom possible. Even so, it is not improbable that such an ownership and such a neighborhood and such an architecture are within man's grasp.

Hyde Park with its five hundred members already is in a position to reach two thousand persons and to help them discover the neighborhood. How about four hundred Hyde Parks in Chicago or New York or Boston, to temper the money motive in trade, and to encourage our urban people, patch by patch, to live together? People's has five hundred members, and possibly three thousand souls. How about a hundred People's in Chicago or any such city, to protect the Negro's economic order, and in the first place to give him the means to begin to build that order for himself? Why not a cool but effective liquidation of those persons who now deny him that order and freedom? The housing project mentioned is a small one. Why not a thousand or possibly up to ten thousand of these? Why should urban people be once for all condemned to work in offices and factories owned by others, ride in trains and buses owned totally by others, buy coal and shoes and meat and beer and groceries in stores owned by others, get insurance and credit from corporations owned by others, get cars and gas and service in stations owned by others, be dependent for recreation on setups owned by others, and come "home" night or morning to houses not planned by themselves, not built by themselves, not owned by themselves, and perhaps not even furnished by themselves?

A WORLD MOVEMENT

1

Co-operation is of vital importance in many lands besides our own. It must be that co-operation is "of man," it takes so well. It must be that it is human-high, that it is man-shape and natural to people. At least, we know that it goes with men of every nation. In some nations, for example, "in Sweden, Norway and Finland, the cooperative sector is a dominating factor of national economy." Its tendency in such places is to regulate private business and to be more effective and democratic than is government in ousting our old friend the monopolist. In some nations, such as France, it has had its ups and downs and has found it hard to keep ahead of a strong and destructive individualism. It is seemingly at home with the Japs and for centuries with the Chinese. It had a good run in Germany, and Russia and Italy too, but with the coming of the dictators it was naturally declared an enemy. Asia, Europe, North and South America—wherever man is at all allowed a breath of freedom, the co-ops find hospitable shores.

Where do they enjoy the greatest success? In China they have their longest connected history, and now feel the stir of a new growth. It is said by the secretary for the Co-operative League of China that in 1942 the co-ops of China were ten million strong in their membership, and therefore they likely were several times that strength in the persons directly affected by them. They are engaged in textile industries, for instance; in making fur coats for the army, and blankets, and also leather goods, and in printing. So says George Hogg in his work on the new China which he sees being made, in notable part with the help of co-ops, by this indestructible people. The Japs are known for their health or medical co-ops, and by 1940 India had more than a hundred thousand co-operative associations, most of them credit societies started by the people and encouraged by missionaries with the hope of outflanking the loan sharks.

If one meant by "success" the healthiest growth rather than size, the reply would be more difficult. Competing for this honor would be the somewhat recent movement in Nova Scotia and, above all, the northern European countries such as Denmark and Sweden and Finland, and China itself with its tradition and the nativeness of co-operation to it. It is a delight merely to review something of what has occurred co-operatively, especially in the past generation or so, among the people of Stockholm, in Sweden. Here is a city with a population now of just over half a million, and its consumer co-operative society, called "Konsum," has within the city 384 separate shops and a membership of 77,000 families. If we were to multiply this number not by four or five but simply by three, we would get as a conservative estimate something like 40 per cent of the people belonging in themselves or the heads of their families to these consumer groups. "More than one-third" is a modest statement. Of course, few families do all their "trading" at such shops, and for that reason the 33⅓ per cent is a reasonable statement. The shops mentioned are of various sorts, some for groceries, some for meats, some for bread and dairy products; a few are shoe stores and a few are furniture stores, and one restaurant and one café are included. In 1935 the set of shops did a business of fifteen million dollars.

From the start Konsum has had its own bakeries, and in 1926 it made a study of prices and quality and the sizes of loaves, and found that one company was then charging 53 per cent more than Konsum for the same product and on the average the unnecessary profit-charge by the private firms was 32 per cent. It is hardly necessary to say that the result was a readjustment of prices for bakery goods in all the shops of the city.

The central society also has its own factory for meat products, and its own savings bank. The capital of the society when it was formed was about twenty-five thousand, and at the end of twenty years it had gone to almost three million. Of course, the consumer society in Stockholm does not begin to tell the story of the Swedish co-ops, which are all over the nation and are concerned with almost the whole social life of the people. Besides, they are of long stand-

ing, and Konsum itself is an amalgam of several earlier independents. They are both consumer and producer. What is significant
about them is that hardly anywhere else do co-ops appear to come
up to the level of the Swedish co-ops in getting a democratic leverage on the total economy. I mean that they have a big percentage
of the nation's economic life, but most of all that they help solve
difficult local and national problems, and they show what one
must regard as great wholesomeness in their general outlook on
man and society. On this last point the inquiry on Co-operative
Enterprise in Europe (1937) says:

> According to Swedish co-operators, the entire consumer co-operative
> business is merely an extension of the family economy, regaining for
> the family, through co-operative action, control over the procurement
> of family needs—a control which the family had lost through indus-
> trialization.
> Employees are given special training to enable them to understand
> and promote this concept.

The number of members is large, and as is usual in such cases
it is not easy to preserve the democratic procedure proper to co-
operation. Probably the Swedes are as successful in this matter as
any people has been to date. They have worked out a system in
Konsum whereby the city of Stockholm is broken into eighteen
districts, and each of these has its annual session in order to go over
the report and balance sheet. Delegates are then chosen for the
general annual meeting, and at this the delegates elect a management council of fifteen members, none of whom may be an employee of the society. It is this council that appoints men to direct
the main departments, that is to say, the grocery, the meat, the
bakery, and the combination shops.

In important ways the great challenge of the Swedish co-ops lies
in the way they have effectively manhandled several big trusts
given to monopolistic practices and abuses. In his very readable
book on Swedish co-operatives, Marquis Childs has made this point
stand out. Certain bodies monopolized the trade in such goods as
electric light bulbs, others in galoshes, others in margarine, or flour
or fertilizer. The co-operators did a wonderful job in busting these
trusts, and in this way of serving themselves and also helping to
free all the people. A national association of retailers had attempted

by "various boycotts" to see that co-operative enterprise would be wiped off the map and kept off it. "Its first attack was on the co-operative margarine trade. When supplies of margarine were cut off, K.F. [the co-operative union] purchased a small independent factory. Prices of margarine were immediately reduced upon the announcement of the purchase of the small factory by K.F., although the cartel had previously refused a price reduction." At the same time the association tried to get banks to allow no credit to the co-operators, but these people then began democratically to collect funds among themselves and to form a savings bank.

More dramatic were the events giving the people a reasonable control over the prices of flour and galoshes and electric light bulbs. The producers of this last commodity were the General Electric people, who formed an international trust, with much if not all their capital supplied from America. They operated in many countries and had the prices quite at their disposal. Research by K.F. showed that the people were being overcharged at least 12 cents a bulb. Childs says: "The price in 1928 for a 25-watt lamp was 37 cents in Sweden, 30 cents in Holland and Germany, 27 cents in Denmark, as low as 18 cents in Hungary, and 52 cents in England." Probably it was as high as the traffic would bear, and bulbs were dumped in some countries. K.F. asked for a reduction in price, and did not get it, and just at that time it happened that G.E. had made trouble with a Swede who was a technical expert. This man then joined hands with K.F., and with the help of an international co-operative setup called "Luma," formed of Swedish, Norwegian, Danish and Finnish bodies, a factory was established. "The success of this undertaking was immediate and far-reaching. Even before the factory was completed, prices of lamp bulbs in Sweden had dropped from 37 cents to 27 cents. Luma was able to price its lamp at 22 cents, a price the trust was compelled to meet. The plant is now able to supply about one-third of Sweden's demand for lamp bulbs." So says the report on co-operative enterprise.

What is significant and vital in the instances of margarine and light bulbs is that the people have in a democratic way managed this considerable problem of trusts and cartels. They have seen to it that these do not any longer rule the economic life and thereby the social and general life of the nation and, on the other hand, they have not waited like children for a collectivistic grandpa to do this task for them. Possibly that is why the Swedes remain free and enjoy such a sound national economy. "According to studies by the International Labor Office, the standard of living of Swedish workers is higher than anywhere else in Europe. Sweden has a higher per capita consumption of milk, creamery products, meat, and eggs than the United States."[1] And when we recall that K.F. and the consumer societies in general are only a part of the total co-operative life of Sweden, that approximately half a million farmers are united in marketing co-ops, and that the people have important co-ops in credit and electrification and housing, we begin to see how considerable is the co-operative movement in this one country. "The Swedes are good co-operators." Certainly we have reason to let this formula stand.

In the line of co-operation, the Swedes have little on their neighbors, the Finns and the Danes. A really big percentage of the Danish people belong, in their persons or their families, to the co-ops, and out of a population that in 1935 fell short of four million it was estimated that, eliminating duplication, the co-ops had four hundred thousand members, which ought to give us a million and a half persons directly served by the movement. Denmark is in the main agricultural, and the story of Danish co-ops is to a great extent the story also of the Danish farmer's freedom from debt and of his security in the possession of his own farm. "Formerly tenants, the Danish farmers now own their own land; over 97 per cent of the farmers are landowners." The Danes have co-ops for collecting eggs and exporting eggs and cattle, for the co-op production of seed, the co-op marketing of almost every commodity; they have co-op fisheries, co-op baking, insurance, banking, electrification, operation of farm machinery, and co-op housing, and also industrial workers' co-op societies or "mechanics' leagues." All this means that much of the Danish economy, so well managed, is handled by the co-operatives. "In the rural areas almost every phase of agriculture is in some way dependent on cooperation. In the cities both the consumers' societies and the workers' productive associations, while not

---

[1] For matters on Sweden, see Childs *Sweden—the Middle Way* (Yale University Press, 1936), and the report of the inquiry on Cooperative Enterprise in Europe (Washington, D. C., 1937).

as large, are of growing importance." One of the most interesting developments anywhere in recent co-operation is that of the co-op canteens started in the 1920's in the area of certain factories. By 1934 there were twenty-two of them, and their yearly turnover was about two-thirds of a million dollars.

The Danish folk schools are well known and are usually thought of in connection with the co-operative movement. The truth is that they are no part of it, nor is it in an official sense tied to them. What their work really comes to is the bringing of an enriched intellectual life, in fact, most of Danish cultural tradition and also appropriate elements in modern science, into the rural high schools. Thus they are not co-op schools. "But they are credited by Danish cooperative leaders with having created the cultural atmosphere in which cooperation thrives. . . . The farm youth who attended these schools 30 years ago are today the backbone of the Danish cooperative movement."

In Sweden and Denmark and Finland and probably everywhere the co-ops stand between the big imperialism of the free enterprisers and the big imperialism of any and every type of collectivistic State. To the American group who in 1937 made the report on co-operative developments in Europe, an official of the Bank of Finland said that the co-op movement reintroduced competition on a basis effective for modern large-scale business, made distribution more efficient, and reduced retail margins. "The resulting almost automatic control of prices, preventing inequitable increases, has 'rendered Government interference with private business enterprise unnecessary.'" So at least our inquirers reported for Finland and also for several of the nations. We mentioned this feature of Swedish and other co-ops in the case of their controlling prices on flour, light bulbs, fertilizer and galoshes. The Danes did the same in the matter of prices on rolled oats. "A large international trust" advertised in a big way, and maintained a monopoly price of 16.7 cents per kilogram. The co-operators, failing to get the prices reduced, started to make their own brand, and found it "immediately possible" to sell the same quality at 12.3, a saving of more than 25 per cent.

For sheer bulk, the British co-operatives, that is, those of Great Britain and Northern Ireland, are certainly the most impressive in

these times. One might think it the number of their members or
of persons directly affected, but it was simply their employees who
in 1935 went above 300,000, and received wages and salaries of
something toward $200 million. The membership then was about
seven and a half millions, the number of retail societies over 1000
with an annual trade of over $1 billion. This amounted to some-
thing between 12 and 15 per cent of the nation's total retail trade.
The people received over $20 million that year as interest on share
capital in the co-ops, and toward $100 million in dividends or
refunds. Since the outbreak of the new wars, the co-operatives in
England have grown at least 12 per cent in business volume and
also in membership, so that the body of members now is over nine
million. Some locals do and some do not allow more than one member from a family, and because British families are small and single
persons become members, it seems an exaggeration to say that the
co-op societies "represent half the population" of Great Britain.
But it is hardly too bold to suggest that they reach in a direct way
fifteen million persons.

Hence their immense importance in the national economy, and
for politics, religion, and education.

The rural societies are not large and perhaps not vital, as they
are in Denmark. This is doubtless because rural life in England
amounts to so much less. What we must emphasize, nevertheless,
is that in the life of the worker and the urban people the co-operative way has been most significant in England. The English people
are patient, they were the first to be generally industrialized and
are now much industrialized, and co-operation as a successful technique in the common man's life was in large part an English discovery. Perhaps it is for such reasons that co-operation has taken
so well with British laborers. Stockholm is surely a great city for
co-operation. But London is like the city of co-operation, when we
consider that by 1931 18 per cent of its millions were in the movement, and even so the percentage is higher in whole counties than
it is in London, running to thirty and above in one instance. The
London membership is slightly less than a million. Before World
War I, London and other large cities were termed "co-operative
deserts." But the growth with that war and ever since has been
phenomenal, and in fact the same is true of the United Kingdom

as a whole. The percentage of co-op membership in the entire population in 1901 was 4.3, by 1911 it was 5.8, by 1919 it was 9.5, in 1931 it was 13.4, and by 1945 we may conservatively say that it was not less than twice this figure.

The British, it is said, are shopkeepers, and the workmen of London and elsewhere have now learned to keep their own shops. What good does it do them? Doubtless it gives them a slight sense of importance and dignity and freedom, a sense of operating as persons in a community of persons. Not, of course, that they are totally freemen when they set up their own shop and make it go, but their doing this is readily embodied in the freeman's economy. It is some economic good too, as is evident in the photo included by Elliott in his story of the English co-operatives. This is a photo of one member's account with a Croydon suburban co-operative. It is not the record of this woman member's debts at the shop, but of her saving through the co-operative. The record opens in 1925 when the woman paid exactly one shilling, or about 24½ cents, to become a member, and that is all she ever paid or ever would be expected to pay. She merely traded at the store. If we may suppose that this store charged the going rates, as is the normal and fairly consistent co-op practice, she was, in terms of expenditure, no better and no worse off than if she traded at a profit shop. But at the co-op, a dividend was each half year coming to her. She chose to let this remain as share capital in the co-operative. At the end of the half year it amounted to seven or eight dollars, and at the end of eleven years, with the interest and the accumulation of dividends and consequent share capital, standing to her credit at the co-op was in our money about $466.46.

Now, that is not a fortune. But for laborers and other poor people, it is something real and considerable, and is much better than for people, presumably paying the same prices, to have a total of nothing standing to their account. Her nest egg she might leave there to protect her, or at any moment draw out for any purpose she pleased. At the same time, she and her husband had also at the co-op a bit of life insurance automatically included in her being a member of the co-op.

The British co-operators provide a great variety of services and commodities. Insurance of the co-op type had by the end of 1935 nearly seven million policyholders. Laundry is commonly done on a co-op basis, and in 1934 the co-op laundry services did a business of about $4,500,000, with a surplus of better than one-tenth that amount. They have penny banks "largely used by children for the accumulation of savings to be used later in buying cooperative membership shares. In 1935 there were 867 societies operating such small savings departments, with a total of £5,631,546 in deposits." These are in effect children's co-ops, and in the total national economy as well as in the building of co-operation, no doubt they can be important.

As is the natural direction and tendency of co-operatives, and as is the experience in every country, the British co-ops moved gradually into wholesaling. This of course is primarily and as a rule exclusively in order to supply their own needs. For instance, the British and the Scottish wholesales, now so well established, farm over thirty thousand acres of tea plantations in India and Ceylon, and also get cocoa and chocolate from those lands.

The Rochdale Pioneers meant to go into manufacturing and they did soon set up a flour mill. In the long run, however, the "workmen's productive societies" in Great Britain, even from the days of the Rochdale Pioneers, have been much more conspicuous for failures than for co-op triumphs. The real success in production came when the factories became consumer owned and made themselves a part of the whole co-operative movement and tied themselves closely to the wholesales. The result is that the British co-operatives now have factories for almost everything. These include biscuit works, jam plants, a tobacco factory, flour mills, a lard refinery, a vegetable oil plant, a margarine factory, printing plants, a rope mill, a colliery, flannel mills and woolen mills, hosiery and corset factories, a paint plant, brush works, shoe factories, glass works, umbrella making, a jewelry shop, a cannery, and shirt factories.

The complaint sometimes made against the British co-ops is that, though they offer democracy of ownership and of control, neither of these is too jealously looked to or too commonly achieved.

The co-operatives in Ireland are of special interest because they were pushed by a modern Irish statesman, Horace Plunkett, and by the poet and statesman, George Russell, or "A.E.", whose work called *The National Being* is one of the greatest books on co-operation, and also because one of the Irish peasant co-operators has produced in *Paddy the Cope* what is to date the most human of all our books on co-operation.

2

When we begin to put together, even in a tentative way, the numbers of co-operators and the volume of co-op business, we may certainly say with the economist Paul Douglas that the growth of co-operation is one of the marvels, in fact one of the unnoticed marvels, of the century. As we said, it is everywhere and is engaged in every enterprise. It is Chinese, and American, and German, and Central European, and British, and Irish, and Italian, and Canadian, and Polish. That is to say, it is human, and natural to man, and possibly, in spite of various dictatorships, it is indestructible. The dictators do and will ban it. But we know now that it is a hardy plant.

What is most challenging of all, it seems to me, is its promise to go a long way, not merely toward managing and controlling an economy or being an economy—though its work in these lines is so important—but toward working out, along with education and religion, into something like a total way of life for a people. This it promises to do in a part of Nova Scotia, and this, I think, it has to a remarkable degree done among the farmers of Denmark, and it is said that it does this also among the Jews who are resettling Palestine. Whatever one may make of the fact, one must remark that it is close to religion in each of these important instances, and that it is integrated with both a religious and a cultural tradition in the case of the Danes and of the Jews. The pages given by Lowdermilk[2] to co-operatives are of interest to those studying the Palestinian question, and likewise to all who are concerned with the welfare of any modern people.

That is what is most elementary, namely, that the co-ops should be worked into a total way of life, a way that is up to our best Western heritage, and is communal and personal. And in our time

[2] Clay Lowdermilk, *Palestine: Land of Promise* (Harper, New York, 1944).

nothing has proved more difficult, and I must say that I for one find it tiring to hear men supposing that because we can study matters of economics precisely as such and as isolated from other phases of life, they can be in fact so isolated. Man is an animal, but he is also a person, a being with intelligence and capable of a Christlike love. For that reason, to try to reduce him, in or out of the co-ops, to a sort of economic machine is to try to change him into an abstraction fit only for a useless theory. That in part is why the co-operative endeavors in such places as Nova Scotia and Denmark and Palestine are likely to prove of even greater importance than some of the bigger ones in England and America: they have regard for man's whole personal and social nature, and they consciously subordinate the economic aspect of co-operation to its fuller human aspects.

Of course it is true that the co-ops have reached a formidable bigness, and this they must do in order to be a great factor in modern life. It was estimated a few years ago that they ran to 100 million members, and some dare to say now that this number is far too small. We know that the International Labor Office in 1939 put the figure for Europe alone at 53 million, and when we take the Americas and Africa and the Orient and translate the membership generally into families perhaps we may safely say that the co-ops are now reaching in a direct way not fewer than 300 million persons. Naturally few, if any, persons are total co-operators; that is, get all their goods and services the co-op way.

It is most likely that the co-operatives will prove to be of vital importance in international reconstruction. This for several reasons: (1) they are in a real sense out of and above politics; (2) they are lovers of peace and were set up at the start for peacemaking and peacekeeping functions; (3) by their nature they are fit to protect us in the rehabilitation era from the dangers of the profit drive; and (4) they have actual organizations reaching into every city and into thousands of towns and villages in the devastated countries.

The co-operators have a committee on reconstruction, and in 1943 this made a study of the co-op facilities available for building up again the European nations. The consumer co-ops of Denmark were judged to have 2,148 retail points and to serve 500,000 families, and her rural marketing co-ops to reach 90,000 farms, and the location of all these co-ops is marked on the published map, and a statement made of the goods and commodities furnished and the total prewar turnover. So also for Norway, Belgium, the Netherlands, and France. As the committee says, the co-operators are not amateurs, and they are not out for gain but for the common good, and experience in our own country during the depression made it evident that funds allocated on a co-op basis go incredibly farther than those left in profit hands and political hands. In California "the Department of Welfare made a study of their costs of relief and found that it cost only one-seventh as much to take care of a family through the self-help cooperatives as it did through a direct dole."

On their own account and aside from rehabilitation problems, the co-operatives plan to move in a big way, in the period of peace, into international trade, and are likely to begin with emphasis on trade in foods and in petroleum products.

Twenty

CO-OPS AND THE LOVE OF GOD

1

OVER and over, as I have had the happiness of going among our co-operators, people have asked me, "How did you get interested in co-operation?" and "Why is a priest interested in co-operation?" In this chapter I want to suggest why this interest on the part of a clergyman, Catholic, Protestant, or Jewish.

The answer may be given in any of a dozen concrete and real ways. For instance, I met in Nova Scotia one day a young medical student from Ohio University who had hitchhiked from Cleveland to see the co-ops. Why did he come so far, and in so hard a way? Why did his eyes nearly jump out of his head when, the next morning, he got a good look at the houses planned and financed and built co-operatively by coal miners for themselves and their families? Why, on his coming from Nova Scotia, did he resolve, and why is he yet resolved, to give his life as a medical man to co-op medicine? He does not want profit; so much is settled. Nor is it likely that he wants prestige. Nothing more strange about the matter, perhaps, than that he believes in God and man.

In a world going out of the frying pan of individualism into the fire of collectivism, youth is starved for a decent human vision. With what socio-politico-economic position in these times can a youthful believer in God and man well ally himself? Unless we are confused, the reply is not evident. But the co-ops, so far as they now go or may in time have it in them to go, may not be an impossibility. At least the words of some young men give me hope, just as the co-ops give them hope. After reading about Nova Scotia, a sergeant wrote from Africa, ". . . a movement, a way of life, a philosophy, a vision. . . And now I'm having 'visions of things that are not.'" I think, he goes on, "wherever it shall be, I will be after the war," I want to be a co-op man as well as a Christian man: they "run up the same hills." From Camp Ritchie in Maryland a lieutenant who, I'll bet, is Protestant, wrote, "Indeed, it is gratifying to know that there are so many good men on this earth of ours; that the future holds so many dormant possibilities to aid these people to acquire their just portion of a divine inheritance. Thru cooperation we can carry on the work that Christ so valiantly and nobly began." A Syrian student at an eastern university writes, "I have found . . . reports on the Nova Scotia movement of very great interest. I would like to acknowledge especially my admiration for the deep insights into the spiritual foundations of the movement, and the beautiful confidence in the practical wisdom and good will of the ordinary man . . . going to mean a great deal in the things I hope to do when I go back to my country."

One may repeat what such statements come to: (1) our best youth hungry for a means to express their faith in God and man; (2) the co-ops possibly a real way to let them have and to let them express a Christian and democratic vision and faith; (3) hardly anything else now in our going world leaving this vision and faith to them in so concrete and real a way.

To put it briefly, a well-developed co-operation—in Chicago or New York, in our mining towns, on our land, in the oil business, the lumber business, the banking business—can be an element in Christian democratism. And we need it now as such an element. For we may continue to doubt that a rugged and humanly ragged individualism can be such an element, at least since it has run so hopelessly into a dehumanized and dehumanizing corporationism. And neither have we any good reason to suppose that the new collectivism, whether in the form of nazi-fascism, or of bolshevism, or of national socialism, can furnish such an element. Yet each of these, the old individualism and some form of the new collectivisms, we will in all likelihood have in almost every nation for a long time to come. Hence the need of some mid-ground, some more defensibly human procedure, at least to temper each of them, if not to save us altogether from them.

That, then, is something of the reason for a clergyman's interest in co-ops. These protect and save people; which means that they could afford the people a way to protect and save themselves. That may seem negative, or at best neutral, but a shying away from evil is always a double negative, and is itself positive. The co-ops, so far as they keep to Rochdale lines, promise to be a constructive element in our economic and social life.

Are they therefore automatically a "Christian philosophy"? Evidently they are not a philosophy at all. Nor are they automatically Christian. In the economic order and again in the social order they are a technique, and in each of these orders they are capable of great good. They are open to Christianity, and Christianity is open to them. But the meeting of the two is not automatic.

Nevertheless, it is beyond argument that Christian life is committed beforehand to co-operation in the broadest and most elemental sense. All men are of one common origin—think of the unitedness and solidarity that are already demanded of us in that fact. We have one common last end, which means that we are by nature and also by grace bound for the same port. Hence again our basic oneness. And we have, as most intrinsic to each of us, the same common human nature, and even if that were the only ground of our oneness, it would bind us to respect and love and go with and work with other men. One common Father we have, too: "Our Father." It is because our nature is one that our destiny is one, and because our nature is one our fundamental needs are one, and our sufferings and joys and hopes and fears are common and are intelligible to all of us. In Christ, besides, we are brothers and are quasi human-divine persons, and through Him we have common beliefs, new common hopes, common rule and common worship. Hence the wrongness of any one who would for a moment think of hating any man, ally or "enemy," white or black or yellow, Jap or Brazilian, Russian or Pole, Jew or Gentile.

The co-ops teach us to work with people and for people, and thus in a real way to love them. For that reason they can be ever so human and ever so Christlike. Nothing at all in their nature to prevent them, in fact, everything to encourage them to go along with what is most human and Christlike in us. I need not ask whether the same is so readily true of individualism as an industrio-economic or as a social technique. As for the collectivisms, has big statism ever in any country made men free or kept men free?

Hence again and again the possible great good of the co-ops. "Good" in the sense of helping to create an economic and social order that is open to what is truly human and Christlike in us.

In spite of its sometimes almost ferocious good will, the collectivistic procedure is mainly destructive of human good. For his part, the profit man has done much human good, and is known on occasion to go out of his way to serve men's general and particular welfare; for instance, to serve as benefactor and philanthropist. Each of these effects, however, is accidental and incidental. What we want is a business-economico-agricultural order that will look directly to the good of our people. And I say without much hesitation that the co-ops best promise to do this. For that reason we may justly declare for a marriage between religion and co-operation. This would be of immense importance to the co-ops, because it would get the whole strength and push of organized religion back of them. It would not be essential to religion, but a great aid to it. What religion must never suffer, if it is to believe in itself, is a severance between the political and economic and industrial and agricultural and cultural life, on the one hand, and its own religious life, on the other: religion here and society there. Yet that is just what at various times tends to happen. One may recall Tawney's powerful summary, toward the end of *Religion and the Rise of Capitalism*. The severance, he says, became real and marked and fatal. That is the modern history of the matter. What we finally got, as he puts it, was—and we may say, is—religion divested of the law, divested of learning, divested of finance and business, and in general shut off from the cultural and social life; and society in general emptied of religion; each is departmentalized, one for Sunday and one for everyday: religion, as he says, robbed of its body and society robbed of its soul.

The co-ops will not become the whole of our social life, nor the whole of our cultural life. But who would not be ashamed to see religion go weak-kneed and be content to bless either our big corporations or any of the collectivisms? That which tempers each of these and tends to protect us from both and at the same time to build up a positive program—this may well be honored by religion. Says Dr. M. M. Coady: "Properly considered, cooperation postulates more, not less religion. We must have charity and justice, which have their foundation in religion . . . if cooperation needs religion, religion also needs cooperation. It is the expression of religion in the economic order. . . The religiously minded man will

use all the good things of God's creation. . . He will be so imbued
with charity, honesty, and courage that he will dare to change a
system that is so hard, cruel, and relentless that it sins against nearly
every ethical principle. He will cut himself off from something
that is vicious and ally himself with something that is better than
anything we have ever had."[1]

2

Take any of a dozen cases we have met on earlier pages, and ask
whether religion is interested in the outcome. The miners and
others at Dillonvale are co-operators on a limited scale. No doubt,
much may be said or at least suggested against them; for example,
they may be somewhat narrow, because at least in their early years
they tended to express only one group. But these co-ops are needed,
and have done good, and with the help of the unions they show
that they have it in them to effect the greatest economic good that
these poor men can effect.

Is religion interested in such a case, and such a cause? It would
be strange if it were not interested, and in fact concerned, in the
sense of being with this local stir toward human betterment, and
also in the sense of being pleased and even elated with the results.

We saw one-fourth of the farmers in Indiana getting rid of
certain dictatorships, and saying that they will be as free as circumstances and their own intelligence permit: rid of dictators in the
matter of their insurance and credit, their coal supply, their lumber
supply, their grain marketing, from start to finish free of Sinclair
and John D. and Texaco, free to manufacture fertilizer and machinery. We saw Finnish farmers at a particular center called New
York Mills making ever so brave and successful an effort to operate
as freemen. What they begin to do at that center may be taken as
typical of what resourceful and wise landmen can do. It is nothing
more nor less than a declaration of economic freedom. "We will
not be the slaves of packing companies, of grain companies, of the
oil men, or of the grocery chains. We will pay no tribute." So the
New York Mills men have in a quiet and firm way said. So too of
men in Chicago and many cities. All around the earth, and no
doubt advisedly, we fight for freedoms. Yet it remains true that

[1] M. M. Coady, *Masters of Their Own Destiny*.

freedom requires a certain vigilance at home. The co-ops work toward this domestic freedom. And the Lord knows they need to work.

Which way does God intend men to be—political slaves, and social and cultural and economic slaves, or freemen? In matters economic, we have seen that the co-ops can in one generation mean the difference between freemen on our land, and an unhappy, crushed, defeated and enslaved herd of men on our land. And in Denmark, we may note, they have helped to give us freemen. May religion therefore stand by, its hands immaculate and tender and timorous, and refuse to take its part in this struggle for freedom?

We saw that the co-op people can, not just as a hope or a threat, but as a matter of fact take over the oil industry. They can at least take over a part of it. This we know, since they have done it. They can take over all kinds of factories. "Most dramatic single factor of the year was the drive into production." This is the report for 1943. Co-ops in this country and Canada have bought a million-dollar plant that is to make machinery. What this means is that the people will own the factories that in any case they pay for, and it means that, as experience shows, they can have them free of charge. Also, since our farmers take these progressive steps, and since English and other laborers take them too, there is no law of logic and certainly no fatal law of psychology forbidding American Labor to take them. Besides, Labor has begun to take them; for instance, at Dillonvale and Granger, and in Waukegan and Racine.

Odd and lagging any religion would be if it were not interested and concerned. In almost all instances the common man, of whom and for whom I speak, is of good will; he is made good by God and given a tendency toward all good, and also, in ways not readily seen or defined, he is blest by grace. He has a basically good intelligence, though he is not in the habit of vigorously using it. Equipped with goodness and with brains, he can work with his fellows toward the building of neighborhoods and communities, toward emancipation from economic peonage and the constant danger of political peonage. He can, in other words, be a freeman in a free community as God intends him to be. He can be. But this freedom is not automatic. Working intelligently and persistently with his neighbors, learning to work with them and for them, and really working with them and for them, this common man can be socially free and economically free, and thus create the factual basis for a possible political freedom. He can have property and a home and perhaps some land; he can have the freedom that goes with these and seldom goes without them. He can have neighbors and be a neighbor. This means that he can actively and effectively love his neighbor, and give some time and hopes and labor for the common economic and social good of his neighbor. Otherwise, we revert to bourgeois individualism, and man is no good at all, and does not live as a human person, let alone as a son of God and a brother of Christ.

That is point Number One. Number Two will be this: Here is a man with ownership and freedom and love for his neighbor. Is religion interested?

We may ask Dr. M. M. Coady to reply. "We can build such a society where these needy brothers will have a chance to live and to contribute to the general good and the greater glory of God, where man, with his marvellous power to recuperate, will find the strength to rise, straighten himself up, throw back his noble head, and gaze into the sun." Dr. J. Henry Carpenter has in effect the same reply in his work called *Peace through Co-operation.*

Men working together, common men, if one pleases, or any men working together, through unions and the co-ops. That is the method. The aims are ownership for every family, and freedom for every man, and also the building up of the community life. At least within certain limits of time and place and materials, these aims are often effected. This we know from a century's history and again from current instances.

Freedom, property, neighborliness. Those are clearly the positive values and I am sure that, without these values, man scarcely operates as a person. We may name, too, as within that freedom the creativeness that is properly man's: his capacity and natural urge to plan and make some things, and to help build a home, a family, a community, a church, an earthly city. To serve that city, also called the State, man needs all the values named. And this common man is not only serving the State, but freeing the State! He and his fellows are unburdening it, taking from its arms and legs yards of red tape and bureaucracy, and taking tons of impossible and unnatural economic burdens off its back. In that way, then, it is true to say that the Rochdale Society of Equitable Pioneers is among our best builders of Church and State, of home and family and community, of man and all his major freedoms.

3

I have been asking, "Is the Church, then, not interested and actively concerned?" But the question is somewhat superfluous, since the Catholic Church and the Protestant and the Jewish Church have in many ways shown that they take the co-ops to be on the side of the angels.

The truth is that, despite exceptions, we have a body of great religious men and great churchmen who are co-op-minded and co-op promoters. In just this connection the man most famous, perhaps, is the remarkable Protestant churchman, Nikolai Grundt-vig. This man is Danish, and a poet, and a priest. But we may claim that in important senses he is The Dane of modern times, the hero and saint of his country, and the voice of his people. Bredsdorf, a compatriot of his, says, "All Danes have met the effects of Grundtvig's life-struggle in our people." Of the well-known folk schools founded under the inspiration of Grundtvig and a layman named Kold, Anders Nielsen writes that "not only the co-operative movement but the cultural position of Danish farmers as a whole" rests on these schools. These two men, he says, are the great modern Danish religious and educational leaders; they have begotten a feeling of solidarity among the people, and taught them to think and work for the common good. The ideal is "freedom with re-sponsibility,"[2] and the work done is one of the major achievements not only of the Danes, but of modern cultural and religious life.

Young men and women learning to work together for the com-mon good, and poetry and religion and history combined with their practical learning—that is what the Danes have learned at the feet of Grundtvig and Kold. In such a matrix, the Rochdale principles become real and lofty and noble.

Of other Protestant leaders in the co-op movement, one must cite, above all, the Japanese Kagawa. This man has given us the

[2] See Peter Manniche, *Denmark, a Social Laboratory*.

most memorable and just phrases for the relationship of co-ops to Christianity. He calls co-operation "brotherhood economics," and says that co-operation is "the love-principle" of economics, and in his lecture tour of our country a few winters ago he inspired many to found co-operatives. One especially mentions also such distinguished churchmen as E. Stanley Jones and James Myers and J. Henry Carpenter. Dr. Myers has for years studied the relation between Labor and religion, and now combines Labor, religion and the co-ops, and Dr. Carpenter has given years to the co-operative movement. I would by no means neglect Henry Wallace, who on many occasions has declared himself for and with the co-ops, nor Congressman Voorhis of California, nor the great moral figure of Dr. Warbasse, who has given his time and energy and money, and we might say his life, to help the co-ops develop in our society.

Among the Catholics we have already mentioned with great honor the priest Virgil Michel, a leader in co-ops and in every live social movement. And certainly we should cite the vigorous statement by the venerable editor Thomas F. Woodlock in the *Wall Street Journal* (Sept. 2, 1942). Says Mr. Woodlock:

> The cooperative movement is today, as it has never been before, a living answer to some of the problems over which logomachy rages— planned economy, for instance, and even democracy itself. It stands . . . against the whole Socialist and Communist motion for the compressing of all men into a rigid "Cooperative Commonwealth" by uniting all who care to join it in a voluntary common effort . . . It stands over against the laissez-faire Capitalism by competing successfully against it. It stands over against all "pressure groups" seeking nourishment at the public trough, by seeking and accepting none for itself. It asks no special laws to protect it; it is not interested in "politics," it has no blocks in legislatures anywhere. . . . There is not the smallest sign that its growth may not continue everywhere there is any freedom for action. It is the democracy of which we are all talking.

The co-op movement in Nova Scotia has for several years had among its leaders the Reverend Nelson MacDonald, of the United Church of Canada, who both in theory and in practice is a remarkably effective co-op man. And the names of M. M. Coady, who is a priest, and of Father Jimmy Tompkins are household words among all Nova Scotia co-operators, and are revered wherever the Nova Scotia movement is known. These men are thorough democrats, full of what some timid and reactionary souls might think a reckless faith in the people. When I had been a while with Dr. Coady and had seen and heard him visiting with the people and awakening them from their apathy, I had this sort of thought: "How that man understands the people and how he believes in them, and how they understand that he is one of them and with and for them!" As for Father Tompkins, all who have been among his people have the same story. It is that this lean little old man gets the people to bring out every constructive and best thing that is in them. In the lives of the people and in the inspired work of young churchmen we already begin to get monuments to these two outstanding educational and religious leaders of our time.

Naturally, Catholics are pleased because for years we have had popes who have labored for the good of the common man and given gladly of their power for the peace of nations and the freedom of every man. Each of these, peace and freedom and the common good, is among the proper co-op products. On the evening of August 31, 1939, the very eve of war, I heard Negro co-operators, visiting Nova Scotia sing:

> There won't be no war no more,
> Down by the river side.

That same week the Pope, after trying to prevent war, had said, "A momentous hour has struck for the great human family." Even when the war came, he did everything at his command to keep the flame from spreading from nation to nation. That action was typical, for I believe we may say that he takes as his problem, above all other problems, the unity and solidarity of mankind. In the thick of the war, with hatred and sects and isolation applauded, he has gone on preaching a gospel of love and peace. All men loving one another, and no man hating any man; that is his platform. And it is just possible that as a real technique making toward world peace nothing is better than co-operation. This is because war is, to say the least, to so great an extent economically determined, that is to say, wars are so commonly started for profit, or to protect some group or some nation's profit and empire; and because, on the other hand, co-operation drops the profit motive.

If co-ops could cut out, or even cut down, profits and monopoly, and in the long run effectively throttle the German-English-American cartels, and also turn our modern economy back from the superstates to the people, they might prove to be the greatest anti-war event in history. Perhaps we might then begin to think of and hope for peace. Just to begin to think of so great a good—war gone! Or wars only reduced, but really reduced in extent, in frequency, in duration, in ferocity, in absoluteness! Persons saving and making themselves, not by destroying the community, but by saving and serving the community, and the nations, too, saving and making themselves, not by destroying others, but by serving the international community. That is what, perhaps, we have a right to begin to long for and to work for, and as we labor and hope we may consider that the co-ops are one of the real techniques looking in that direction.

If in this connection the co-ops have any constructive good in them, then every man, and most of all the religious and Christian man, will be happy to pay tribute to them. On that ground, no doubt, the co-ops would be near the heart of Pius XII.

As a matter of fact, his predecessor gave vigorous expression to the principle that is basic to co-op philosophy and co-op practice. This he did in 1931 in the encyclical called "Quadragesimo Anno," or "Forty Years After," and first he paid tribute to Leo XIII's "Rerum Novarum" (1891). Leo had laid down principles for handling "the difficult problem of human solidarity," and he had got results. Even so, said Pius XI, workers today usually remain without property and a few men are so wealthy that most of our family men are lacking in means, security, freedom, and confidence. This condition should not and cannot continue. We used to have a variety of institutions linked together in an organic way, but because of individualism and its evils, these have been "all but ruined, leaving thus virtually only individuals and the State." So we get statism, and the State is loaded down with unnatural burdens once carried by associations "rendered extinct by it," and as a consequence the State is "submerged and overwhelmed by an infinity of affairs and duties."

Can man do anything about the matter? He might, if he had the intelligence and courage to return to the basic principle that is here violated. This is the principle: It is a mistake to give up to the community what the person can do, and "it is an injustice, a grave evil and a disturbance of right order for a larger and higher organization to arrogate to itself functions which can be performed efficiently by smaller and lower bodies. This is a fundamental principle of social philosophy. . . The State should leave to these smaller groups the settlement of business of minor importance."

That at any rate is what Pius XI said, and it is what every co-operator from 1844 to 1944 says. The principle stands: negatively put, it is that individualism, like collectivism, is reactionary and a dictator; and positively, it is that persons and groups should be free to perform whatever functions they can efficiently perform. Caveat dictator! Whether he is the old economic imperialist or the new political imperialist, let him be careful not to allow freedom to the people. He must have slaves; that is his protection and his glory.

Pius XI therefore is not far from affirming the ground on which co-ops stand, and when in recent years I have frequently gone again over his encyclical it has seemed to me that the co-op is the kind of association he sought for the concrete, real order. The end is "right order," and the task is to save the person, the family, and the association—exemplified in our time by the private school, the labor union, and the co-op—and also to save the State. The Pope is asking, Where is the vital and necessary group that stands between individual and State? The co-op, so far as it goes, qualifies, and on papal teaching, as well as on simple logic and on much experience, the co-op is approved and is something to acclaim.

This same Pius XI, through his secretary who became Pius XII, blessed a particular body of co-ops. In 1938 a letter signed by that secretary came from Pius XI to the bishop of Antigonish. The letter said that in those days the Pope found events that did not make greatly for his happiness. But in Nova Scotia he did find cheer. For here he saw the co-ops in action, encouraged by St. Francis Xavier University, and he saw bodies of men who by pulling their oars together were able, though men of "slender means," to make a certain headway. As if to complete the thought, Pius XII said on September 1, 1944: "Small and medium holdings in agriculture, the arts, trade and industry must be guaranteed and supported. Co-operative unions must provide them the advantage of big business."

These overt statements may be taken as a boost not only to Nova Scotia co-ops, but to those Catholics who are still looking for means to make concrete and real the principle affirmed in 1931.

A further effective statement on religion and co-operation came to me directly from the common man in Nova Scotia. Here are four of these, each so pat and so strong and fully human-divine that the people there must be not only good co-operators, but not bad philosophers and theologians. On a rocky road over the Bay of St. Lawrence, an Acadian put the matter in terse terms. He said, "The man who is only good for himself is no good. That's what I think." Another day in a miners' study club the question finally was, Can we do this really hard thing? A black Scot slid from his place and said, "Of course we can do it, if every man has his neighbor in his heart." A French miner in a neighboring group was quiet, but when it was suggested that a certain man was an excellent co-operator the modest man said, "We're not sure. We think maybe he's in it for his own good. And that's not co-operation. This co-operation is kinda on God's side." The fourth was a young man, a Scot and a farmer, a thinker but not a lively talker. Taking time and care he said, "It could be a better system if enough people got into it and stayed in it long enough." Possibly that is asking a great deal of people. But the young Scot was sure that people have good reason, even a divine reason, for going thus together in the co-ops. He said, "Isn't that the way we're supposed to be? Isn't that the way God meant us to be—not fighting one another, but loving one another?"

Index

DATE DUE

1987